THE MIRACLE & TRAGEDY
OF THE DIONNE QUINTUPLETS

THE MIRACLE & TRAGEDY OF THE DIONNE QUINTUPLETS

BY SARAH MILLER

schwartz & wade books · new york

Grateful acknowledgment is made to the following for permission
to reprint previously published materials:

Archives of Ontario: Excerpts from letter of July 3, 1935, by Fred Davis; diaries of 1934
and 1935 by Yvonne Leroux; handwritten draft entitled "Quintuplets" by Yvonne Leroux;
and handwritten draft entitled "The Five Unluckiest Children" by Yvonne Leroux.
Used by permission of the Archives of Ontario. All rights reserved.

Berkley, an imprint of the Penguin Publishing Group, a division of Penguin Random House LLC, and
Carole Hébert: Excerpts from *Family Secrets: The Dionne Quintuplets' Autobiography* by Jean-Yves Soucy
with Annette, Cécile, and Yvonne Dionne, translated by Kathe Roth.
Original title: *Secrets de Famille,* copyright © 1995 by Editions Libre Expression. English language
translation copyright © 1996 by Stoddard Publishing. American edition copyright © 1996 by
Penguin Random House LLC. Used by permission of Carole Hébert and Berkley, an imprint of the
Penguin Publishing Group, a division of Penguin Random House LLC. All rights reserved.

Kathryn Brough: Excerpts from *We Were Five: The Dionne Quintuplets' Story from Birth Through Girlhood to
Womanhood* by James Brough (New York: Simon & Schuster, 1964), copyright © 1964 by James Brough.
Used by permission of Kathryn Brough. All rights reserved.

Doubleday, an imprint of the Knopf Doubleday Publishing Group, a division of
Penguin Random House LLC: Excerpts from *The Dionne Legend: Quintuplets in Captivity* by Lillian
Barker, copyright © 1951 by Lillian Barker. Used by permission of Doubleday, an imprint of the Knopf
Doubleday Publishing Group, a division of Penguin Random House LLC. All rights reserved.

Visit us on the Web! GetUnderlined.com

Educators and librarians, for a variety of teaching tools, visit us at RHTeachersLibrarians.com

Library of Congress Cataloging-in-Publication Data is available upon request.
ISBN 978-1-5247-1381-2 (trade) — ISBN 978-1-5247-1382-9 (lib. bdg.) — ISBN 978-1-5247-1383-6 (ebook)

The text of this book is set in 11.8-point Dante MT Pro.
Book design by Stephanie Moss

Printed in the United States of America
10 9 8 7 6 5 4 3 2 1
First Edition

TO SARAH NICOLE,

who has a smile like Marie Dionne's

CONTENTS

We don't feel anyone can be fair to
both sides and tell the truth.
—THÉRÈSE DIONNE

Children are the riches of the poor.
—PROVERB

PROLOGUE

In an empty nursery, behind two woven wire fences topped with barbed wire, five nine-year-old girls waited for their father. Five suitcases sat alongside them. Five smiling Shirley Temple dolls were clutched in their arms. Yvonne stared out the window at the yellow brick mansion up the hill. Annette quietly seethed, pretending not to be afraid. Cécile sat in a corner, rocking her doll. Émilie prayed that it was all just a bad dream. Marie tried to tell a silly story, but no one laughed.

At the sound of their father's footsteps in the hall, all five sisters hugged their Shirley Temples closer to their chests. The moment they dreaded had come.

For the first time in their lives, the Dionne Quintuplets were going home.

Oliva Dionne did not speak as he and his five identical daughters walked through the hospital's guarded gate, down the road, and through another gate that led to the colossal Georgian house that was to be their new home. He did not lead them up the steps to the grand front door. Instead, he entered through a service door into the kitchen. Yvonne followed first, trying to be brave for her sisters' sake. Though Yvonne was no more than a few minutes older than Annette, Cécile, Émilie, and Marie, she had acted the part of the little mother since she was a toddler.

For nine years Mr. Dionne had battled with the government to unite his family under a single roof. Now that his triumphant moment had arrived, the man who had once crawled through a drainpipe to elude hospital guards just so he could glimpse his five famous babies through a window spoke a single sentence.

"The little girls are here," he told his wife, and continued into the house, leaving his daughters standing in the unfamiliar kitchen with their dolls and suitcases.

"Bonsoir, Mom," Yvonne, Annette, Cécile, Émilie, and Marie said, greeting their mother in a mixture of French and English.

"Supper will be ready soon," Mrs. Dionne replied in French, then called for two of her elder daughters. "Show the little girls around the house," she instructed.

Without a word, "the little girls" followed as their big sisters pointed into one doorway after another. The living room, the den, the sewing room, their father's office. Redolent of fresh paint and filled with pristine furniture, the house felt new and sterile, more sterile by far than the hospital that had been their home since they were four months old.

Then they reached the dining room. Like everything else in the house, it was big, in this case big enough to seat fourteen—Mr. and Mrs. Dionne, Yvonne, Annette, Cécile, Émilie, Marie, and their seven brothers and sisters, Ernest, Rose-Marie, Thérèse, Daniel, Pauline, Oliva Jr., and Victor. An archway divided the room in half, with a table on each side. "This side is for our family," the little girls remembered one of their elder sisters saying. "The other side is for your family."

Not one of the bewildered nine-year-olds knew what to say.

PART ONE

---

1 IN 57,000,000 BIRTHS

MAY 28, 1934–MARCH 15, 1935

CHAPTER 1

Quintuplets Born to Farm Wife

NORTH BAY NUGGET, MONDAY, MAY 28, 1934

The knock at the back door roused Douilda Legros from her bed. "Auntie, please hurry and dress and come over," Oliva Dionne called. "Elzire, she is very sick. Please hurry," he said again.

Auntie Legros was on her way in minutes.

It was only a short drive across the road to the Dionne farm, but it was long enough for Douilda Legros's worries to unreel through her mind. Poor Elzire had never had such a difficult pregnancy. Headaches, dizzy spells, vomiting. Painful legs and feet swollen to twice their normal size. A finger pressed into her skin left a deep dent. Now and then the edges of her vision went black.

Two, perhaps three weeks ago it had become so bad Elzire had finally consented to let her husband, Oliva, consult the doctor in spite of the cost. The doctor had ordered Elzire off her feet entirely, but that was next to impossible on a three-hundred-acre farm with five young children to care for.

And now? The urgency in Oliva's voice could only mean something worse yet. Perhaps the worst thing of all—the baby, coming too soon.

Auntie Legros let herself in the front door without waking Ernest, Rose-Marie, Thérèse, and Daniel, asleep upstairs, and made her way to the bedroom at the back of the house. Eleven-month-old Pauline slept in a crib at the foot of the big wooden bed where Elzire lay. Her niece's black eyes peered up out of a pale and puffy face. "Auntie," she said weakly in French, "I don't think that I will be able to pull through this time."

Auntie Legros could hardly contradict her. Even by the light of the kerosene lamp, it was clear that Elzire was ailing badly. The young mother's legs and feet were so distended, her toes had nearly disappeared. She could neither stand nor walk. There was a bluish cast to her fingernails. Her labor pains had woken her sometime near midnight—mild at first, steadily advancing until there could be no doubt that the baby was insisting on being born.

Nevertheless, Auntie Legros did her best to comfort her niece. "Don't you worry, my dear. I will stand by you now as I always did before," she promised. This child would be the fifth Dionne she had helped bring into the world.

Elzire asked for her rosary, and the two women paused to say a prayer to the Blessed Virgin. Elzire kissed the feet of the crucifix and recited aloud the Ave Maria. Both women cried a little. Then Auntie Legros set to work.

Herself a mother of nine, Douilda Legros had been helping deliver her neighbors' children for eighteen years, sometimes assisting the midwife or doctor, sometimes working alone. In all that time, she'd lost only one baby—a premature infant, born with the umbilical cord around its neck. And now Elzire's baby was coming two months too early.

O God, inspire me in my work, Auntie Legros prayed.

Nothing was prepared. No clothing, no diapers. Elzire should have had most of the summer to sew new baby things and accustom little Pauline to sleeping upstairs with her brothers and sisters. But that could not be helped now. Auntie Legros did what she could. She lit the wood stove and put a pan and a teakettle on to boil. She found a stack of newspapers to spread over the mattress, easing Elzire back and forth as she rearranged the bedding for the birth. Elzire was too weak to move without assistance, but the prayer, to Auntie Legros's relief, had bolstered her niece's spirits. Douilda Legros had never before seen Elzire discouraged or fearful, even during the most difficult of her deliveries, when Thérèse had been turned the wrong way.

Just the same, Auntie Legros herself was growing more ill at ease as Elzire's suffering increased. The prospect of losing another newborn was difficult enough; the memory of that failed premature delivery still haunted her. But to lose Elzire? Though they were not related by blood (Elzire was Douilda's husband's niece), Elzire had been like a daughter to her since she was a little girl. Auntie Legros had taken Elzire in after her mother's long illness and death—until the eleven-year-old was compelled to leave school and return home to help her father care for a houseful of brothers. She had seen Elzire married to Oliva Dionne at sixteen, and watched her become the mother of six children before turning twenty-five. Hardest of all, she had supported Elzire when her fourth baby, two-month-old Leo, died of pneumonia.

After all that, Auntie Legros would take no chances with Elzire's health. Within an hour of her arrival at the Dionne house, she sent Oliva a mile down the road for Madame Lebel.

To the French Canadians of Corbeil, Ontario, *midwife* and *Madame Lebel* were interchangeable terms. A large "weather-beaten" woman with "a heart as big as a washtub," Madame Lebel had borne eighteen children of her own and delivered her neighbors of at least three hundred more, most of them without a doctor's assistance. She never expected so much as a penny for her services—something that endeared her more and more each year to the small rural community, now that times were harder than anyone could remember.

Madame Lebel recognized the gravity of the situation at once. Warmth and color were draining from Elzire's body as the frequency of the pains increased. She ignored Elzire's requests not to send for the doctor. "Elzire's pulse is bad," Madame Lebel told Oliva. "So is her general condition. Get Dr. Dafoe here quick as you can."

Oliva obeyed instantly.

With her rosary pressed tightly to her heart, Elzire begged Madame Lebel to hurry the baby's arrival. Though the Dionnes were one of the few families in Corbeil who were not receiving relief payments from the government, Elzire knew there wasn't a cent to spare for the doctor. Since the Depression had hit, their savings had "melted away." Not a day went by that she wasn't thankful for Oliva's $4-a-day job as a gravel hauler, but with a $3,000 mortgage on the farm and seven—soon to be eight—mouths to feed, $20 a week stretched barely far enough. Dr. Dafoe's last visit had spread them tissue-thin; another might cost as much as a week's wages. Elzire's lips were white as she formed the request.

Fewer than three miles separated Oliva Dionne from the doctor's neat brick house in Callander, but it was dark, rocky going, more a rutted lumber trail than a road. Aside from the priest, not another man in the Corbeil parish had the good fortune to own an automobile, but it still might not get him there in time.

When he reached the house with its plaque reading *Dr. A. R. Dafoe,* Oliva pounded on the door and rang the bell.

Dr. Allan Roy Dafoe himself answered, wearing a pair of pants under his rumpled nightshirt. The doctor was an odd-looking man at any hour of the day—short enough that folks called him "the Little Doc," with hands so small he had to buy gloves in the children's department. Yet his head was so large he was rarely able to find a hat that fit properly. And he stuttered. The next day would be his fifty-first birthday.

At first, the doctor could make little sense of Oliva Dionne's presence on his doorstep. Elzire Dionne was not expected to deliver until late July. Besides, it was something like four o'clock in the morning, and Dafoe had had less than three hours' sleep. Returning home from a delivery well after midnight, he'd sat up past one to read a detective story.

"My wife is very sick," Oliva said in English. (The doctor, like most who lived outside the tiny Catholic community of Corbeil, did not speak French.) "I think she soon have a baby. Can you come right away, Doctor?"

"You go on back," Dafoe told the worried father. "I'll dress and come along in my own car."

Oliva had to know how long he would be.

"A few minutes," Dafoe answered, and shut the door.

If the doctor was short with Oliva, it was not only because of the stutter that obliged him to get straight to the point. Dr. Dafoe had warned the Dionnes about Elzire's condition, and they had not complied. She ought to have been in bed these last two weeks. No housework, no farm chores. Get a hired girl to take over Elzire's work, Dafoe instructed Oliva, or else start looking for a new wife. Yet when the doctor visited the Dionne farm the next day, there was Elzire, waddling around the kitchen on feet puffed up like bread dough, aggravating the swelling as well as her blood pressure. The results of the test he'd conducted indicated the beginnings of toxemia—a condition better known today as preeclampsia, guaranteed back then to be fatal to mother and baby if it progressed—but Dr. Dafoe seems not to have bothered to explain all that to the Dionnes. He took it for granted that a doctor's orders would be obeyed, regardless of whether his patient understood why.

Now that their ignorance had made things worse, they wanted him to hurry. And, of course, he would.

The doctor was already too late. Around ten past four, Elzire's baby was born.

Between them, Auntie Legros and Madame Lebel had delivered hundreds of babies, but the size of this infant left the two midwives terror-stricken. Arms barely bigger around than sticks of chalk, and every bit as breakable. Fingers that seemed too tiny to contain bones at all. Bruise-colored skin so thin and tender, it might as well have been cellophane. Lamplight glanced off the shining outline of her delicate ribs. The whole of the baby's torso fit within Madame Lebel's palm; a bulbous head the size of a small orange wobbled on a frail neck. Like an insect's, her head and belly were entirely out of proportion with her long, spindly limbs.

Everything about the tiny little girl looked raw and unfinished, with one startling exception: a beautiful set of long black eyelashes.

She was not breathing.

The midwives rubbed her back and chest and blew into her mouth, desperate to inflate her lungs. Precious seconds ticked by as the two women struggled to make her live without injuring her impossibly fragile body. Suddenly a mewling sound rose from the thin blue lips.

A moment's exultation, then the realization: a child so small could not live more than a few minutes. Auntie Legros dashed to the kitchen pump for a dipper of water. "Ego te baptizo in nomine Patris et Filii et Spiritus Sancti," she murmured as she sprinkled the water over the child's silky dark hair. *I baptize you in the name of the Father and of the Son and of the Holy Spirit.* They could do no more than that. The midwives tied off the cord with a length of cotton thread from Elzire's sewing basket, wrapped the baby in a torn bit of wool blanket warmed before the oven door, and laid her near her mother, certain that death was imminent for one or both of them.

Within minutes, Elzire's pains returned. But instead of the afterbirth, out came another baby girl, smaller yet than the first. Again Auntie Legros and Madame Lebel persuaded the baby to breathe. Immediately they baptized her, too, and laid her next to her sister, who, miraculously, was also still breathing.

Madame Legros and Auntie Lebel had no time to congratulate themselves before yet another infant's head began to emerge. Not twins, but triplets! At almost the same moment, Dr. Dafoe arrived. "Good God, woman, put on some more hot water!" he exclaimed as he headed to scrub up in the kitchen basin.

The third baby, delivered by the midwives before the doctor had taken his coat off, was even smaller, even more reluctant to breathe than her sisters. Undaunted, Dr. Dafoe and the two women worked her over until they coaxed her into making that strange but encouraging mewling. Auntie Legros baptized her, and she joined the widening row of dark-haired baby girls at the foot of the bed.

By now Elzire was so exhausted, she appeared to be unconscious. What little of her strength remained, she devoted to pressing her rosary beads to her heart and praying silently to herself. She desperately needed rest. But her body had not finished its work.

"My God, there are still more there," Madame Lebel said to the doctor.

"Gosh!" he exclaimed. Realizing that Elzire had become too weak to bring yet another child into the world without assistance, Dafoe put "a little pressure" on her abdomen, and a fourth baby made its way into the lamplight. "Gosh!" he said again as a fifth followed two minutes later.

Through the transparent walls of the unbroken amniotic sacs, Dafoe could see arms and legs moving: two more miniature baby girls, these the smallest of all. In his sleepy state, the scene was "unreal and dream-like," he remembered, "but I mechanically went about the business of looking after the babies."

Madame Lebel and Auntie Legros were every bit as stunned. Five babies in a single hour! "We just looked at each other with amazement," Auntie Legros recalled of the fifth birth. And the last two were born in "angel veils"—an uncommon sign of good luck. It was clear from their size that this pair would need every ounce of luck imaginable.

Quickly, Dr. Dafoe ruptured the sacs and got the last two babies breathing. Auntie Legros baptized them. (Or perhaps it was the doctor. Maybe both—certainly both remembered doing so.) Madame Lebel swaddled the infants in napkins and sheets and laid them alongside the first three. Then a warmed blanket was spread over all five babies.

"Auntie, have I twins, this time?" Elzire asked.

"Yes, my dear," Madame Lebel answered, "twins and three more." She held up her fingers and counted off five daughters—"Cinq fillettes."

Elzire burst into tears. "What will I do with all them babies?" she wailed.

✦ ✦ ✦

Satisfied that the birth was finally over, Auntie Legros ran home for supplies. Into a butcher's basket went an old woolen blanket, a bottle of olive oil, and some flatirons. When she returned, everything had changed. Elzire had gone into shock. She was cold to the touch. Her fingertips were black, her pulse nearly imperceptible. Frightened, Auntie Legros called the doctor in from the yard.

Dr. Dafoe injected Elzire with pituitary hormone to raise her blood pressure, and ergot solution to slow any internal bleeding. A little color appeared in her face. Her pulse quickened, but not enough to bring her out of danger. For forty-five minutes, Auntie Legros and the doctor worked to keep her from slipping away. When Elzire looked no better, Auntie Legros told Dafoe it was time to send for the priest. Dafoe agreed—he had been thinking the same thing.

Auntie Legros went out to the living room, where Oliva was pacing the floor. "My God, what am I going to do with five babies!" he exclaimed, just as Elzire had done. In the space of an hour his family had doubled, leaving his wife on the verge of death. He felt as though he had been "punched." The news put Oliva in such a frantic state of nerves, Auntie Legros did not trust him behind the wheel. Instead, it was Dr. Dafoe who left Elzire's bedside and sped off to Corbeil to alert Father Routhier. There was not much else Dafoe could do for her.

Elzire had watched the doctor's face and heard his grave tone as he spoke with the midwives in English. She did not need to understand the words to guess what he was telling them. Elzire had never felt so feeble and helpless in all her life. She tried to say Oliva's name. She wanted to touch her babies once while they were still living. But she was too weak to speak, too weak to lift her hand.

✦ ✦ ✦

In the time it took Dafoe to return, Elzire had rallied somewhat. He left a prescription for her and instructed the midwives to administer it if she had any more pains. He had done everything he knew how to do. If that was not enough, the priest would be along soon.

"As we did not anticipate his return, I asked Dr. Dafoe what to do with the babies," Madame Lebel recalled. In all the commotion over Elzire, hardly anyone had given a thought to the five infants at the foot of the bed. Every last one of the "little mites" was still living.

"All we can do is to keep them warm and quiet," Dafoe answered. "Leave 'em alone, except to give them a few drops of warm water every couple of hours—if they live."

What about bathing them in warm olive oil? Madame Lebel wondered.

"He told her to please herself," Auntie Legros remembered, "as he did not think there was much use in her troubling herself a great deal as the babies would all die." Perhaps the biggest one might have a chance, he conceded, but certainly not the others. No set of quintuplets had ever lived before, and he had no reason to hold out hope for these five. Twenty-six years earlier, Dafoe had assisted at the birth of a set of quadruplets; all four were dead within a week. "However, you can please yourself," he repeated.

Madame Lebel warmed flatirons on the stove. The midwives positioned two chairs before the open oven door and balanced the basket across the two seats while one at a time they sponged each of the infants with warm olive oil. Careful to preserve the order in which they had been born, Madame Lebel and Auntie Legros arranged the babies in the butcher's basket from biggest to smallest.

By the time Oliva came in to see his five daughters for the first time, they were back in the basket on the foot of their mother's bed, with hot flatirons propped near their toes and a big wool blanket draped over the top.

Elzire lay watching as her husband approached on tiptoe, hesitating in the bedroom doorway. His brown-black eyes were red from crying. She knew what kind of tragedy or sorrow it took to bring Oliva Dionne to tears. "Realizing this, near death as I was," Elzire remembered, "I made up my mind to be as brave as possible. So when Oliva grasped my hand and asked me how I felt I replied: 'Not too bad.'"

Oliva glanced at the butcher's basket. Then he took a few steps to the end of the bed. Elzire watched him stare into the basket. She could not guess his feelings. He looked sheepish, embarrassed, bewildered.

"What do you think of . . . of . . ." Elzire stammered. She could not bring herself to say *our five babies*. It still seemed too much. ". . . of them?" she finished.

Oliva did not take his eyes from the basket. "I don't know what to think, Elzire," he answered slowly, "for the unheard of has just happened to us, hasn't it? But I do know that I never could have imagined any babies so small. Aren't they the tiniest things to be alive and breathing?"

"They're still alive and breathing, all five of them?"

"Yes," Oliva answered, "I'm watching them breathe."

It was a miracle, she decided. A miracle from on high. That was the only way Elzire could explain it to herself. But already Elzire knew better than to expect anyone else to see it the same way.

"What will people say when they find out about this?" she wondered aloud. Only animals gave birth in such numbers. "They will say we are pigs."

CHAPTER 2

Canadian Woman Gives Birth to Five Girls; All Are Doing Well

DOTHAN EAGLE, MONDAY, MAY 28, 1934

News of the extraordinary birth began to spread the moment Dr. Dafoe stepped from the Dionnes' porch. When he spotted Oliva's brother, Leon Dionne, driving up to the barnyard to collect a load of manure for his garden, Dafoe did not miss the opportunity to inform Leon he'd just become an uncle again, five times over. To Leon Dionne it seemed "either a mighty joke on Oliva, or else the worst kind of hard luck."

Dr. Dafoe was not nearly done reveling in the astonishment. Down at the post office in Callander, he teased the postmistress, "Saw something this morning you never saw."

She was used to his jokes and stories. "You're always seeing things I've never seen, Doctor," she scoffed.

"No, I mean something real. I've just seen five babies."

"Goodness me! Did you have five cases last night?"

"No, I m-m-mean five babies from one mother," Dafoe boasted, finally taking her by surprise.

"Say, that's something!" she exclaimed.

(Some bystanders that morning claimed to remember hearing him call the Dionne babies "five little French frogs." It was an insult—*frog* was, and still is, a derogatory term for a French person—and one the Dionne family would not forgive.)

In the sort of happenstance that occurs only in the smallest of towns,

Dafoe also crossed paths with the babies' grandfather Olivier Dionne as he left the post office. "Did you know you are the grandfather of five new babies?" the doctor asked.

The old French Canadian was as thunderstruck as anyone else. The number was preposterous, the date too soon. "What do you mean—five baby?"

"Why, Oliva's wife has just had five little girls. They're all still living— but I don't think they can m-m-make it."

"Mon Dieu!" Grandpa Dionne cried. *My God!* "What will my poor son do?"

Dafoe told a store clerk, too, who thought the doctor ought to call the newspapers. There Dafoe drew the line. It wouldn't be quite pro- fessional, he decided. Businesslike again, he went home and made the world's tersest record of the birth in his journal: "Oliva Dionne—5F."

But it turned out that Uncle Leon Dionne had already snatched up the chance to tantalize the papers with his family's remarkable news when he rang up Eddie Bunyan, editor of the nearest paper, the *North Bay Nugget.*

"How much would it cost to run a birth notice in the paper announc- ing the birth of five babies at one time?" he asked. Would it be more than the usual fee for just one?

"You're kidding me, aren't you, Leon?" Bunyan asked.

The question sounded like a joke, but the news itself, Bunyan soon discovered, was absolutely authentic. Bunyan got the details, assured Uncle Leon that there would be no charge at all, and whipped off a dis- patch on the Canadian Wire Service:

> *North Bay, May 28th:*—Mrs. Oliva Dionne, residing
> within a few miles of Callander, nine miles south of
> here, gave birth to five girls today. All were healthy,
> said Dr. A. R. Dafoe, Callander attending physician.

Mrs. Dionne is 24 and had previously given birth to
six children.

The story continued to whirl just as quickly through Callander,
spreading by word of mouth. One four-year-old boy came running home
from school to beg his mother to get him one of the Dionnes' babies.
There were so many, he was afraid they might be drowned, the way folks
sometimes drowned kittens when there were too many to feed. Yvette
Boyce, a schoolgirl at the time, heard the news from a friend who lived
near the Dionnes. "We couldn't believe it. Five babies—one mother?
So away we went." The two girls trudged a mile to peep at the babies
through the back window. "It was fabulous!"

By midmorning, a reporter and a photographer from the *Nugget* had
arrived at the Dionne farmhouse. Auntie Legros let the two *Nugget* men
inside and, in disregard of Dr. Dafoe's advice to avoid unnecessary handling, allowed them to arrange the five newborns on the bed beside
Elzire for a photo. They were barely six hours old. Dafoe's injections
and a visit from her priest had apparently done Elzire a world of good;
the newsmen could hardly tell she'd been on the verge of death only a
few hours before. As the camera flashed, she laughed and joked with the
midwives. Mindful of the physical ordeal she had just endured and limited by their own lack of French, the visitors troubled Elzire no further.

With Oliva, they were not as sympathetic. The reporters met him
just as he walked in from the morning chores. Oliva, who could only
have been surprised to find two strangers emerging from his bedroom,
obliged them at first. They wanted to know the babies' weights, so he
found an old potato scale and helped measure his new daughters, again
overriding Dr. Dafoe's recommendation to "leave 'em alone." The biggest registered 3 pounds, 4 ounces; the smallest, a pound less. Together
the five little girls totaled 13 pounds, 6 ounces.

"Well, do you feel proud of yourself?" the *Nugget* reporter wanted to know. Something about the question, or perhaps the way the man asked it, touched a nerve. It struck Oliva as just the kind of insult Elzire had feared—as though the reporter were implying there was something dirty or shameful in having more than one child at a time.

"The way you talk, people would think I ought to be put in jail," he retorted. At least, that is what Oliva Dionne forever insisted he'd said. What the *Nugget* printed was "I'm the kind of fellow they should put in jail," introducing him to the entire world as though he were indeed ashamed of himself. The offense Oliva took from that single question and answer would taint his dealings with the media for the rest of his life.

The photo the *Nugget* snapped of Oliva that morning was only a little more flattering. He sat, brow furrowed and gaze fixed dazedly ahead, with Pauline in his lap, holding Daniel by the arm. Ernest, Thérèse, and Rose-Marie looked warily over his shoulder at the camera. "He had not slept all night and had not thought to shave," his children remembered. "His thick, dark hair was uncombed, his eyes were tense, his lean face was gray with fatigue and concern."

That was the world's first glimpse of Papa Dionne, as he came to be called in the papers: a small, disheveled man on the verge of hysteria. The very idea that this thin, nervous young farmer had it in him to father five children all at once struck the public as though it were a joke. As with most first impressions, it would prove difficult to shake.

Unbeknownst to anyone at the Dionne farm, the five newborns were still very much on Dr. Dafoe's mind. He had told everyone that they could not possibly live, yet almost immediately he began taking steps to assure that they might at least have a fighting chance to survive. By nine-thirty that first morning he was at the Red Cross outpost in Bonfield, ten miles south of Callander. If those babies were going to make it, they needed a nurse—ideally one who spoke both French and English fluently. French-speakers were very much in the minority in Ontario, but as luck would have it, Dafoe knew a newly graduated bilingual nurse personally. Before the day was out, the Red Cross had enlisted twenty-one-year-old Yvonne Leroux. The daughter of Callander's only taxi driver, Nurse Leroux had grown up just two doors down from Dr. Dafoe.

"I'm so tired I could drop," she'd jotted in her daybook at three o'clock that afternoon at the hospital in North Bay. "Two septic and two lung cases." Then, added at the bottom of the page: "Out to country on case—wonder what it is."

At five o'clock, Nurse Leroux arrived at the Callander bus station. Dr. Dafoe explained the case as he drove her up the road to the Dionne farm. "Dr says Quintuplets—I had never dreamed of such a word," she marveled to her diary.

"Do whatever you can," Dafoe advised her; "keep them warm and keep them quiet. Feed them sterilized water drop by drop from an eye-dropper. Try to keep them alive. Do your best and I'll be with you as much as I can."

"To this day I don't recall a thing about the drive to the Dionne farm. I must have been in a daze," Nurse Leroux wrote later. "I will never forget the picture that met my eyes in that farmhouse—five incredibly tiny creatures in a butcher's basket, covered with a white blanket that smelled of moth balls." They had no names yet, only the labels A, B, C, D, and E on their diapers, wrappings, and the pads of cotton batting they slept upon.

The conditions were daunting, supplies almost nonexistent. No telephone, water, heat, or electricity. More than once, Nurse Leroux made note of the dingy farmhouse—"no decent dishes, no screens, doors, or cleanliness"—perhaps unaware that Elzire Dionne had been too gravely unwell for the past two weeks to keep up with her chores. A scrawled daybook entry from Nurse Leroux's first twenty-four hours on the Dionne case gives a sense of the overwhelming task before her:

What have I here—
Quintuplets (and a mother)—

premature—7 mon
Rickety—
Hungry—about 3 drops fill them to the top—
Mosquitos—dirt—flies—and neighbors—
Nothing except above
oh-oh

Yvonne Leroux sat up all night long, feeding, warming, and reminding the babies to breathe. They were acutely sensitive to temperature. Too cold and they went blue around the nostrils, their breaths speeding to a fearful rate, while too much heat made them flush and struggle for air. Nurse Leroux had brought her own hot-water bottle, which had to be rotated among the five babies and constantly refilled from a pot on the wood stove. "The largest seems to have difficulty holding her own—was anxious several times—turns blue," she recorded. "The littlest one seems all right. She breathes, looks good, and seems satisfied to just live. 2nd largest holds her own splendidly, two next were very hungry—cried more than others." Their voices were so small and weak, Nurse Leroux could hardly distinguish between the babies' cries and the whine of the mosquitoes circling her legs.

CHAPTER 3

Country Doctor Struggles to Save Lives of Canadian Mother and Quintuplet Girls

PITTSBURGH PRESS, TUESDAY, MAY 29, 1934

Dr. Dafoe's telephone woke him at 5:30 a.m. Considering that it was his fifty-first birthday, he might have indulged himself and rolled over, but he did not. He had given instructions to be notified if "one or two" of the Dionne babies died.

Instead, it was long-distance—Chicago. Harry Reutlinger, assistant city editor of the *Chicago American* newspaper, was on the line with a torrent of questions: Were the babies still alive? What chances did they have of surviving? How was the mother? And the father?

The moment that conversation ended, another ring rattled the telephone. Now it was the *New York Journal* with the same barrage of questions. Dafoe had just gotten back to bed when the phone rang once more. Chicago again, a Dr. Bundesen this time, wanting to know if the babies were alive. When Dafoe answered yes, as far as he knew the babies were still living, Bundesen said he didn't believe it. Dafoe's temper sparked. He told Bundesen he could go to hell and hung up.

Dr. Dafoe didn't make it up the stairs before the ringing started all over. Bundesen had called back. This time he introduced himself properly: Dr. Herman N. Bundesen, commissioner of the Board of Health of Chicago, expert in premature babies. How could he help with "these marvelous Quintuplets"? What did Dafoe need?

Need? Dafoe said he needed everything. "There was nothing in the house to work with—except babies."

For the next thirty minutes, Dr. Dafoe stood barefoot in his nightshirt while Bundesen told him what the Dionne babies would require to survive. Breast milk, for starters. Dafoe informed him that Elzire Dionne had never been able to nurse her children for more than a few days; even if she had, she hardly stood a chance of nourishing five babies single-handedly. The health commissioner cleared that hurdle instantly—if Dafoe couldn't get any mother's milk, Bundesen would have some flown in.

The other critical factor, Bundesen counseled, was warmth. The temperature in that house must not drop below 85 degrees. What they needed was an incubator. Dafoe agreed, but the problem was bigger than simply shipping one in. An incubator wasn't any good without electricity, and the Dionne farm was two miles from the nearest electrical current.

Dr. Bundesen had no immediate solution to that quandary. Maybe, he suggested, they could make do with hot-water bottles. "And good luck, and God bless 'em all," he said.

Nurse Leroux met Dr. Dafoe at the door when he arrived at the Dionne farm a little after seven that morning.

"How they doin'?" Dafoe asked. The young woman was "hollow-eyed and worn from her long night's vigil, but there was a look of triumph on her face."

"They're still alive," she said. "I thought some of them wouldn't make it—but they have." The news defied every bit of medical history Dafoe knew.

The doctor went into the bedroom and peeked under the wool blanket covering the basket-crib. All of them were breathing, just as Yvonne Leroux had promised. "Bien, très bien," he said to Elzire. *Good. Very good.* It was almost all the French he knew.

Elzire spoke rapidly to him. Nurse Leroux translated. Would they live? Would they be all right? Wasn't it a miracle of the Blessed Virgin herself?

Dafoe didn't promise much as he examined her. For Elzire he ordered nothing more than rest, and plenty of it. As for the babies, if they were going to insist on living, it was time to give them something to eat. They could not be made to wait for Dr. Bundesen's promised breast milk. Dafoe improvised a formula of seven ounces of cow's milk, twenty ounces of sterilized water, and two spoonfuls of corn syrup. His instructions to Nurse Leroux consisted mostly of his specialty: common sense. "Give them this from the eyedropper every two hours. Keep the babies warm at all costs." They were not to be handled more than once a day, and must be left in a position so they could breathe easily.

What about the sinking spells, Nurse Leroux wanted to know, when they seemed to forget to breathe? Dafoe didn't have a ready answer, but he wasn't stumped for long. Rum was the thing, he decided—one or two drops mixed with ten drops of water. Whenever one of the little mites turned blue around the mouth and nose, he ordered, give her a drop or two of this "cocktail."

Feeding them proved a tedious, painstaking process. Their mouths were too tiny and weak to suck from anything bigger than an eyedropper. Swallowing seemed to exhaust them. Two droppersful constituted a meal, but squeezing out more than a droplet at a time risked smothering them. By the time the fifth baby had finished her ration, the first was mewling for her turn again.

And then of course they must be changed and bathed. "Well, these tiny little bits of humanity must be cleaned," Nurse Leroux mused. "Kitchen stove best place, I guess. Paraphernalia: a saucer of olive oil, some soft rags, larger pieces of the cleanest and warmest cloths I can find, boracic acid, and a prayer."

Nurse Leroux shooed everyone from the kitchen and placed the basket full of newborns in front of the open oven door. The temperature in the room, she guessed, was 100 degrees. Balancing each baby on her knee, she daubed their nearly transparent skin with warm olive oil rather than soap. "Babes fought against the exposure—wouldn't be surprised if they did live," she wrote that night.

From the beginning, Nurse Leroux was adamant that the little girls possessed the mettle to survive in spite of their almost terrifying appearance. One early observer called them "scrawny, spider-legged, horrible, yellow, pot-bellied specks of half-humanity." Dr. Dafoe was more succinct. Asked what the newborns looked like, he replied, "Like rats."

No one except Yvonne Leroux expected the babies to live, but Oliva Dionne could think of nothing else during those first stupefying hours. If they did make it, how would he support ten children, feed them, clothe them? You did not have to be a doctor to see that these newest five were going to need a great deal of costly medical care. He had been getting by without government relief payments, but just barely. And there was still $3,000 to pay off on the farm. All Oliva could do was pray for guidance.

The babies were just over twenty-four hours old when a potential answer to those prayers arrived. "Green the Greek," a Callander shopkeeper, pulled up to the Dionne farm in Georges Leroux's taxicab at around eleven o'clock on the morning of May 29. A long-distance telephone call had come to his store for Oliva, Green explained, all the way from Chicago. Oliva listened as Green relayed a bewildering message; then he went inside to speak to his wife.

"Green's come out here from Callander with a message from a Chicago promoter by the name of Spear," Oliva began. According to Green the Greek, Ivan Spear had proposed that Oliva bring their quintuplets to Chicago, to display them at the World's Fair, seven hundred miles away. In exchange for letting the public view the babies, Spear was promising fabulous sums of money, as well as expert medical care.

Elzire shuddered at the idea. Yet she realized the bind Oliva was in.

He was "frantic with worry," she could see. "The thought of exhibiting the babies was abhorrent to Oliva. On the other hand, the realization that he was unable to give them the expensive care we both knew they would require was maddening."

Oliva Dionne got into his car and followed Green the Greek down to Callander to hear for himself what Spear had to say.

Oliva was still in town when the first newsreel cameramen found their way to the Dionne farm. Crews from two different companies arrived almost simultaneously—one by way of Michigan, the other from Montreal. Ross Beesley of Associated Screen News was among them.

"We knocked on the door but Miss Leroux, the nurse, told us that Mr. Dionne wasn't at home," he remembered. "So we sorta stood around in the front yard and then this car drove up and it was Dr. Dafoe—roly-poly little fella—and he said, 'Oh, you want to see the children? Come on in.' And there were the five little rascals crosswise in a basket." Dafoe was just telling the cameramen he didn't expect the babies to last until the next day when the door flew open.

It was Oliva, back from Father Routhier's house, where he'd gone to seek his priest's advice about the Chicago proposal. "He says, 'Get out, Get out, Get out!'" Beesley recalled. "And he started bawling out Dr. Dafoe for letting us in. So we got out."

Oliva panicked and bolted from the farmhouse. The eager newsreel crews all piled into one car and followed him back to town, setting up their tripods on Routhier's lawn. "We thought we had him nailed down for sure," Beesley said.

"Will you fellas please go away and leave Mr. Dionne alone?" Father Routhier implored. The men wouldn't budge. It was a public street, they retorted.

The standoff lasted another thirty minutes while the cameramen watched Oliva through a window, tripods at the ready. Finally, Oliva made a dash for his car. "He couldn't get the car started—looked very excited, and we were cranking away by the side door there when he finally backed away," Beesley said of his triumphant moment.

When Beesley's footage played in theaters, it was edited to fool moviegoers into believing that the close-up of Oliva's startled face had been captured just after his five daughters were born. *When Mr. Dionne heard the news,* the movie said, *this was his reaction.*

It would not be the first, nor the last, joke at Oliva Dionne's expense.

The newsreels were not the only ones scrambling to get in on the story from Callander. When Charlie Blake of the *Chicago American* walked into his editor's office around ten o'clock that same morning, his boss told him, "Dig up an old-fashioned baby incubator somewhere, Charlie. It's for those five kids up in Ontario, and it's got to be run by something besides electricity."

The assignment wasn't exactly Charlie Blake's style. Word was that he had dined with Chicago's most notorious criminal, Al Capone, and carried a wallet pulled from the corpse of a gangster. Nevertheless, Blake realized that those Canadian babies had the potential to shape up into a human-interest story the likes of which had never been told before. As long as all five survived, that is. If even one of them gave out, there would be no quintuplet story, and without an incubator it was almost certain that the smallest of the quintet didn't have a chance. Searches for an old-fashioned incubator in New York, Detroit, Montreal, and Toronto had already come up dry, and the last train to Canada left at seven p.m.

Charlie Blake dove in headlong. He called the World's Fair. Plenty of incubators there, but all electric. He called hospitals. Nothing. He called the health commissioner, Dr. Bundesen, who "gave him all the leads he could think of." Blake hung up and started dialing medical supply houses. "Sure you haven't got one tucked away in the back end of a storeroom or attic?" he asked the skeptical president at Sharp & Smith. The fellow didn't think so but promised to look anyway, and told Blake to call back. Blake continued working his way down his list until nearly five o'clock, then dialed Sharp & Smith again. Jackpot. It was full of dust and cobwebs, but the Sharp & Smith man had come across "an old-timer" shoved into a far corner. It was an 1895 model.

"Get it downstairs and clean it up as soon as you can," Blake told him. "I'll be over in ten minutes for it."

By seven that night, Charlie Blake and his incubator were on the train to Toronto.

CHAPTER 4

Progress of Quintuplets Amazes Medical World

Toronto Globe, Wednesday, May 30, 1934

Nurse Leroux was exhausted, but like the babies themselves, she was holding her own. Her forty-eight-hour vigil over the butcher basket had taught her to look for "the telltale white lines along the nose" that signaled a sinking spell. Before the tiny face turned blue, she was fighting back with rum and hot-water bottles.

She had more than one to wield now. A basket had arrived from the Women's Institute of Callander, filled with flannelette, diapers, absorbent cotton, and more hot-water bottles. With the absorbent cotton, Nurse Leroux fashioned little sleeveless, buttonless "Red Riding Hood dresses" for the babies to wear.

Two days old, and they'd still had almost no proper food. Every two hours, like clockwork, Nurse Leroux squeezed a few drops of Dr. Dafoe's corn syrup concoction into their wide-open birdlike mouths. The three smallest, she noted, had to be "coaxed along." "Very thin," she wrote. Late the previous afternoon, the Red Cross nurse from Bonfield had brought two precious ounces of mother's milk to the Dionne farm. Her patients had donated all they could spare. A grateful Nurse Leroux divided it among the three smallest babies. Yesterday they'd been known only as C, D, and E. Now, though, all five had names. From biggest to smallest they were Yvonne, Annette, Cécile, Émilie, and Marie. All were named after nuns the family was fond of, except Marie. Fearing for her survival most of all, Elzire had dedicated her tiniest daughter to the Blessed Mother.

The Dionnes' house was beginning to bulge at its seams. Ernest, Rose-Marie, Thérèse, Daniel, and Pauline were often underfoot, since they had been forbidden to play in the yard for fear of kicking up dust that would harm their fragile sisters. Oliva's sister Alma had come to lend a hand with the housekeeping. Aunt Laurence Clusiaux cooked and did laundry. One uncle, Leon Demers, chopped wood all day long, while another, Lias Legros, "efficiently, punctually, and quietly" hauled load after load into the house to keep the big stove fueled day and night.

That stove was vital to the babies' survival. Not only was it the sole source of heat in the house, but water also had to be kept boiling all day long, to sterilize the eyedropper, sanitize diapers—dozens upon dozens of diapers—and keep the hot-water bottles up to temperature. The stove was also a hazard. The night before, it had overheated the plaster ceiling, nearly causing a fire. But the babies could not make do with less heat, any more than they could stretch the meager ration of mother's milk.

Warmth and food. That was what Yvonne, Annette, Cécile, Émilie, and Marie needed most for a chance to survive. If they could only hold out for the incubator and breast milk from Chicago, they might continue to defy the incredible odds against them. Marie in particular desperately needed that incubator. Simply keeping warm was a bigger task than her two-pound body could manage. "Well, will just have to keep up," Nurse Leroux told her diary.

At the train station in Toronto, Charlie Blake was hung up in the Canadian customs office. His incubator, a hulking old thing three feet long and two feet high, had the customs officers flummoxed. Should they allow such a contraption into the country? How much duty should they charge? Every minute they hemmed and hawed put Marie Dionne's life at greater risk. Finally, they agreed to let Blake pass with a duty payment of $3.75. Blake rented a car, strapped the incubator to the trunk, and sped north. He still had two hundred miles to go.

Every hour his daughters survived, the more urgently Oliva considered the Chicago proposal. Help was rushing in by plane and by train, by car and by mail, with no indication of how long it would last, or what it might cost. Dr. Dafoe was coming two and three times a day. Nurse Leroux had been on duty close to forty-eight hours straight. Where was the money going to come from? No one but Ivan Spear had suggested a viable solution. The Chicago deal promised everything the babies would need—expert nurses, modern equipment—and all of it paid for with cash to spare.

Still, Oliva hesitated to jump at Spear's offer. He was a man who preferred to "turn any question over and over in his mind, searching for flaws, avoiding hasty decisions like the plague." He was also acutely aware of being watched. Callander was a small town, and everyone knew Oliva Dionne was mulling over the prospect of tens of thousands of dollars. "As long as he lived, Oliva Dionne would remember that experience," a friend wrote later. "The looks on those people's faces, staring at him as though he were a circus freak. He felt like a man in a fog, all mixed up, and the more he thought about his responsibilities, the more mixed up he became."

A decision this momentous could not be made alone. Oliva had already consulted Father Routhier, who had agreed to act as his business manager should Oliva decide to meet with Spear. In addition, Oliva sought Dr. Dafoe's opinion.

Dafoe's exact words have not been preserved. Nor is it known whether he said them to Father Routhier or to Oliva Dionne himself. In typical Dafoe style, the essence of his response went straight to the point: *Make what you can, while you can.* A complete set of quintuplets had never survived more than four days. In 1866, a single quintuplet in Portugal had managed to live for a record fifty days, but that was it. If Oliva meant to accept the Chicago offer, he had no time to lose.

Oliva summoned Nurse Leroux's father, Georges. Together with Father Routhier and Green the Greek, Oliva Dionne climbed into Georges Leroux's taxi and headed toward Orillia, 130 miles to the south, to meet Ivan Spear's plane.

The eyes of the continent were beginning to turn toward Corbeil as minute by minute, Yvonne, Annette, Cécile, Émilie, and Marie defied five centuries of medical history simply by continuing to breathe. That Wednesday morning of May 30, they were front-page news in Toronto, Ottawa, and Winnipeg. *Country Doctor Battling to Keep Quintuplets Alive,* said the headlines. *Progress of Quintuplets Amazes Medical World.* Readers in Pittsburgh, New York, Detroit, and Chicago memorized their names and weights, panting for the next update.

Dr. Dafoe, just by being willing to speak with the press, was quickly becoming the centerpiece of the newspaper stories. Bruised by his initial encounters with the media, Oliva Dionne was more guarded, often coming off as brusque and defensive. As one article put it decades later, "no one could have been more poorly designed by nature . . . to become a superstar." Dafoe was his opposite in every way. Congenial, accommodating, and unassuming, the doctor had rarely refused a chance to show off the basketful of babies to reporters and photographers as though he were the proud father. Already Dafoe had instinctively, or perhaps even accidentally, grasped the power of publicity and harnessed it for the babies' benefit. Treating the reporters like pals and feeding them any little tidbit on the newborns' progress kindled the public's interest, which in turn motivated the press to lend a hand in Yvonne, Annette, Cécile, Émilie, and Marie's struggle for survival. After all, the longer those five babies lived, the more newspapers would sell.

◆ ◆ ◆

At three o'clock in the afternoon that same Wednesday, a car with "a funny-looking box strapped on behind" pulled up to Dr. Dafoe's curb.

"My name's Charlie Blake," the driver told Dafoe. "I'm from the *Chicago American*. Am I too late with my incubator?"

"You're just on time," Dafoe said. "Let's go right out to the house. Guess you'd like to see the babies?"

At the Dionnes', things were already looking a little brighter. Dr. Bundesen's shipment of breast milk had arrived on the morning train, packed in dry ice. It was frozen, but Nurse Leroux thawed and sterilized it, and for the first time in their short lives, all five babies enjoyed a full meal of human milk.

Nurse Leroux pounced on the incubator. Within minutes, she had scrubbed it out and lined the inner compartment with gauze and cotton. That compartment was something like a boat. Its walls and bottom were hollow, so that hot water poured in at the top filled the reservoir underneath, then gradually rose up the walls, surrounding the occupant with heat from all sides without using a spark of electricity or a drop of kerosene. It was built for just one infant, but the Dionne sisters were so tiny, the Chicago incubator could hold the three smallest if they were laid crosswise.

"Those babies don't know what they owe you," Dr. Dafoe told Charlie Blake as Nurse Leroux transferred Marie to the soft, clean nest and then added Émilie and Cécile for good measure.

From that moment, the lives of the Dionne Quintuplets were inextricably bound with the press, for Charlie Blake and the *Chicago American* had almost certainly just saved Marie Dionne's life.

CHAPTER 5

Star Sends Assistance to Mother and Five Babes

Toronto Star, Thursday, May 31, 1934

The *Toronto Star* could hardly stand the thought of a Chicago paper becoming the Dionnes' hero. The *Star*, as a matter of fact, was rarely content to simply cover the news if there was the slightest chance that the paper itself could play a role in the story. So the *Star* called up Dr. Dafoe's kid brother, Dr. William Dafoe—a skilled Toronto doctor who just happened to specialize in delivering babies—to find out what kinds of supplies the Dionnes might need. Dr. Will gave the newspaper a list as long as his arm: everything from soap and safety pins to bunny blankets and a bathtub. To this bounty, the *Star* added a tissue-wrapped basket of delicacies assembled "with particular thought to what might be tempting to the young mother's appetite." Bramble jelly, strawberries, cantaloupe, tomatoes, celery, biscuits, sponge cake, and cream cheese, topped off with a box of candy for "the other little Dionnes." Reporter Keith Munro and photographer Fred Davis were assigned to ferry the carload of gifts to Callander. Accompanying them was "a pretty little nurse with fair hair and soft capable hands" named Jean Blewett.

Two hundred miles later they arrived at Dr. Dafoe's doorstep and were welcomed inside by the Little Doc himself, who was "pathetically grateful" for the mountain of supplies. "He was dressed in baggy pants innocent of crease, and a sweater coat," Keith Munro remembered. "He had a pipe in his mouth. I've often thought that he must have been born with a pipe in his mouth." They talked well into the night, there in Dafoe's book-lined study, and got the whole story of the birth straight from the doctor's mouth. "The Little Doc was a newspaperman's dream," Munro marveled. "He just told you everything and relied on your sense of decency not to let him down. I don't think we ever did."

Keith Munro and Fred Davis were up at four o'clock Thursday morning, May 31, and on their way to the Dionne farm, eager to see the quintuplets while there were still five of them to see. The night before, Dr. Dafoe had told them, "I don't see how they can live, but they're living." Little Marie in particular still had him worried.

"Our first impression of the place was of lines and lines of diapers hung out to dry," Munro remembered. "The diapers almost obscured the tiny, unpainted clapboard house where the Dionne family had lived for a couple of generations."

He and Davis spoke to Nurse Leroux and loitered outside the house. Just as Dafoe had predicted, Marie had almost not made it to first light. Only the rum, it seemed, had compelled her miniature heart to keep beating. The men waited and schemed, desperate to get their camera into that house long enough to snap a photo. They watched with envy as Dafoe arrived and went in. In a few minutes, he was back out. Before Munro and Davis had mustered the nerve to ask, the Little Doc said, "Do you want to see the babies?"

"We piled into the house and got one of the big thrills of a lifetime," Munro remembered. Nurse Leroux lifted the lid of the incubator as though it were a box of cigars. "She rolled back the white coverlet and there, blissfully asleep, were three babes. In a big basket to their left were the other two."

"There was something terribly exciting about those babies that made thrills run up and down my spine," Keith Munro said of his first glimpse of Yvonne, Annette, Cécile, Émilie, and Marie. "I can't explain it." He wasn't the only one. Charlie Blake dubbed the phenomenon "the Quin-tuplet Disease."

With Dafoe's and Elzire's permission, Fred Davis set up his camera and began snapping away. "It was like taking nature pictures," he said. "Birds in a nest. Little skinny red nestlings." And then something happened that would frighten Fred Davis every time he thought of it for the rest of his life.

A flashbulb exploded.

"Shattered glass flew all around the little room," said Munro. "It seemed to me that a whole shower descended right on the basket with the tiny heads."

The *Star* men were mortified at the thought that Marie might have died from the shock. But Elzire and the staff took the incident in stride, staggering Munro with their kindness. "The doctor even made some little joke about it," he remembered. Fortunately, the bedroom was so small that Davis had set his tripod just outside the doorway; none of the shards actually fell in range of Elzire and the babies.

The *Star*'s story included interviews with Elzire, Dafoe, and, as an uncommon bonus, the two midwives. It would be one of the few times Dafoe gave Auntie Legros and Madame Lebel full credit for their critical role in the delivery.

"Didn't you get the shock of your life when all this happened?" the *Star* asked Dafoe.

"Shock? No, I was too busy."

"And you had no help?"

"Certainly; excellent help; Mrs. Lebelle [sic] and Mrs. Legros."

"But no other medical help?"

"What do I want other medical help for? Things went along pretty good, didn't they?" That was Dafoe's style—to make light of things if they turned out right.

Madame Lebel was more forthright. "I'd rather have a baby myself than go through that again," she declared. Auntie Legros agreed. "I think it was the worst experience of my life," she told the *Star.*

"What did you think when Mrs. Lebelle [sic] handed you a second baby, and then a third?"

"I didn't think. I was too busy to think anything but that I must get those babies to breathe. You see, we were all alone. The doctor hadn't come yet. . . . I am not very strong, but I seemed to get strength from somewhere that night."

The *Star*'s in-depth article was one of the first to let the public truly savor the story's drama: the miraculous birth, the wonder of seeing the babies themselves, all told firsthand. The appetite it whetted would prove to be bottomless.

CHAPTER 6

Quintuplets May Go on Exhibit at Chicago Fair

FRESNO BEE, THURSDAY, MAY 31, 1934

One hundred thirty miles to the south, in Orillia, Oliva Dionne had come face to face with the man from Chicago who had promised him so much. Ivan Spear was the very image of a promoter from the big city—"very colorful, very adept, very resourceful, with piercing eyes and a quick smile." Tight suit, slick wavy hair, and a pencil-thin mustache. With him were two other men: Spear's business partner, Ted Kopelman, and their lawyer, Luis Kutner.

The terms of the contract they presented to Oliva were every bit as fantastic as Spear had offered on the telephone. In exchange for exclusive rights to install Oliva's five daughters in the fair's Life Exhibit, Spear was prepared to make the Dionnes' financial worries evaporate. The contract promised to take up the responsibility for Yvonne, Annette, Cécile, Émilie, and Marie's medical expenses immediately, before they ever left Canada—up to $100 per week for as many as six weeks. Spear would also arrange for the babies' medical care en route to the United States, as well as on the return trip. Upon their arrival in Chicago, the girls would reside in a "luxurious private ward," staffed by experts, furnished with the most modern equipment available, and outfitted with windows similar to a hospital nursery, so spectators could admire the children without disturbing them or interfering with the doctors and nurses. Kutner went so far as to pledge to recruit Chicago's commissioner of health, none other than Dr. Herman Bundesen, to oversee the babies' care. Housing, meals, transportation, and more would be provided for the entire family for the duration of the Dionnes' six-month stay at the fair, and Elzire Dionne would have the right to approve the conditions under which her babies would be exhibited.

Spear and his team had anticipated and addressed a parent's every tangible concern. All that remained was the moral hurdle: exploitation. Was it right or wrong for a father to exhibit his daughters in a glorified sideshow attraction for the sake of their health and financial welfare?

"Ivan had a cheque made out," Kutner remembered, "and he did a very good thing psychologically. He gave the cheque to Dionne to hold while we drafted the agreement." The $100 check—worth over $1,400 in US currency today—was the equivalent of more than a month's wages for Oliva, yet it represented only a fraction of the riches Spear dangled before him. As an advance against ticket sales, Oliva would be entitled to receive $250 a week for every week he and his family lived in Chicago—$250 above and beyond their living and medical expenses, to tuck away in the bank or spend as he pleased. That meant $1,000 a month, guaranteed, with the promise of much, much more when they divided up the profits in December, just for letting people peer through a pane of glass at his five baby girls.

If Oliva harbored any revulsion about putting his daughters on display, the practical benefits quickly began to obscure the psychological drawbacks. Before signing, however, Oliva insisted that a clause protecting his babies' health be included in the contract. The promoters readily agreed. The third paragraph of the agreement stated that the Dionne family would not be expected in Chicago until "the physicians in charge of the quintuplets decide that they can be moved without possibility of injurious effect."

One task remained: negotiating how to divvy up the profits from ticket sales. The promoters offered 10 percent to Father Routhier as business manager and 20 percent to Oliva. Luis Kutner remembered, "They were talking back and forth in rapid French and very meaningful overtones. Ivan Spear and Ted Kopelman and I looked at each other and thought we'd blown the whole deal. We thought, well, maybe we should've offered more."

They needn't have worried. Oliva and Father Routhier came to their own agreement between themselves: 23 percent for Oliva, and 7 percent for the priest.

Oliva Dionne signed.

Back home, the babies were losing weight. From 13 pounds, 6 ounces total they had dropped to 12 pounds—with their clothes on. Newborns often shed a few ounces in the first few days, but Yvonne, Annette, Cécile, and especially Émilie and Marie, had none to spare.

"Babes holding their own and that's all," wrote Nurse Leroux. "All kinds of blue spells."

The problem was more than a matter of getting enough food in. Not enough was coming out, either. The mixture of cow's milk and corn syrup that had undoubtedly kept the babies from starving for the first fifty-two hours of their lives was proving difficult for them to fully digest. Their diapers were wet, but that was it. On the surface, fewer soiled diapers was a mercy, for it meant less work. It also meant that waste was gradually building up in the babies' bodies. Their skin was turning yellowish, their movements languid. Dr. Dafoe ordered magnesia added to their formula, hoping it would loosen their sluggish intestines. "Praying every minute," Nurse Leroux wrote.

CHAPTER 7

Quintuplets' Father to Get $100 a Week While All Live

TORONTO STAR, FRIDAY, JUNE 1, 1934

Reporters. Cameras. Gawkers. By the time Oliva returned from Orillia on Friday, June 1, a full-fledged media circus had erupted outside the Dionne farmhouse.

"I don't know what this town did before the babies were born," a seventeen-year-old Callander girl told the *Pittsburgh Press*. "We must have been completely dead, because no one for miles around is talking, thinking or wondering about anything but the Dionne babies and whether or not they'll live."

Folks who a scant few days earlier had never heard the word *quintuplet* now fancied themselves worthy of becoming intimately acquainted with "the quints" or "the quins." It was "a constant fight," Dr. Dafoe remembered, to keep everyone from long-lost cousins to perfect strangers from swarming the place. "They simply could not be made to understand why they might not hold the wonderful quintuplets, examine them minutely, even kiss them!"

Yet reporters were still allowed in, and plenty of them. "Newshawks," the *Toronto Star* called them, from Chicago, New York, Cleveland, Pittsburgh, and Detroit. Some were downright deceitful, such as the two French-speaking nuns who were admitted to the house to pray for the babies, only to be exposed as reporters when Oliva caught them gloating in English about the trick they'd played.

An agent from Ripley's Believe It or Not! "Odditorium" was said to be courting the Dionnes in hopes of adding the five babies to its world-famous collection of human anomalies. A nightclub owner offered no less than $500 a week for the chance to display Mrs. Dionne and her daughters for twenty weeks.

Oliva could not even walk to his outhouse without being filmed by newsreel crews. "We wanted some more shots of Papa Dionne if we could," cameraman Ross Beesley said, "so we focused on the walk down to the privy; we figured this poor guy would have to go eventually to the outdoor biffy, but he never did."

"Our little world was topsy-turvy," Oliva said of that time, "and I knew not which way to turn for the quietness and seclusion I had been accustomed to."

Signing the Chicago contract had not relieved Oliva's worries. If anything, the scrutiny had intensified.

Ivan Spear had not wasted a moment to begin publicizing the quintuplets' impending appearance at the World's Fair. Before Oliva was back in Corbeil, Spear had broadcast the news of his spectacular contract, and by Friday morning the figures were in all the papers. Anyone in North America could see exactly how much Oliva Dionne stood to gain by exhibiting his daughters, and the numbers were dazzling. Every weapon of modern medicine would be at their disposal, too. But could the babies withstand the seven-hundred-mile trip?

"Father of Five Babies, Doctor Split over World's Fair Offer," the *Pittsburgh Press* announced, making it sound as though Papa Dionne and Dr. Dafoe were squaring up for a fight.

The truth is not so clear-cut. Early reports from the *North Bay Nugget* present a Dafoe unruffled by the Chicago deal. "Told of the contract Dionne has signed, Dr. Dafoe was glad to hear that the family would get some money," the *Nugget* reported. "Asked as to when the mites could be moved, Dr. Dafoe said, 'Their condition and progress govern the entire matter.'"

In the big-city papers, however, Dafoe came off as vehemently opposed to the Chicago scheme. The *Toronto Star* reported him calling the idea of moving the babies anywhere before they were six weeks old "preposterous." The Little Doc spoke only of their health, making no moral judgments about exhibiting Yvonne, Annette, Cécile, Émilie, and Marie.

"As long as I am boss, there will be no trip anywhere for those infants, the father can go if he wants to, but not the babies," one American paper quoted Dafoe. "Public opinion wouldn't stand for it," he told the *Chicago Tribune.* "As their doctor I have the absolute authority right now to prevent their removal." Such adamant refusals gave the impression that Dafoe and Dafoe alone was standing between the Dionnes' daughters and death at the hands of greedy showmen. No one bothered to acknowledge that the power Dafoe wielded had come at Oliva Dionne's insistence. Without the protective clause Oliva had demanded, Dafoe would have had no authority to blockade the babies' trip to Chicago. But with nothing but the doctor's blunt comments to go on, it became all too easy to assume that Oliva Dionne regarded his daughters as a cash crop.

Few papers appear to have sought out Oliva's side of the story. His emerging reputation for reluctance to speak to the press certainly did not encourage them to try. (*Father Silent About Plans to Show Babes,* an Iowa headline read.) One reporter, Helen Allyn of the *Pittsburgh Press,* told her readers that Oliva was "still in a daze over the sudden increase in his family. When he talks about his children he classifies them as the 'new' family and the 'old family.'"

"Who wouldn't be worried with ten children to feed?" Oliva was quoted. "They offered me $50,000, but the doctor says it may mean the death of a child. What am I to do? Whichever way I guess, it would be wrong."

Hardly twenty-four hours after signing, Oliva Dionne was ready to wash his hands of the whole affair. Not only was the attention unbearable, but the contract itself was losing its luster. With the babies unable to be moved, Oliva realized that responsibility for their medical expenses would fall right back into his lap in six weeks. If Ivan Spear got impatient, nothing in the contract prevented him from firing Dafoe and hiring doctors who might declare the babies fit to travel in spite of the enormous risk to their health. Even if Yvonne, Annette, Cécile, Émilie, and Marie all survived the move, what if no one bought tickets to the exhibit? The whole family could end up on the next train back to Ontario without a dime to show for it. Oliva telegrammed Ivan Spear that he wanted out.

Spear's response read, "Nothing doing. You are signed to a legal document."

Oliva returned Spear's $100 check and declared that since Elzire hadn't signed the contract, it wasn't legal. "I will never go to the Chicago fair," he told the *Toronto Star*. "I am a farmer and I will stay on the farm where I belong."

None of the hoopla over the Chicago deal would matter if even one of the babies did not survive, and as Friday, June 1, drew to a close, things were looking grim.

Nurse Leroux had pushed herself beyond the brink of exhaustion. Even with Nurse Cloutier there from the Red Cross post, she hardly dared sleep. Yvonne and Annette had improved, but Cécile, Émilie, and Marie were no better. The littlest two were failing fast. Their empty diapers and bloated bellies indicated they were being slowly poisoned by their own waste. Nurse Leroux had every reason to believe they were dying. When Dr. Dafoe arrived, he touched his fingertips to their foreheads and agreed. All Dafoe could think to do was to rinse their clogged bowels with warm water—an enema. For three premature newborns already at death's door, the risk seemed lethal. The dilemma was twofold: not only whether to do it, but *how*.

Dr. Dafoe did what he did best—he improvised. He combed through his bag until he found a tiny, two-inch glass syringe and a narrow length of rubber tubing. Nurse Cloutier watched with horrified fascination as he fitted the tube over the end of the needle and filled the syringe with a warm saltwater solution. The equipment was so small, "he might have been filling a fountain pen."

"Doctor, if you do that it will kill them," she warned.

"If I d-d-don't do it, they'll die."

One by one, Nurse Leroux laid Cécile, Émilie, and Marie across her knees so he could perform the simple procedure. Out came one yellowish-black pellet after another.

"I think they deserve a little rum for that," Dafoe said afterward, trying to make light of it.

"What a job," Nurse Leroux wrote in her daybook when it was all over. "I'm still scared."

As the babies rallied from their latest brush with death, "the faint dawn of something that had been in Dr. Dafoe's mind suddenly rose, hard and clear." Yvonne, Annette, Cécile, Émilie, and Marie were not necessarily doomed, Dafoe realized. Every time a chance to survive was extended to them, their matchstick fingers had grasped it. "Living had become a habit with them and they seemed to like it." The odds were still stacked heavily against those five babies, but if they had it in them not just to linger but to live, well then, it was time to stop showing them off and start guarding what precious little strength they had.

"At that moment the world's greatest 'no' man was born," reporter Keith Munro said.

The shift in the doctor's outlook was immediately apparent. "The next morning when we arrived at the Dionne home we were greeted by 'No Admittance' signs," Munro remembered. "Of course that couldn't mean us, we argued." They'd earned the right to go in, and Charlie

Blake, too, with the diapers and incubator. "But when we tried to get in the gate Grandfather Dionne appeared, pitchfork in hand, and sternly bade us scram."

The reporters wheedled, reminding him of the bushels of supplies they'd brought all the way from Toronto. Grandpa Dionne stood firm. Orders were orders, and his came straight from Dr. Dafoe.

When the doctor drove up, Munro and Davis thought for sure they'd be let in. They were pals, weren't they? They'd sat in the Little Doc's living room and shared a drink with him. The change in Dafoe was impossible for Munro to miss. "He looked us right in the eye and said quietly, 'These babies need quiet. I value their lives ahead of anything else in this world.' Then he walked away, leaving us all feeling cheap as hell."

Now Dafoe had only one thing to tell the reporters: "They are alive— that's about all I can say."

Dafoe's new approach had a galvanizing effect on the media. "What had merely been a mildly sensational story," Fred Davis recalled, with the reporters half expecting the story to die with one of the babies, "suddenly became a world story, a riot, a mass attack with tanks, bribery and corruption and conspiracy, with a little country doctor on one side of a door, and the newspapers of the world on the outside, hammering, keyholing, shoving things through the crack of the door. Love, money, highsigns, oratory, whispering campaigns, nothing would open that door."

CHAPTER 8

Home Turned into Hospital

New York Times, June 3, 1934

In the space of five days, life as the Dionnes knew it had become barely recognizable. "The first week," Dr. Dafoe said, "was a nightmare, with the frequent alarms and innumerable trips."

Five-year-old Thérèse Dionne had developed bronchitis and so was sent to Auntie Legros's house to shield her fragile baby sisters from infection. To Elzire's dismay, the little girl left in tears, treated "like an orphan," she thought, at the hands of Dr. Dafoe. Soon Ernest, Rose-Marie, Daniel, and Pauline would all follow as the sickness spread through their upstairs quarters.

Downstairs, they were still battling to keep the bedroom warm at night, mostly for the sake of Yvonne and Annette, who were getting by with hot-water bottles pinned to the sides of the butcher basket. Auntie Legros had sent her coal stove over to be set up in the living room and the flue had promptly caught fire, hardly five feet from Elzire and the babies.

Nurse Leroux was diligent and dedicated but inexperienced. She was also worn-out, both from constantly tending a quintet of newborns and from persuading Elzire, who saw no reason to stay in bed any longer than she had after her previous births, not to get up.

The entire situation had turned into "a task for a giant." One name, and one name only, came to Dr. Dafoe's mind: Louise de Kiriline.

According to the people of Corbeil, "never was there a woman up here like Madame de Kiriline." Descended from Swedish aristocracy, Louise de Kiriline had danced in royal ballrooms and nursed wounded soldiers in Russian prison camps. She spoke half a dozen languages, including French, and was equally adept at driving a dogsled and removing an appendix. After immigrating to Canada, she had served six years at the Red Cross post in Bonfield, where Dr. Dafoe had come to know and rely on her uncommon fortitude. That spring of 1934, Nurse de Kiriline had not only resigned from the post, but had treated herself to a holiday in Toronto. Desperate for help, Dafoe tracked her down by telephone on Saturday, June 2.

"We've got five babies out here," Dr. Dafoe said when he got her on the line. "I want you to get on the job as soon as you can. You're b-b-badly needed."

Nurse de Kiriline answered without hesitation. "I'll leave in half an hour."

Five hours later, she pulled up to Dr. Dafoe's redbrick house in Callander. Dafoe had just two sentences for her before she continued up the Corbeil road to the Dionnes' farm: "Go out and get order into that business out there," he instructed. "Most important, two-hour feedings, you know that."

"No more was needed," Nurse de Kiriline recalled. The two of them had worked side by side for half a dozen years. She was used to his terse instructions, and he trusted her skill and judgment.

Now Nurse de Kiriline made her way through the throngs of gawkers and to the Dionnes' back door, "conscious only of a fleeting feeling of slight annoyance, natural to nurses, over the presence of so many unnecessary people."

As she peered down at the infants for the first time, Nurse de Kiriline wondered to herself, *Are they really alive?* The look of their dark, wrinkled faces and still, small bodies put a catch in her throat. "Then one tiny creature moved a little and, bending closer, I heard a sound like the mewing of a very feeble, very new kitten. Yes, they were alive. But that was about all."

Louise de Kiriline found herself nearly as daunted as Nurse Leroux had been. Every inch of the house was cramped and ill-lit. The bed stood barely a foot and a half from the wall. "Pressed into the corner on the other side of the window stood a dresser still ornamented with odd knicknacks, porcelain statues of the Holy Virgin, china trays for buttons and pins and dry palm leaves. On one of its corners enough room had been made for a small tray with the babies' feeding implements, sterilized and covered with a clean cloth." In the parlor, an upright piano and pink marble-topped table had been shoved aside to make room for an iron bedstead for the nurses. The big living-dining room was a shambles of boxes. So many gifts and donations had arrived that some of them had not even been opened. They covered the floor and rose, teetering, toward the ceiling.

The house, in her opinion, was "upset beyond recognition." She hardly knew where to begin straightening it out. Beneath the chaos lay a perfectly respectable northern Ontario farmhouse, but absolutely nothing in such a farmhouse was suitable for the care of premature babies.

One fact at least was clear: the house must be cleaned. Such fragile newborns had virtually no resistance to infection, making a sterile environment essential to their survival. Nurse de Kiriline rolled up her sleeves, trusting that a plan would emerge as she banished the winter's accumulation of dust and woodsmoke.

That initial uncertainty was imperceptible to everyone in the house. The next morning Nurse de Kiriline commandeered the front parlor and scrubbed it floor to ceiling with warm water and soap. Nothing less than "surgical cleanliness" would do. Out went the bed, the piano, the marble-topped table, and the chairs. In came a neighbor's dining room table. This she covered with "a shining white sheet" and padded with cotton wool. Since there was no space for washstands, Grandpa Dionne built wooden shelves and nailed them to the walls for Nurse de Kiriline to line with clean white cloths and fill with bottles, basins, soap, and disinfectant. Even the boxes of Kleenex were nailed to the walls to save space. She opened each and every gift box, sorting and organizing everything that was immediately useful, and stowed the rest in the cellar. Last of all, she took down the red tufted curtains from the parlor doorway and replaced them with mosquito netting and fresh white sheets.

In the space of one day Nurse de Kiriline transformed the parlor into "the babies' sanctuary." When she moved Yvonne, Annette, Cécile, Émilie, and Marie into the spick-and-span little room, she thought triumphantly that "their eventual survival was brought within the realm of possibility."

Yet in her zeal for protecting the babies' health, Nurse de Kiriline simultaneously managed to shame and alienate Elzire and Oliva Dionne almost from the moment she walked through their door. The vigor with which she scoured their walls and floors made it clear what this "arrogant taskmistress" thought of their housekeeping. "We gave Madame de Kiriline and Mademoiselle Leroux the living room, the best room in the house, because we wanted them to have the best," Elzire said. But obviously, their best was not good enough. Nurse de Kiriline's relief and satisfaction at whisking the newborns out of the "chaos of the upset little home" and into the sterile oasis of the parlor-nursery stung Elzire deeply. Worse, she was still confined to bed, unable to cross through the doorway of Nurse de Kiriline's domain. Elzire was so distressed at being separated from Yvonne, Annette, Cécile, Émilie, and Marie that Grandpa Dionne was compelled to cut a small window into the wall between the two rooms so she could at least glimpse her daughters from her bed.

Dafoe dubbed himself "Boss Number One," Nurse de Kiriline "Boss Number Two." Behind them, the whole country was mobilizing itself like an army to save the Dionnes' babies. The Red Cross stepped up to guarantee the nurses' salaries, and a portable bungalow was assembled behind the house for them sleep in. The *Toronto Star* sent another, larger incubator—"the only five-baby incubator in all the world"—and was having three more built from antique blueprints. Twenty-eight ounces of fresh breast milk arrived every morning by train, courtesy of the best-known pediatrician in Canada, Dr. Alan Brown of Toronto's Hospital for Sick Children. The district relief officer came and took a list of everything the nurses needed, from window screens to sheets and towels. The attorney general's office ordered two constables to keep gawkers and promoters from disturbing Elzire and her newest daughters, while a mile and a half from the Dionne farm, two hundred men fought to keep a brush fire from coming within range of the infants. Dr. Dafoe's brother, Dr. William Dafoe, visited the babies and recommended oxygen rather than rum to pull them from their sinking spells. The eighty-pound oxygen cylinders arrived the very next day.

"They are a wonderful thing," Nurse Leroux marveled. A small funnel placed over the mouth and nose delivered a gentle stream of 95 percent oxygen and 5 percent carbon dioxide, which proved far more effective than the eyedropper of diluted rum, reviving the babies almost instantly. The nurses nicknamed these oxygen cocktails apéritifs.

Even with aid pouring in, the sheer volume of labor necessary to keep Yvonne, Annette, Cécile, Émilie, and Marie alive was staggering. A day's work at the Dionne farm, said Aunt Alma Dionne, was "worse than seven funerals."

Keeping up the supply of hot water remained the most labor-intensive chore. "I'll say they need water," said the hired girl, fifteen-year-old Eva Gravelle. "I have to pump about two pails every fifteen minutes."

Each of the incubators built by the *Star* was heated by three hot-water crocks. Every hour, one crock from each incubator had to be poured out and refilled with fresh hot water. "If all crocks were changed at the same time the air inside was likely to become too hot," Nurse de Kiriline explained, "and later, when they cooled all at once, undesirably cold." The babies were still remarkably sensitive to changes in temperature. If the thermometer began to creep above 92 degrees, they flushed and panted. When it dropped below 90, their breathing faded as they turned blue around the nostrils.

"Just to keep those five 'blue,' choking little creatures warm and breathing was a twenty-four-hour job," Dr. Dafoe said of those early days.

CHAPTER 9

Parents of Quintuplets Dazed by Sudden Fame, Offers, Gifts

Kokomo Tribune, June 11, 1934

By Yvonne, Annette, Cécile, Émilie, and Marie's one-week birthday, a semblance of order had descended on the Dionne farm, in no small part because the "No Admittance" policy had acquired the force of law. To appease the curious public, a signboard was put up outside the gate where Dafoe posted daily bulletins on the infants' weight.

The only glimpses to be had of the five babies were through the parlor windows. *Toronto Star* reporter Keith Munro nosed up to the glass on the morning of Monday, June 4, and witnessed a scene he'd remember forever. "It was one of the banner days of my life," he proclaimed.

The spectacle was nothing more than bath time.

As Munro peered through the pane, Nurse de Kiriline lifted a "tiny roll of white" out of an incubator and carried it to the big table in the middle of the room. Nurse de Kiriline knew full well the reporters were watching and was willing to humor them as long as they followed the rules. With a smile toward the window she called out, "This is Émilie."

To Munro's delight, Émilie roused in the unfamiliar sunlight. "All of a sudden she opened her mouth and yawned prodigiously. Then she stretched. Actually stretched. Arms the size of your little finger went out straight, and her tiny legs did the same. Even the minute fingers and toes wriggled."

That was the magic of the quintuplets—the infants were so impossibly small, and there were so impossibly many of them, that the most ordinary happenings had the power to enthrall grown men. Munro recorded every blink and breath as Émilie was daubed with warm olive oil and laid atop a hot-water bottle on the scale.

"Émilie weighs one pound, thirteen ounces," Nurse de Kiriline announced—down from her scant birth weight.

Munro watched, no less fascinated, as the procedure was repeated on Cécile, Annette, and Yvonne. Then came Marie. Munro knew she was supposed to be littlest of all, yet it was difficult to conceive of a smaller baby than he had already seen. "The clothing was unwrapped and there she lay, absolutely motionless and oh so small. Her sisters were small, but this mite was tinier. All her body was wrinkled."

Marie did not stir as Nurse de Kiriline bathed her face and eyes. "Even the nurse seemed disturbed by her lack of movement," Munro noticed.

"Marie, Marie," Nurse de Kiriline crooned.

"Movement began in one of the arms which was drawn up to the face as though to shield her eyes from the sun. A leg kicked. Both legs kicked, and there was a wail so weak as to be almost inaudible. Marie is alive. In fact, she is livelier than usual, the nurse softly states as she bathes her. As she holds her up, the little body comes between the watcher and the sunlight. One could almost swear that she is transparent."

The public's appetite for these glimpses of the quintuplets was insatiable. So was Elzire Dionne's. She could get no closer to her babies than the reporters. Stranded in her bed, Elzire "grieved over the loss of her doll-sized roommates."

Though some pitied Elzire Dionne, assuming that any twenty-five-year-old woman with ten children must be the victim of a "brute of a man," Elzire's feelings were entirely to the contrary. "I'd be lost without a baby in my arms," she said many years afterward. "I can't imagine myself without a baby." As a child she had loved to dress in overalls and play first baseman on her brothers' baseball team, yet by cutting coupons from soap wrappers and sending away for prizes, the little tomboy built herself a family of ten dolls. They were so precious to her that as a bride of sixteen, Elzire smuggled the entire collection into a closet in her new home. The distress she now felt at being separated from her ten living, breathing children hardly compared. Days dragged into weeks, and still Dr. Dafoe and the nurses insisted she remain in bed, thanks to a fever and an inflamed vein in her leg.

Elzire bided her time by making five down comforters for her new daughters, each a different color, carefully selected for each of her ju-melles. (That was her pet name for them—that and petites. Petites means "little ones," and jumelles is French for "twins," no matter how many.) Pink for Yvonne, yellow for Annette, green for Cécile, lilac for Émilie, and blue for Marie.

Elzire's situation barely improved when she was finally allowed to leave her bed more than a month after giving birth. The Dionnes' parlor had become "a super-death-fighting laboratory," and Nurse de Kiriline's vigilance over it was absolutely rigid. Like everyone else, Elzire dutifully donned mask and gown and scrubbed her hands before entering what Nurse de Kiriline dubbed the "Holy of Holies."

All Elzire was permitted to do was gaze at her daughters through the lids of the incubators for a few minutes each day, the *Toronto Star* reported. "She always remarks on how cute they look," one of the nurses told the *Star*. "She thinks they are getting the very best care and never tries to interfere with them at all."

The papers made her sound meek and obedient, but underneath, Elzire was throbbing with frustration. According to Dr. Dafoe, the care of Yvonne, Annette, Cécile, Émilie, and Marie was "too highly specialized" for Elzire to lend a hand in. That was one thing. His order forbidding her to hold or cuddle her babies was quite another. "The nurses won't let me in to touch them and get close enough to them so that I can really see them," Elzire told a French-speaking reporter from the *Toronto Star*.

"Doctor Dafoe's heart was made of stone," one of his admirers bragged. "Doctor Dafoe knew that a stray microbe from their own Mama Dionne could kill them just as neatly, just as quickly, as any bug breathed onto them by their worst enemy." Dafoe himself didn't touch them if he could avoid it—didn't even enter the nursery any more than he had to, for fear of carrying in germs from any of his other patients. That was no consolation to the babies' mother.

"I long to hold my little jumelles and sponge them off just like the nurses. But they don't even want me around," Elzire said. "They don't want Oliva around, either. We are outcasts in our own home."

Holding in her temper and not back-talking to Dafoe and de Kiriline became a full-time job for Elzire. It was not easy in such small quarters, for she was not half so shy as she appeared to the English-speaking reporters who rarely pried a word out of her. Those who knew her well knew that Elzire Dionne was "quick-spoken where her children were concerned, for all her timidity with strangers."

Elzire did not dare defy the nurses openly—she could see better than anyone that her daughters' lives depended on the staff—but she was also not about to let them deprive her babies of a mother's love and protection. At times she crept into the nursery, slid the glass lids of the incubators aside, and sprinkled Yvonne, Annette, Cécile, Émilie, and Marie with holy water. The little vial had been sent to her by a sympathetic mother from the grotto at Lourdes, the French shrine where the Blessed Mother had appeared to Saint Bernadette. Elzire knew the nurses would never approve of such a thing. They would doubtless think it unsanitary, seeing as how they were forever plunging everything but the babies themselves into vats of boiling water. But to Elzire, nothing could be more pure.

Oliva advised Elzire to do her best to get along with the staff. "They're doing everything for the babies," he said. "And bossy as Dr. Dafoe is— even if he does treat us like dirt under his feet—"

"We'll just have to take his dirt," she finished.

It wasn't that they were ungrateful. For years to come, Oliva and Elzire would state time and again how much they valued the care and attention lavished on their babies. More disconcerting to the Dionnes than the staff's attitude was the sense that their family was being splintered. Yvonne, Annette, Cécile, Émilie, and Marie were turning into a family unto themselves, with Dr. Dafoe and the nurses as their parents.

Even the "old family" had been fractured by Dafoe when he shunted Ernest, Rose-Marie, Thérèse, Daniel, and Pauline from their home. "We were helpless," Thérèse remembered. She and her siblings had never been away from home without their parents. "We begged to go back to them." But in the weeks Elzire was bedridden, the elder Dionne children appear to have been allowed back into their house for a single visit. Little Pauline's first birthday passed while she was living with her aunt and uncle; when she finally returned home for good after almost two months, she did not recognize her own mother.

CHAPTER 10

Too Many Showmen After Quintuplets

TORONTO STAR, JUNE 15, 1934

Held captive by their daughters' helplessness, the Dionnes choked down their frustration and carried on as best they could. They confined themselves mostly to the hot summer kitchen and the bedroom so that the nurses might have more elbow room in the big living-dining room. Elzire cooked the nurses' meals and served them "like ladies," but she went about her tasks "with the abstracted manner of a woman who is not mistress of her own household."

Oliva had it a little easier, for he could escape outdoors to be "master in the cow barn and hay field," but he was still being bombarded with moneymaking offers from would-be entrepreneurs. Morning after morning he was accosted at the train station when he came to pick up his daughters' daily shipments of breast milk. Some hoped to rent a square of Dionne land to sell postcards and hot dogs. A pair of Americans offered to pay him thousands for the bed the quintuplets were born in. There was no escaping the attention, even at home. The *No Admittance* signs made the otherwise nondescript farmhouse conspicuous, effectively pointing the curious straight to the Dionnes' front door. Cars with license plates from as near as Quebec and as far as Oklahoma made their way up the Corbeil road, and not all of the visitors were courteous. "We have had no trouble with the Canadians," Grandpa Dionne told the *North Bay Nugget*, "but some of the Americans have been too inquisitive." Indeed, the American promoters were swarming so thickly and so persistently that local officials were exploring the possibility of having some of them deported.

"There have been so many other promoters rushing in and out of the Dionne home that they have become suspicious of everybody," Ivan Spear's lawyer complained. "These other promoters attempted to point out loop-holes in our contract, and poison the minds of the family against it," he claimed.

Dafoe was just as fed up with being approached by sideshow managers. "They have offered me money and everything else if I can get the family signed up," he told the *Toronto Star.* "I won't have anything to do with it at all." A story was making the rounds that Dafoe had even threatened to abandon the Dionne case entirely if the showmen didn't ease up. "I'm not denying it; I'm not saying it's true," he said. "My interest is those children and keeping them alive. I'm not in the least interested in any scheme to take them somewhere to be exhibited."

Most worrisome of all was the Chicago deal. Despite "strenuous efforts to break the contract," the agreement remained binding, and that knowledge hung heavily over Oliva Dionne's head. He couldn't eat. The tension gave him chronic headaches. His anxiety kept him from taking any pleasure in his daughters' birth and made him snappish with reporters.

Grandpa Dionne was more cordial to the press, often chatting with them over the fence as he stood guard at the gate. "You know, Oliva has been alone here for ten years, and was always able to look after his business dealings in a capable manner," he praised his son. "But he wasn't thinking clearly when he signed that contract . . . it wasn't fair to ask him to act at such a time. The contract must be cancelled." They were not accepting the $100 weekly payments for the babies' expenses, Grandpa Dionne explained. "As fast as money arrives from Chicago, we send it back," he said.

◆   ◆   ◆

On Friday, July 13, Ivan Spear arrived in North Bay, allegedly to compromise with the Dionnes. "We are quite willing to be reasonable, and are not trying to force the issue," Spear's lawyer told the *Nugget*. What happened next baldly contradicted that statement.

The negotiations between Oliva Dionne and Ivan Spear happened behind closed doors, but whatever was said prompted immediate action. By Monday, the Ontario attorney general's office had come up with an unprecedented strategy to thwart Spear's contract and keep Yvonne, Annette, Cécile, Émilie, and Marie safe in their Canadian nursery.

The plan hinged on the fact that although Oliva was still bound to the terms of the contract, the government of Ontario was not. If Oliva and Elzire were to sign over custody of their babies to the Red Cross, Spear could not touch them. To ensure that the little girls would have every chance to grow into normal, healthy children without interference from Spear and his ilk, the attorney general proposed a custody term of two years. More extraordinary still, the Red Cross intended to oversee the construction of a fully staffed private hospital to house the Dionnes' newborns across the street from their farm, complete with every modern convenience the farmhouse lacked.

Oliva was dumbstruck. It was an ironclad solution, guaranteed to keep his fragile daughters free from the grasp of showmen and hucksters, and yet it violated his every instinct as a father. To guarantee them the care and protection they so desperately needed, Oliva and Elzire would have to live apart from their five baby girls for two years. In their place, a board of four handpicked guardians would function as Yvonne, Annette, Cécile, Émilie, and Marie's legal parents.

As Oliva told it, the conversation took a disturbing turn when he tried to discuss his reservations about the guardianship proposal with Dr. Dafoe. "Turning over custody of our babies to the Red Cross would mean surrendering our God-given rights as parents," he protested. "My wife would never consent to it."

"You'd better talk it over with her and see," Dafoe replied, "and if you don't do what I say, I'll walk out on the case. I've told you before I would quit. I'm telling you this again for the last time. And that's not all. The Red Cross will withdraw the nurses and take away all nourishment and supplies. That includes the shipments of mother's milk."

Could Dr. Dafoe have handed down such a cruel ultimatum? Everything about it goes against his image as the benevolent country doctor adored far and wide as the savior of the Dionne Quintuplets. It's tempting to shrug off the story as the fabrication of a desperate and angry father.

Yet it is a fact that Dafoe could be startlingly blunt and "more than a little gruff." He was bullheaded, too. If a flu-stricken patient disregarded his orders for fresh air in midwinter, he'd been known to smash a windowpane to guarantee his instructions would be followed. "In a sickroom he was a tyrant in sheep's clothing," his biographer said, who "had no time or patience for sentimental twaddle." Dafoe's relationship with the Dionnes was no exception. "He treated them with disdain," the doctor's secretary admitted. And hadn't there been rumors in the newspapers, when Dafoe was being badgered by promoters, that he'd threatened to quit? Outrageous though Oliva Dionne's claim may seem at first, this less-than-saintly side of Dafoe's personality suggests it is not outside the realm of possibility.

Regardless of whether any threat was made, what is certain is that the guardianship proposal left Oliva more helpless to the extraordinary circumstances of his daughters' birth than ever. If there had been so much as a hint from Dafoe or the Red Cross that a delay in signing might cease or even slow the shipments of breast milk, the possibility amounted to a death warrant for Yvonne, Annette, Cécile, Émilie, and Marie. No father could take such a risk. The prospect of letting his daughters' welfare fall into the hands of Ivan Spear was equally out of the question. Oliva's sole option was to sign half of his family over to the Red Cross. Not only that, but he must convince his wife to sign away her two-month-old daughters as well.

◆ ◆ ◆

"We were raking hay," Elzire remembered of the day he broke the news to her. It was heavy work, but she welcomed the escape from Dafoe and the nurses, and the feeling of being "an alien" in her own home.

Oliva hardly spoke. *Yes* or *no,* he muttered as they worked, and that was all. Elzire sensed something was wrong. "His face looked as though the world had come to an end." Finally, Oliva set down his hay rake and took Elzire's from her. "Brace yourself for a shock, my dear," he warned. Elzire did her best to prepare herself, but as Oliva described the terms of the proposal, her vision dimmed and her legs threatened to give way.

"Why, with such an unnatural arrangement, our house would be divided," she cried.

"It's already divided, Elzire," Oliva said. "What control have we over the quints?" The truth of it was so cutting, Elzire broke down and wept. Oliva said no more.

For the sake of her babies, Elzire knew she could not fight. "To me they were five little human flowers—delicate hot-house flowers that required the most constant and careful and expert attention. Costly attention for which we had no money to pay," she said. Yet everything in her resisted. While the nurses were out on the porch, Elzire smuggled herself back into the parlor-nursery and sprinkled her five daughters with holy water. "If I live to be a hundred I'll never forget how awed I was, how overwhelmed by my sense of responsibility to my premature incubator babies," she remembered. "How can I accept it?" she asked herself. "How can I?"

There was no time to resign herself to the idea. Lawyer H. R. Valin and Mr. Alderson of the Red Cross arrived with the paper for her to sign that very day. Elzire sat at the kitchen table with the handwritten document before her, a blur of English swirling around her as the two men discussed the details with Oliva. Elzire could not comprehend a word of it. (Since French did not become an official language of Canada until

1969, no one was legally required to present or even explain the document to Elzire in her own language.) "Then there was an ominous lull. And silence. Deadly silence, and next thing I knew Oliva was signing the memorandum."

In another second I will have to put my name below Oliva's, she thought. *In just another second, I, too, will have to sign that paper.*

There was no other way. Even the government had looked for alternatives. The Children's Aid Society was willing to step in, but ironically, the excellent care Yvonne, Annette, Cécile, Émilie, and Marie were receiving from their nurses and Dr. Dafoe made it impossible. "As far as we are aware they are being well cared for and are in no danger of being neglected," the Society stated. The Dionnes were deemed "fit and worthy parents," and if there was no neglect, the Society had no authority.

Elzire's hand "shook like a leaf" as she set her name to the paper. This date, she knew, would be written on her heart when she died. As she signed, Elzire was already imagining how she would eventually explain to her daughters why she and Oliva had done such a thing. "I would tell them that we had placed their welfare above every other consideration," she vowed.

CHAPTER 11

Dionnes Now Have to Guard Quintuplets from Tourist Horde

CHICAGO TRIBUNE, AUGUST 2, 1934

By midsummer, so many cars had worn down the ruts in the Corbeil road that it was being rebuilt. It had also been unofficially dubbed "Dionne Highway" and "Quintuplet Drive." When visitors asked for directions, they no longer bothered with the name of the town, the *Chicago Tribune* reported. "They want to know 'How far to where the quintuplets live and which way do we go?' "

Letters addressed to "Mrs. Oliva Dionne, the Miracle Mother, North Woods, Canada" had no trouble finding their way to the Dionnes' mailbox. Newspaper readers tracked every fraction of an ounce Yvonne, Annette, Cécile, Émilie, and Marie lost or gained "with the excitement of a sporting event." They celebrated as one by one the babies graduated from oil baths and incubators to soap and water and white enamel cots; rhapsodized over their two-month newspaper portraits; and bit their fingernails while Marie received a radium treatment to shrink a spongy, blood-filled growth the size of a quarter from her thigh.

"What is there about these babies which has enchanted half a world and back again?" a *Pittsburgh Press* editorial asked. "Why is it that when they sneeze, the press of a continent calls attention to it?"

In part it had to do with a public aching for good news. Column after column of the papers was saturated with grim headlines. Drought. Fire. Starvation. The whole world was struggling to make ends meet. Hundreds of thousands of men were out of work. One of every five Canadian families depended on government relief payments for their survival. Men, women, and children alike felt small and helpless in the face of the Great Depression. And then came the Dionne Quintuplets, five baby girls who personified an entire continent's fears for its future. Nothing could be smaller, more helpless, or more determined to thrive than those babies. "Of course, they have no right to be alive at all," Dr. Dafoe said. "But they are and that is the wonder of it." Hardly anyone could watch their grip on life slowly but surely strengthening without feeling encouraged.

Marie in particular became the world's darling. "Not 'How are the quintuplets?' but 'How is Marie?' is the universal question," said the *Toronto Star.* "She is so tiny, so weak, she gets into your heart," Red Cross nurse Cloutier confessed.

The nurses were every bit as susceptible to the babies' appeal as the public. Despite the constant repetition of their duties, Nurse de Kiriline explained, attending to Yvonne, Annette, Cécile, Émilie, and Marie "never could lose its entrancing novelty and its intense fascination. And mingled with this, deepening the experience, came the inevitable growth of affection and love for the five little lives, which made the hours away from the babies seem all too long, the time to re-enter the nursery a moment of delightful anticipation and the hours spent with them exquisite enjoyment."

Already, glimmers of individuality were beginning to shine in each of the five baby girls. As newborns, they looked so much alike that the only surefire way to tell them apart was by weight. Their skin was too tender for ID bracelets or necklaces; only the incubators were labeled, and so the nurses had taken utmost care to handle one baby at a time, and to put each back in her proper place.

"I remember one of the first times I placed all the babies in a proud heap on the table," said Nurse de Kiriline. "My heart suddenly stood still when I realized their extreme similarity to each other as they lay softly cooing and contentedly blinking." Until then, she'd only really known them by their charts—which was the heaviest, which the weakest, the most prone to blue spells or anemia. Nurse de Kiriline was not entirely sure she'd returned the babies to the correct incubators until they were weighed the following morning. After that, bracelets with engraved nameplates were ordered, to be absolutely sure no mix-ups occurred.

"But gradually," Nurse de Kiriline noticed, "there began to be characteristic differences in the babies, each small personality became subtly unique."

Yvonne, being the biggest, was not difficult to distinguish from her sisters. Yet in spite of her size, she was not the hardiest. She was more prone to sickness as well as skittishness. "In many ways I would say she was more sensitive and easier to frighten than the others," Nurse de Kiriline said. Changes in routine were apt to provoke a reaction from Yvonne. Sometimes it even seemed she was frightened by her own imagination. Her face was larger, her neck shorter. The most curious of the babies, the sight of something interesting made her mouth pop open. She was Nurse Leroux's special pet.

Annette was in many ways an ideal baby. "A more perfectly shaped child could hardly be conceived than Annette," Nurse de Kiriline proclaimed, and no one contradicted her. Despite the sisters' breathtaking similarity, something about Annette's looks drew extra attention. Mentally, physically, and emotionally she was also the most robust, "well-balanced, harder to frighten and more difficult to upset."

Cécile's face was only "a shade rounder" than Annette's, making the two of them easier to mix up than any of the others. The truer contrast was in their personalities. Cécile's "nature was a distinctly placid one." Where Annette's gaze was quick and bright, Cécile's was calm and deep, her movements less lively. She cried the least of all her sisters, and was "pathetically patient" when sick.

Émilie was still frail enough that it was hard for Nurse de Kiriline to paint a picture of her personality. Fortunately, her most distinctive trait was being an obliging feeder, as she was almost fatally anemic. Later, when she grew sturdier, Émilie "acquired the disposition of a slightly temperamental but adorable imp."

Marie's size alone made it simple for anyone to single her out, for she was consistently the smallest. There was more to it than that, though. Her solitary demeanor gave Marie the air of "a small duckling in the midst of a flock of lively yellow chickens," Nurse de Kiriline said. "She rarely laughed or even smiled; she cooed to herself, when at last she mastered the trick, in an absolutely detached way, perfectly alone, not at all in the company of the others." The staff soon took to calling her "the little Madonna."

While nurses reveled in their twenty-four-hour shifts with the babies, the Dionne family was still making do with glimpses through the small indoor window. Every morning the elder Dionne youngsters piled onto their mother's bed to clap and exclaim with delight each time a nurse held up one of their baby sisters for inspection.

To the nurses, the daily ritual presented a charming scene. From Oliva and Elzire's point of view, it illustrated all too literally their greatest objection to the guardianship agreement—the formation of a wall between the "old" and "new" families. Even under one roof, their children were divided. How would they continue to be a family when Yvonne, Annette, Cécile, Émilie, and Marie were moved to their own private hospital?

Oliva and Elzire's misgivings were impossible to mask. "Parents are not quite sure what everything is about and are getting very suspicious of everyone," Yvonne Leroux noted after the guardianship agreement was signed.

The nurses' eagerness for the new hospital was every bit as apparent as the Dionnes' dread. "The hospital is under way," Nurse Leroux recorded on Monday, August 6. "The excavation is started and everyone is excited wondering what it's going to be like."

◆　◆　◆

That same week, the inadequacies of the Dionnes' farmhouse made themselves clearer than ever. In the wee hours of Tuesday, August 7, Nurse Leroux was awakened by "a jumbling noise at the window." Someone was trying to raise the pane from outside. Elzire heard it, too, and together they hurried into the nursery. Nurse Leroux lifted the curtain and peered into the darkness. She saw nothing but thought she heard a movement in the pasture to the east of the house. Another of the babies' caretakers "heard the noise of someone running and a bit later the sound of a motor car down the road," the *Toronto Star* reported.

Although the incident was blamed on an overly curious tourist, it left the household badly shaken. Grandpa Dionne, "the watchdog of the household," was furious. "The grandfather quivered with rage as he told of the marauding visit," the *Star* observed. "He would, he repeated over and over . . . enjoy laying hands on the miscreants."

Everyone's thoughts flew to kidnapping, and ransom. Two years earlier, the baby son of America's most famous aviator, Charles Lindbergh, had been snatched from his crib. The little boy's body was found within six weeks, but the kidnapper, who'd demanded a $50,000 ransom, remained at large. No one said it aloud, "but that dread was in everyone's mind." Immediately, there was talk in the papers of adding a six-foot barbed-wire fence to the hospital, as well as a private telephone line direct to Dr. Dafoe in Callander so that the nurses could raise an alarm. It was rumored that the premier of Ontario himself would appoint a night watch over the farmhouse in the meantime. "Underneath the routine in nursery, front yard, kitchen, farm ran a current of fear," the *Star* reported. Perhaps that collective nervousness led to what happened next.

"Calamity in nursery," Nurse Leroux recorded on Wednesday. While puncturing holes in a fresh set of nipples for the babies' bottles, Nurse de Kiriline tipped over the alcohol lamp she'd been using to sterilize the rubber. The alcohol spilled across the table and instantly ignited its soft cotton padding into blue flames. "She grabbed them all to her breast and ran out. I didn't know what had happened till I heard her call 'Yvonne!' "

Nurse de Kiriline's uniform had caught fire. Yvonne Leroux snatched a bedspread from the bed and beat the flames from Nurse de Kiriline's arms and legs. "Boss Number Two" suffered painful burns to her hands and ankle, but her instinctive reaction had saved the babies, and perhaps the entire Dionne household. It was over so quickly, no one in the house had been aware of what was happening.

That night, the prowlers returned. The farm's isolation and lack of electricity made Nurse Leroux keenly aware of their vulnerability. Without streetlamps it was impossible to see anyone approaching, and so by Friday, a gas-powered Coleman lantern bright enough to illuminate an acre of field hung at each of the four corners of the Dionne farmhouse. "Any prowler daring those lights has a lot of nerve," gloated Nurse Leroux. No chances would be taken with Ontario's miracle babies. Two special constables were sworn in the next day, providing Yvonne, Annette, Cécile, Émilie, and Marie with twenty-four-hour protection.

But even the constables could not guard against Dr. Dafoe's latest worry: whooping cough. An epidemic had broken out in the district that week, and if Dafoe got his way, Oliva, Elzire, and their five elder children would be evicted from their own home to eliminate the slightest chance of their carrying the deadly sickness into the nursery. "The older, singly born Dionne young ones are being watched," the *Pittsburgh Press* reported. "Two of them coughed last night. The sound created a minor emergency in the circle around the quintuplets. At the first whoop, out will go the older children and, indeed, the whole family." It was against Dafoe's wishes that Ernest, Rose-Marie, Thérèse, Daniel, and Pauline had returned to their home at all after their bout with bronchitis. "He grumbles daily about the possibility of infection in the crowded quarters of the story-and-a-half cottage," the papers said. From where Dr. Dafoe stood, it was evident that every day the babies spent in a nursery with a sheet hanging across the doorway as their only barrier from germs put their lives at unnecessary risk.

CHAPTER 12

Quintuplet Hospital Started Near Home of Parents

EL PASO HERALD-POST, AUGUST 9, 1934

On August 13, 1934, a delighted Nurse Leroux helped lay the cornerstone of the hospital that promised to alleviate all their worries. "Can you imagine just how thrilled we will all be to have a decent place to work in and not always be bumping into each other," she wrote to her diary.

Oliva and Elzire did not share her excitement. Nor did they attend the cornerstone ceremony. Instead, they watched the festivities from an upstairs window that would become known as "the observation tower." The public for the most part frowned on Mama and Papa Dionne's absence, construing it as ingratitude. Few seemed to appreciate that the Dionnes were in an impossible position: indebted for the support that was continually saving their babies' lives, yet already mourning their impending two-year separation from Yvonne, Annette, Cécile, Émilie, and Marie. They were also dismayed to learn that the building would be named for Dr. Dafoe rather than their daughters: the Dafoe Hospital for the Dionne Quintuplets.

"L'hôpital temporaire," the Dionnes called it instead—*the temporary hospital*.

Every day, Ernest, Rose-Marie, and Thérèse clustered around the window under the eaves to watch the bungalow-style building take shape. The nine-room structure was a monument to the public's boundless affection for their five baby sisters. Funds for its construction had come almost exclusively from a subscription drive sponsored by the Red Cross. Even families with virtually nothing to spare were proud to contribute. Nine-year-old Clair Aubin of Rhode Island put a nickel in the mail with a letter to Dafoe saying, "Dear Doctor: I am sending you five cents to put in the Dionne Hospital Fund. Would love to send you more but Daddy works only three days a week to keep us five going."

Donations of lumber, log siding, roofing, insulation, plasterboard, hardwood flooring, and brass bathroom fixtures poured in from companies across Ontario. No convenience was spared. Wires for electricity and telephone service were strung from Callander all the way up the Corbeil road. Water pipes, too, complete with a private well and septic field. Red log cabin siding added a rustic touch to the otherwise thoroughly modern facility.

For some, contributing to the construction wasn't enough—they actually wanted to own a piece of the hospital they'd helped build. "Scraps of wood and stone were speedily carried away as souvenirs by the many daily visitors," the *Toronto Star* observed on a visit to the grounds in late August. The pebbles and splinters were more coveted than the picture postcards of the babies Grandpa Dionne offered for a quarter apiece.

When the curiosity-seekers dispersed and the workers went home for the night, Elzire Dionne crept across the road and quietly slipped Sacred Heart medals into the hospital's unfinished walls.

The next crisis seemed to come out of nowhere. "Look here!" Nurse Leroux said as she and Nurse de Kiriline were putting the babies to bed on September 11. "Feel how hot Yvonne is." By nine o'clock her temperature registered 104.3 degrees. Cécile's was creeping upward, too, and a rash was developing on both babies. The nurses sent Oliva into town for the doctor.

"We'll give the baby an enema and put her in the Chicago incubator,"

Dafoe decided after examining Yvonne. Her temperature peaked at 105 that night. Nurse Leroux and the night nurse, Pat Mullins, sponged her nervous, perspiring little body in hopes of staving off convulsions.

The next day, Cécile's and Émilie's temperatures shot up. Marie and finally Annette followed suit the day after that. Their fevers were frightening, their diapers filled with green curdles. Dr. Dafoe diagnosed intestinal toxemia.

Dafoe and the nursing staff were confounded. "I became convinced that our aseptic technique had slipped badly," Dr. Dafoe remembered. But how? They had taken every precaution to keep germs from crossing the nursery threshold. Finally they pinpointed a most unlikely culprit: the babies' clean laundry.

Their diapers ought to have been boiled—every one of them. But with eighty diapers a day to launder, someone had opted for a shortcut. Only the soiled diapers were being properly sterilized. The wet ones were scrubbed in soap and hot water. Then all of them, boiled or unboiled, were stacked in a cardboard box without a lid. In the nursery, that open box would have posed minimal risk. In an outdoor shed, with the windows propped open and flies passing freely between the barnyard and the babies' laundry, it had become a breeding ground for disease.

For three days and nights the nurses battled to keep Yvonne, Annette, Cécile, Émilie, and especially Marie from losing all the ground they'd worked so hard to gain over the last three months as the infection wreaked havoc on their miniature bodies. At 7 pounds, 11.5 ounces, Yvonne was barely more than half the size of a normal three-month-old. Marie, at 5 pounds, 4.5 ounces, was still smaller than a typical newborn. "Babes are all losing weight and look so deathly ill," Nurse Leroux wrote on September 12. The next day, Marie would not eat at all. Annette, usually the hardiest, frightened the nurses more than any of her sisters when her fever blazed to 105.1 degrees.

"That whole time was a nightmare," Nurse de Kiriline remembered.

"The senior Dionnes paced the floor outside the nursery and bombarded us with anxious questions. We pitied them but could give them no assurance."

"Babes still sick; the smallest ones look dreadful," Nurse Leroux reported on September 14. "They are waxen and their faces are drawn. If they *only* pull through this." It was the day of the hospital's dedication ceremony. Across the street, a crowd of several hundred listened to Dr. Dafoe thank everyone from Mrs. Dionne to the government of Ontario for making the hospital possible, while inside the Dionnes' parlor the nurses silently despaired. "The situation did not bear discussion," Nurse de Kiriline recalled, "but on every face you saw the same thought written. Would we ever carry these babies to their new home?"

Three days later, the Dionne household breathed a collective sigh of relief. It was clear that all five babies would recover, though they had lost weeks of progress in a matter of days. Thin, weak, and anemic, the infants, with their feeble immune systems, had been taxed to the limit. "It was evident to us all that the babies must have fresh air, safety from the sources of infection, and sunshine if they were to survive," Nurse de Kiriline said.

A week after the dedication ceremony, Dr. Dafoe looked the babies over and said to Nurse de Kiriline, "We've got to move them today."

"Do we dare?" she asked. There had been talk of it the day before; some of the babies' things had even been moved across the street in anticipation, but now it was raining, and the furnace was not up and running.

"We don't dare keep them here," Dafoe answered. "There's a chance for them over there. Get everything ready."

Oliva and Elzire resisted. "Naturally, they were afraid," Nurse de Kiriline said. "They, too, had seen the shadow of death in those five little faces. They knew as we did that the hospital was not ready." There was no furniture, no pots or pans to thaw the babies' milk and sterilize their bottles. The water and electricity had not been hooked up yet.

Dr. Dafoe held firm. It was a bold move. If anything happened—if one of the babies suffered or died after being transferred out of their warm home and through the rain to the unfinished hospital—the whole world would be at his throat.

The Dionnes and the nurses fretted while plumbers and steamfitters hustled to connect pipes and light a fire in the furnace across the street. At one o'clock, word came that the nursery needed just one more hour to heat up. "The radiators began to warm the air and, with the chill off, everybody's spirits shot up," Nurse de Kiriline remembered.

Everyone except Elzire and Oliva, that is. The separation they had dreaded since July was suddenly upon them. Elzire could not bear even to watch the nurses begin folding up her babies' clothes. She begged Oliva to take her out of the house until it was over.

"It was a cold, rainy, miserable day," Oliva recalled. "The sky wept and we wept. Where we drove I do not know."

While the Dionnes motored aimlessly up and down the sodden countryside, Nurse de Kiriline directed the final preparations, ensuring that a hot-water bottle was tucked into each waiting cot at the hospital while Nurse Leroux stayed behind to ready Yvonne, Annette, Cécile, Émilie, and Marie. The babies did not have the vitality to resist the strange breach of routine. They lay without fussing on the big table while Nurse Leroux wrapped them in blankets, leaving only their faces showing, then did what she could to return the Dionnes' parlor to its former state.

Around two o'clock, two cars with the heat roaring at full blast pulled to a stop in front of the farmhouse. Nurse Leroux picked up Yvonne. Nurse de Kiriline carried Annette. Aunt Laurence Clusiaux and Uncle Lias Legros took the bundles that were Cécile and Émilie. "The Little Doctor followed with the fifth roll. He had reserved for himself the privilege of carrying Marie."

"We stood at the door a moment—the doctor, the housekeeper, we three nurses—each with a baby so carefully swathed that it resembled a cocoon more than a baby," Nurse de Kiriline said of that pivotal moment. "We looked back once at the dreary room in which we had spent such anxious months and then we carried the quintuplets out into the open."

When the Dionnes returned to face the empty nursery, Elzire was so choked with emotion, she felt as though she were suffocating. Standing in the doorway with "eyes that had been wrung dry," she told her husband, "This will never seem like home again—without our petites. It is a house divided."

"If we had expected drama," Nurse de Kiriline said of the nerve-wracking hundred-yard journey across the Corbeil road to the Dafoe Hospital, "we did not get it." All five babies slept through the entire trip without so much as blinking as they were slipped into their warm cots.

Instead, the nurses were the ones who were shocked by the change. The lighting in the Dionne house had been so poor, de Kiriline said, that looking at the babies in the bright new nursery was like seeing them for the first time. "Those children were as pale as poor little ghosts. Marie and Émilie were even worse than pale. Their color was a ghastly green." All at once the nurses realized how perilous the situation had been.

"For Dr. Dafoe to move those babies just when he did was the bravest thing I ever knew a doctor to do," Nurse de Kiriline later said. The way the nurses would eventually tell it, Yvonne, Annette, Cécile, Émilie, and Marie were on the verge of death when he decided they must leave the farmhouse. "The day of the moving they were hot with fever, their faces were of a livid paleness, they were indeed sick, almost dying babies," Nurse de Kiriline claimed in 1936. Only a last-ditch effort to whisk them into the fresh, sterile hospital could save them from the ravages of intestinal toxemia, so her version went.

It was a dramatic story, a satisfying story complete with a heroic doctor and a miraculous ending in which the babies' fevers broke just hours after crossing the hospital's threshold. "As if by the touch of a fairy's wand," the usually levelheaded de Kiriline wrote, within a week the five critically ill infants "turned the corner towards blossoming bright-eyed babyhood." Most importantly for the doctor and nurses, it was a story that left no room to doubt the necessity of removing the children from their family's home. There was just one problem: it wasn't true.

No one, not even Oliva and Elzire Dionne, would deny that the hospital played a tremendous role in reviving their daughters' health, but the fact of the matter is that by September 17, all five were considered "much improved," "fine," or "very good." Still, Dafoe waited four days more before risking the hospital transfer on September 21. "In general their condition is satisfactory," he told the *Nugget* that afternoon.

What prompted the move more than anything was the resurgence of the local whooping cough epidemic. With infection sweeping the countryside, Dr. Dafoe realized he could not chance keeping five fragile premature infants in the Dionne home any longer, especially not in their weakened state. Though Yvonne, Annette, Cécile, Émilie, and Marie were not dying that day, they were stranded in a sort of no-man's-land, too feeble to do anything but simply exist.

The hospital granted the babies the opportunity to truly thrive for the first time in their lives, and true to form, Yvonne, Annette, Cécile, Émilie, and Marie grasped it eagerly. "In short," Nurse de Kiriline said, "they took up life again after so nearly giving it up forever and the happiness in their new little log house was a thing that could be felt."

The front room, stretching the full width of the building, belonged entirely to the babies. Sunlight poured in through a row of six tall southern windows, illuminating the apple-green walls and ivory trim. A line of five small bed tables and five ivory cots painted with pink wreaths and hung with holy medals took up the center of the room. A little wooden "pet" was clamped to the bars of each crib: a puppy for Yvonne, a squir-rel for Annette, a rooster for Cécile, a rabbit for Émilie, and a goose for Marie. To one side of the front door stood the nurses' table, with its new padding and white enamel bowls full of bathing and diaper-changing supplies. Stacks of diapers, dresses, and shirts warmed on a radiator within easy reach. On the other side was the big new sun bunk Nurse de Kiriline had contrived. It looked rather like a drawer on stilts, with a cushioned bottom broad enough to hold five babies at once, and sides seven or eight inches high to keep them from tumbling out onto the floor. The nurses irreverently christened it "the rats' nest."

All day long, Yvonne, Annette, Cécile, Émilie, and Marie sprawled in this play box, drenched in sunshine from the open windows. As if fresh air and sunlight were a kind of tonic, the five-month-olds "soon became vigorously kicking youngsters with an omnivorous curiosity for every-thing within sight and later on within reach." Their cheeks turned "the exact shade of the old-fashioned cinnamon rose," and their plumping limbs "a light biscuit-tan." It was a beguiling sight, that brimful box of squirming babies "with their dark velvety sparkling eyes and their rosy glow of healthfulness," the five of them as alike as a string of paper dolls.

Their budding personalities were emerging ever more strongly. The most flirtatious of the babies, Yvonne had developed a particular enthu-siasm that set her apart from the others. "Whatever she does is done with all her might, from tantrums to pat-a-cakes," Nurse de Kiriline said of her. Usually the first to learn new tricks—like wrinkling her nose—she practiced them all by herself. Nurse Leroux had also discovered that Yvonne had three extra-long hairs they could use to distinguish her from her sisters if all else failed.

Annette was the fearless one, most inclined to "scrap" with the others. "She is interested in everything and likes innovations. She is also intensely interested in the effect on others of what she does," said Nurse de Kiriline. Nurse Leroux still considered Annette the prettiest, finding something inexplicably appealing in the squareness of her jawline.

Round-faced Cécile remained the most serene and the least likely to cry—even when Annette tussled with her. "Almost the most upset she ever got was when she couldn't pick the red roses off her quilt," Nurse de Kiriline recalled. It was in Cécile's nature to become engrossed in a problem, working at it until she'd seen it through.

Émilie's liveliness earned her the position of "athlete of the crowd," always eager to join in whatever her sisters were doing. "She never needs more than the merest invitation to play," Nurse de Kiriline observed. "She screams with laughter at the very suggestion of a frolic." According to Nurse Leroux, Émilie had the pointiest chin.

Independent and imperious little Marie was Émilie's opposite. She always seemed a bit separate from the busy flock of babies, either taking her own sweet time, or demanding that her desires be instantly fulfilled. The glow of bright lights or bright objects could captivate her contemplative soul for hours. "To make her laugh and frolic was a hard job but we succeeded in doing it," said Nurse de Kiriline.

As the babies bloomed, so did the nurses' affection for them. "You felt as though you wanted to give them the moon," Nurse de Kiriline confessed. "I have often been asked if any one is my favorite. I answer that the last of those babies you pick up is your favorite, but perhaps I picked up oftenest Annette and Émilie." Nurse Leroux still favored Yvonne, while relief nurse Pat Mullins had a soft spot for Marie.

Dr. Dafoe delighted in the babies every bit as much as the nurses. "Hello, bums!" he called out to them as he entered the nursery each day. "How's my gang this morning?" As one journalist who reported regularly on the goings-on at the Dafoe Hospital recalled, "his voice, his smile, his eyes made the words more affectionate than a dictionaryful of 'dears' and 'darlings.'"

"I know of no greater treat in the world," Dafoe himself said, "than the one I receive when I enter the Quintuplets' nursery every morning and see such a rare collection of smiling, healthy babies." Thanks to the pictures in the papers and the newsreel films in the theaters, the whole world could see just how healthy Yvonne, Annette, Cécile, Émilie, and Marie were growing, and they worshipped Dafoe for his part in it. "It never occurred to us that they belonged anywhere else but in what we considered to be a lovely little hospital right across the street," said quintuplet fan Genia Goelz. "We accepted Dr. Dafoe, and the whole way that the thing was managed, absolutely. In fact, we admired it."

While the hospital ministered to the babies' physical well-being, the board of four guardians—Dr. Dafoe, local merchant Ken Morrison, William Alderson of the Red Cross, and Grandpa Olivier Dionne—were seeing to it that Yvonne, Annette, Cécile, Émilie, and Marie would enjoy lifelong financial security as well. Together the guardians were managing a trust fund that was growing as fat and as promising as the babies themselves.

Every newspaper snapshot and every frame of newsreel footage meant money in the bank. That summer of 1934, Fred Davis, the *Toronto Star* photographer, negotiated an exclusive contract to photograph the five sisters for the Newspaper Enterprise Association. The $10,000 the NEA paid to the quintuplet trust fund guaranteed that no one else in the world—not even Oliva and Elzire Dionne—would be permitted to photograph the Dionne Quintuplets for the next year. Pathé News deposited between $12,000 and $15,000 in royalties to the trust fund for every quintuplet newsreel it made. The right to print a single magazine photograph cost $150—the modern equivalent of $2,500 in US currency. Everyone from Lysol to Karo corn syrup, Carnation milk, and Palmolive soap wanted Yvonne's, Annette's, Cécile's, Émilie's, and Marie's darling faces on their advertisements, and was willing to pay thousands of dollars for the privilege. The Madame Alexander Doll Company's Dionne Quintuplet Dolls were such fiercely coveted Christmas gifts that the girls' share of the profits—just 5 percent of the total sales—easily amounted to over $25,000. By the time the five little girls turned twenty-one, the guardians confidently predicted, they would be millionaires.

CHAPTER 13

Parents of Babies Plan for Future

TORONTO GLOBE, NOVEMBER 3, 1934

Across the road at the Dionne farmhouse that fall and winter, the mood was entirely different.

"That was a sad time," neighbor Yvette Boyce recalled. "I remember my mom saying that Mrs. Dionne would cry every day for the girls." Sometimes, if the wind was just right, Elzire could hear her children's voices drifting across the road.

Elzire missed her five baby girls right down to her bones, yet, as she herself said, "I would sooner do a big washing than go to the hospital." Official policy was that she and Oliva were welcome to visit their daughters at all hours of the day or night, anytime they pleased, so long as no one in their own household was ill. In reality, the Dionnes never felt welcome on Dafoe's turf. The hospital, in the words of a sympathetic reporter, was "a luxurious fortress," and the doctor and his staff focused with such intensity on keeping Yvonne, Annette, Cécile, Émilie, and Marie safe and healthy that they seemed to have no regard for how their rules and attitudes would affect the babies' family.

Security procedures made no exceptions for Oliva and Elzire. The babies' parents had to ring a bell at the gate and wait for the guard to let them inside. Once in the nursery itself, they were never granted private time with their children. A nurse always remained in the room, probably due more to lack of tact on the part of Leroux and de Kiriline than to any concern for the babies' safety. Nevertheless, their constant presence unnerved Elzire by exuding the impression that she could not be trusted with her own children—"like we had committed some crime," as she put it.

When at last she was permitted to lend a hand with her daughters' baths, Elzire was so intimidated by the nurses' stern gaze that her usually capable hands fumbled. "She looked down at the adorable children she had brought into the world and she asked herself, 'Are these really my children?'" her husband recalled. Thinking such a thought was enough to overwhelm Elzire's emotions, and she'd flee to weep and pray in privacy. "She could only approach them timidly, in fear, like a stranger," Oliva said.

Tourists, on the other hand, were not the least bit timid about approaching the Dafoe Hospital. They came by the hundreds, parking along the fence and peering through the woven wire in hopes of catching a glimpse of the famous babies. Signs along the Corbeil road reading *No Admittance to the Dionne Quintuplets* did not discourage them. Every day, no matter the temperature, Yvonne, Annette, Cécile, Émilie, and Marie were bundled into pink chinchilla coats and wheeled out onto the porch in their draft-proof carriages for a fresh-air nap, and anyone lucky enough to snag a front-row spot on the fence line could see it happen. Folks drove out of their way just to stop and see five frosted curls of breath rising up from the carriages, Nurse de Kiriline remembered.

It was not unusual for Elzire to have to elbow her way through a crowd on her way to and from the hospital, a phenomenon Elzire felt magnified the distance between herself and her daughters. "They belong to them," she said of the tourists, "not to us."

Oliva did his best to comfort her. "That is not so," he said. "These people are friends who come to see our children. Perhaps in time they will know how we feel, how hard it is for us."

The mobs of curious visitors hardly showed the Dionne family common courtesy, much less any sympathy. Locked doors and drawn shades just barely held them at bay. One man smashed a kitchen windowpane and reached inside, badly frightening little Pauline as she sat playing on the floor by the sink. "Kodak pests" constantly angling to snap pictures made it impossible for Ernest, Rose-Marie, Thérèse, Daniel, and Pauline to romp in the yard, so Oliva converted the old milk shed into a playhouse for them. He also rigged up Elzire's clothesline with a pulley that reached into the house, so that she need not face the hordes of strangers to hang her wash out to dry. On the rare occasions when she ventured out, Elzire hid behind a clump of bushes in the kitchen garden while Ernest flung clods of dirt at the perpetual crowd of fifty or more tourists who shouted questions through the gap beneath the twelve-foot fence. Oliva fell into the habit of simply not looking at anyone. "He keeps his eyes downward and tries desperately to see as little as possible of what is going on around him," noted the *Boston Globe*. His demeanor made Oliva appear so unapproachable that his closest friends stopped greeting him on the streets. Even Auntie Legros's visits to the Dionne farm tapered off.

"As the weeks passed our despondency increased," Oliva said. "It was not only we who were now so definitely cut off from the babies. Our other children felt, too, that there was a barrier between them and their little sisters, and they were puzzled."

Each time she went to visit the nursery, Elzire left five disappointed children behind. "Dr. Dafoe says our other children have chronic colds, and shouldn't visit the quintuplets," she said. "But Dr. Dafoe hasn't made any effort to treat them for these colds. The children often ask to go see the babies. We have to tell them no." It did not matter how much they begged and cried. The antigerm edict was so strict that Ernest, Rose-Marie, Thérèse, Daniel, and Pauline were not allowed inside the nursery—not even to help their baby sisters celebrate their first Christmas. They could only peep at Yvonne, Annette, Cécile, Émilie, and Marie through the big observation window in the office, where select visitors were permitted between two and three o'clock each afternoon.

Their efforts to glimpse their sisters made for a heartbreaking sight for Oliva. "Crowds came to see the quintuplets, and the quintuplets' brothers and sisters stood outside the fence that surrounded the new house with them—wistful little boys and girls, the poor kin of wealthy relatives."

The Dionnes placated themselves with the knowledge that the situation was only temporary. "It is only for two years. We had to do it," Oliva told himself.

When they did come home, though, what then, Elzire wondered? "In order to house them properly—to build a modern, up-to-date house large enough for us all with special nursery equipment for the little ones—and to provide the same expensive scientific care of which the babies had become accustomed and which we realized they might require indefinitely, Oliva and I knew we must have money." But their daughters' fattening trust fund was inaccessible.

Once again a Chicago man came to the Dionnes' rescue with a proposition—this time a theater agent by the name of Max Halperin. His scheme centered on a vaudeville tour of Chicago, South Bend, and Detroit. All the "wonder parents" had to do was stand onstage for a minute or two, just introduce themselves and thank the public for its interest in their babies. That was it. No performance, no act. For those few minutes, the papers reported, they'd be paid upward of $1,700 a week. Halperin would book them a presidential suite in Chicago and pay all their expenses. They'd call it a "goodwill tour," lest anyone consider it in poor taste for the Dionnes to be capitalizing on their extraordinary parenthood. "We just want to show them a real good time and let them see some bright lights," Max Halperin assured the *North Bay Nugget*. "This is just a visit," he told another paper, "nothing commercial about it."

The Dionnes screwed up their courage and, together with their business manager and two relatives to act as interpreters, boarded a train for Chicago on February 3, 1935. Grandpa Dionne stayed behind to look after Ernest, Rose-Marie, Thérèse, Daniel, and Pauline. It had the potential to be a grand adventure, for this was the first time Oliva and Elzire had been away from home since their 1925 honeymoon.

"But as we got nearer and nearer to our destination," Elzire said, "recurrent attacks of pre-stage fright became more and more violent and I recall saying to my husband: 'If I'd had only myself to consider no amount of money could have lured me from home onto the stage—any stage anywhere.'"

Oliva knew just how she felt. "I am sure, if it had been possible, we would have left the train and run back home," he said.

Their apprehension was unmistakable. As Halperin whisked them from nightclubs to department stores, beauty parlors, the fairgrounds, and the stockyards, Oliva and Elzire tried to smile for the multitudes of cameras that greeted them, but the effort showed. Their eyes often shifted downward from all the attention, making Oliva appear stiff and awkward, Elzire shy.

"Events followed one another in nightmarish order until we stood blinking on a stage, and would have been glad if the floor had opened and swallowed us," said Oliva. Chorus girls nudged each other and giggled at them backstage. Elzire held Oliva's hand, trying to be brave as they waited in the wings, and he wrapped his arm around her waist.

A film of their daughters flashed up onto a screen. The band played "Baby Your Mother Like She Babied You." Then an announcer told the audience, "These are not actors, folks. They are just pioneers, frontierspeople. Ladies and gentlemen, the world's most famous parents!"

Oliva had memorized a single line. "Mrs. Dionne and myself are glad to have the opportunity to thank the people of the United States for their interest in our babies," he recited. Elzire stepped up to the microphone and managed to add, "Merci beaucoup et que Dieu vous bénisse." *Thank you very much and may God bless you.*

They delivered the simple greeting five times daily. In between, Elzire played solitaire and hummed hymns while Oliva paced the stuffy dressing room and chain-smoked.

Audiences cheered at every performance. The spectators, in fact, were the only ones enjoying the Dionnes' tour. Just two days into the trip, Elzire was homesick for her babies and cried to return to Corbeil. Oliva was slapped with a $1-million lawsuit by Ivan Spear for breach of contract. (The contract Oliva had signed the year before granted Spear the exclusive right to exhibit and exploit the entire Dionne family, and entitled Spear to 70 percent of any profits.) By week's end, Max Halperin was regretting his promise to pay all the Dionnes' expenses. The tour, he claimed, was $900 in the red. Halperin blamed it largely on the Dionnes' appetites. The food bill had reached $456 in four days—though he neglected to mention that was for the entire party of five, not just Oliva and Elzire. He groaned to the press about the quantities of ginger ale and ice cream they consumed, and the thirty-five-cent cigarettes he said Oliva was constantly borrowing. Their fondness for out-of-season strawberries alone was running Halperin seventy-five cents to a dollar a bowl. "They eat them three times a day," Halperin complained. "They've never had lobster before but they ordered it for dinner and baked ice cream at a dollar a throw."

The newspapers, likely resentful of Oliva and Elzire's habit of dodging photographers and wincing at the sight of reporters, followed Halperin's lead and took to making fun of them. No aspect of their appearance or demeanor was out of bounds. *That Little Shrimp There, Yep, That's Papa Dionne,* one headline pronounced. Fascinated by the physical contrast between husband and wife, the article went on to remark that the size 44 dress Elzire admired in a department store "would never be big enough." Another called Papa a "stooge" and discussed Mama's underwear purchases. Papers in Canada and the United States alike seized every opportunity to mock the Dionnes' plain tastes, taking particular delight when Elzire grimaced at her first taste of caviar, then scoffing when the "backwoods" couple ordered six bottles of strawberry soda pop instead of champagne. *Dionne Tour a Flop,* the *Toronto Globe* decided. The *Pittsburgh Press* dubbed the whole affair a "circus tour."

No one was more displeased with the trip than Ontario's premier, Mitchell Hepburn. "It's nauseating to Canadians, it's disgusting, revolting, and cheap," he declared, seemingly unable to find enough adjectives to condemn it.

Oliva and Elzire insisted that they'd undertaken the stage appearances for the purest of motives. "I want my babies to have the best possible chance in life," Elzire told a reporter. "We must have more bedrooms in our house. There is to be electricity—a new bathroom. It will cost much money!"

Premier Hepburn was not convinced. "They are far from destitute," he told the press. "If two of those babies died where would they be? They would be forgotten in no time," he asserted. "They have no value except as parents of the Quintuplets." As he saw it, Oliva and Elzire's repeated susceptibility to promoters' schemes, coupled with their new willingness to appear onstage for money, was a glaring danger signal. "You can rest assured these children are not going to be put on exhibition to the detriment of their health. That stands, whatever happens," the premier said, and he had every intention of putting his full power behind that promise.

CHAPTER 14

Parents' Wishes to Be Ignored

NORTH BAY NUGGET, MARCH 11, 1935

Premier Hepburn made good on his vow to protect Yvonne, Annette, Cécile, Émilie, and Marie immediately. "We returned to Corbeil," Oliva remembered, "and just then a new calamity overwhelmed us."

By the first of March, a bill that would make the Dionne Quintuplets special wards of His Majesty the King until their eighteenth birthday was headed to the Ontario Legislature. The Canadian government intended to seize custody of the girls until adulthood—without their parents' consent.

The news left Oliva and Elzire reeling. "Elzire could not speak," Oliva recalled. "I could not speak. The children gathered around us wondering what had happened. 'Is anything wrong?' they asked. 'Is it les petites?'

"We could not answer them. This seemed the end. We had been given five wonder children; but because they were wonder children they had been taken from us."

The Dionnes had hardly dared to voice objections to the first guardianship arrangement with the Red Cross. In March of 1935, they broke their silence. For the first time, Oliva Dionne granted extensive interviews with the press, protesting the government's intrusion into his family in no uncertain terms. "They can do that in Russia," he told the *Toronto Star,* "but they can't do that here." To the Dionnes, the premier's insistence that their babies' health must be legally safeguarded was ludicrous, for Oliva and Elzire were confident their daughters had already been blessed with the ultimate protection. "Do you think the quintuplets could have lived if it had not been God's will?" Oliva challenged. "No doctors or nurses on earth could have saved them but for that." Furthermore, he told the press, God had singled them out as parents for these babies; no man-made edict had the authority to overrule that.

When the government did not budge, the Dionnes tried a compromise, conceding that the Dafoe Hospital was the best place for their babies for the time being. If they retained their rights as parents, they would not remove their daughters from the hospital. "I know that we are not the smartest or most worldly wise of people," Oliva said, "but as parents we have a certain responsibility to all our children. It is our duty to give them all a good education, and equal advantage, and the parental care they have a right to."

Premier Hepburn remained unmoved. On March 8, the bill went before the legislature for its first reading. The bill designated the minister of public welfare of Ontario, David Croll, as the babies' "Special Guardian." Oliva would be recognized as his daughters' "natural guardian," but all decision-making power rested with Croll and a board to be appointed by the government.

Oliva vehemently opposed the welfare minister, for David Croll seemed to believe that the Dionnes saw nothing but dollar signs when they looked at their daughters. According to Oliva, Croll had instructed him "to go back to my farm and forget about the babies until they are eighteen, and then we would have a million dollars." But the core of the issue was not money, Oliva insisted—it was the sanctity of his family as a whole. All of his children should have the same opportunities and upbringing, Oliva said, flatly refusing to accept Croll's promise of wealth as a substitute for allowing half of his children to be raised as "state babies."

"All we want is a chance to prove that we can raise our babies," Elzire echoed. "We've never had a chance to show just what we can do. The babies were taken away from us, and now we are like two separate families, and if this bill passes the government we will always be two separate families."

To Croll, it was incomprehensible that anyone could oppose an act that had precisely one purpose: "to prevent professional, quick-talking exploiters and so-called impresarios from exhibiting these children in penny arcades.

"These children are our own royal family," he argued as the bill was debated during its second reading before the legislature. "To ballyhoo them under a tent would be an insult to the babies and their parents. We want to make it possible for them to lead normal lives at home with their brothers, sisters and parents."

His reasoning sounded contradictory, for granting custody of Yvonne, Annette, Cécile, Émilie, and Marie to the government would almost certainly widen their separation from their family, but the welfare minister's point was that a guardianship act would put an end once and for all to Ivan Spear and his million-dollar lawsuit, along with anyone else who might try to follow in Spear's footsteps. "We don't want them exhibited between some sword-swallower and bearded woman on the Chicago midway," the premier reiterated.

That was the one element everyone from Oliva and Elzire Dionne to Premier Hepburn could agree on. Some more conservative members of Parliament, however, thought Hepburn's solution overstepped the government's bounds. "You must protect the father and mother as well as the children," Ontario's former attorney general insisted. "I never saw such drastic legislation."

"Extreme cases require extreme measures," Premier Hepburn replied. If he were Mr. Dionne, Hepburn said, he would welcome the bill's passage.

"Who would like to have their children taken away?" Oliva retorted in the press. "All other Canadians look after their children, why can't I?"

No one opposed the bill more strongly than Elzire Dionne. The day before the vote she announced, "If the bill goes through, I'll go to the hospital and take my babies myself, even if I have to die on the spot."

The animosity between the two sides was palpable from Toronto to Corbeil. Again and again, Nurse Leroux bemoaned in her diary the "hateful" undercurrents flowing through the nursery. The two sides seemed to be making no attempt to understand each other. Louise de Kiriline remembered hearing one of her fellow nurses remark, "I often wonder if it would not, after all, have been fairer to the babies to have left them alone when they did not want to breathe."

In spite of "bitter controversy," the bill moved through the legislature with astonishing momentum. "The Dionne quintuplets nearly caused a riot on the floor of the Ontario Legislature today," the *Pittsburgh Post-Gazette* reported on March 15, the day of the vote. Nevertheless, the Dionne Quintuplet Guardianship Act passed. Legally speaking, Yvonne, Annette, Cécile, Émilie, and Marie belonged to the government of Ontario until they turned eighteen.

Oliva and Elzire took immediate action. In protest, they packed their bags and marched across the street to the Dafoe Hospital, determined to show that no act of Parliament had the power to keep them from their children.

"What a mess," Nurse Leroux lamented to her diary. "The Dionnes moved in today. He & She came over with trunks and walked in and sat down."

Though the standoff did not breach the nursery itself, its nine-month-old occupants were not immune to the incredible tension inside the hospital. "The trouble is that all this emotional upset is a terrible strain on us and the babies sense it and become difficult to handle," wrote Nurse Leroux.

Persuaded by the "eloquence" of a provincial police constable, Oliva and Elzire consented to return home two hours later. The crisis had come to an abrupt halt, but its reverberations would echo through the nursery for years to come.

PART TWO

QUINT-MANIA

March 1935–May 1943

CHAPTER 15

Ontario Adopts Five World-Famous Little Girls

Newsweek magazine, March 1935

Everyone in the world wanted nothing less than the best for the Dionne Quintuplets. Their lives had all the makings of a real-life fairy tale, if only the people most devoted to Yvonne, Annette, Cécile, Émilie, and Marie could have agreed what "best" meant. On one side stood Oliva and Elzire Dionne. On the other, Dr. Dafoe, the nurses, and the board of guardians. Though Oliva himself had a seat on the board, its other three members—Dafoe, Welfare Minister Croll, and Joseph Valin, a respected French Canadian judge from North Bay—outvoted him so consistently that Oliva soon gave up attending the meetings at all.

As a result, Dr. Dafoe enjoyed complete control of daily life in the nursery. Or so it appeared to the public. For all his growing fame as a miracle worker, Dafoe was in truth an "extraordinarily adequate" physician, and he recognized how small a role his skill had played in his five most famous patients' survival. "You know it is only just good luck that the babies are alive," he'd told Nurse de Kiriline. "I mean—don't let's kid ourselves. . . ."

In reality, Dr. Dafoe had a trio of experts prescribing his every move. Dr. Alan Brown of Toronto's Hospital for Sick Children, "the continent's best-known baby doctor," was the ultimate authority on the babies' health. Dr. William Blatz, director of the University of Toronto's Institute of Child Study, oversaw their mental and emotional development. For daily advice on less consequential issues, Dafoe telephoned his brother, Dr. William Dafoe. Armed with their recommendations, he instructed his staff.

And so it fell to the nurses to enact the experts' directions on a day-to-day basis. While Dr. Will's and Dr. Brown's instructions dictated what to do for the children, Dr. Blatz's ideas were perhaps most influential, for he told them *how* to do it. How to act and how to speak every minute of the day as they fed, dressed, and bathed their little charges. "To the whole world these children represent childhood," Dr. Blatz said. "They need protection, they command the affection and sympathy of the multitude."

For starters, "bickering or misunderstanding" between those in charge was not permitted anywhere within earshot of the nursery. Such disruptions made the little girls "peevish and petulant," even as infants. "Now there is the strictest rule that only smiles are allowed around the children," Dr. Dafoe said. He prided himself on "not only the physical hygiene but the moral hygiene of our ideal nursery."

No less than perfect serenity and ironclad firmness was expected of the nurses. It was a daunting combination to pull off. "It is necessary to control even your voice, your expression with a baby. That's not easy," one of them admitted. "Sometimes you forget. But you ought never to scowl and say sharply, 'Émilie, don't do that!' You can use those very words, only speak them firmly, not crossly."

Discipline was gentle, yet absolute. From infancy Yvonne, Annette, Cécile, Émilie, and Marie were trained to eat, sleep, take their baths, and swallow their daily doses of cod-liver oil without the slightest fuss, and no exceptions. "The babies were never picked up after lights were out," Nurse de Kiriline boasted of the nighttime routine. "There was no walking the floor with them at any time to induce them to sleep. There was no rocking to and fro of a disturbed baby, they were never put to sleep in our arms. If any one of them did not fall asleep at once or woke up to cry, the cause of the discomfort or the disquietude was carefully ascertained and eliminated."

Despite their devotion to such strict routines, the nurses were not coldhearted. Rather, they had been tasked with creating "a kind of gold standard of childhood and child care." With the most up-to-date scientific equipment, knowledge, and methods available to them, with twenty-four-hour control and no outside interference, every nurse in the Dafoe Hospital faced expectations that amounted to an infant utopia. "There, surrounded by a retinue of trusty guards and servants, [the Dionnes] have been shut away from the dangers, diseases and debasements of this imperfect world," wrote the *New York Times* of the hospital. Behind its gates, the babies' "starched and expert nurses" were "watching and presumably improving every curl of their hair, every tone of their voices."

Remarkably, the staff appeared undaunted by such lofty goals. Indeed, they were committed to Dr. Blatz's belief "that the care and effort that is expended on a childhood returns dividends in the form of a happily adjusted adult," and had every intention of giving Yvonne, Annette, Cécile, Émilie, and Marie the best possible start in life.

Not even the tiniest seed of a bad habit was allowed to take root. No thumb-sucking. No picky eating. No crying for attention. When the babies discovered the ticklish places between their legs, their pajama sleeves were tied to the bars of their cribs to keep their own curious fingers from straying into their diapers while they were supposed to be sleeping.

The staff had a profound horror of bad habits. Once, Nurse de Kiriline admitted, she nearly gave in to the temptation of putting Annette's favorite toy into the crib with her. "Then all at once the enormity of what I had been about to do struck me. In my thoughtless desire to please Annette, I had nearly committed the sin of starting her on the path of an undesirable habit—to go to bed with toys." For de Kiriline, the greatest shock was how easy it was to succumb to such a mistake, "deftly disguised into an act of loving tenderness, if one relaxes into thoughtless indulgence of a momentary desire."

This constant vigilance, even with the noblest of intentions, was inevitably exhausting. Advocates claimed that although the nurses' work was unrelenting, requiring the sort of round-the-clock devotion more typical of nuns in a convent, they never uttered the words *sacrifice* or *complaint.*

"The work was made easy by the sweet nature of the children," one of the staff confirmed. "I adore these children. I was taken by them the first moment I saw them and I love them with all my heart."

Critics took a less rosy view of the staff's situation. "The hospital is a sanitary glass cage for the babies and for the nurses it has become almost a prison," one writer concluded, with ample reason.

"We had to be cautious who we spoke to," a nurse remembered. "If we went out through those crowds, if anyone talked to you, you just ignored them. They'd question you about the Quints and quote you, and it would get to the newspapers. . . . When we went out of the grounds, our name was put down and the time we left the grounds. And when we came back the time was logged by the guards. And they'd put down any visitors to your residence: the time they came, the time they left, and how many and who they were. . . . We were under constant pressure from the family, the board of guardians, the public—everybody."

Tension between the staff and the Dionne family in particular was ever-present. Oliva and Elzire had not spoken to Dr. Dafoe since the first guardianship arrangement was passed. The doctor, in turn, was "no longer friendly," according to Oliva. "He has the stiff neck when he drives past to the hospital," Oliva said.

Nurse de Kiriline, who was largely responsible for touching off Oliva and Elzire's earliest hostility toward the medical staff, was still incapable of making any allowances for their feelings. As long as Louise de Kiriline was at the helm, the children's health came before their parents' wishes, regardless of the consequences. In May of 1935, she demonstrated that stance all too vividly.

Just four days before the babies' first birthday, Elzire's cousins from Montreal paid a visit. After dinner, they asked to see their five famous relatives. It was not visiting hour, but Yvonne, Annette, Cécile, Émilie, and Marie were napping in their carriages on the hospital's little front porch. Elzire led her guests up the front walk, rather than toward the office door on the side of the building.

When she smiled up at Nurse de Kiriline, who had come out onto the porch, the nurse warned, "Don't you come up those steps."

Elzire stopped.

"But we only meant to take a little peek," one of the cousins protested. "See, they are asleep, and the wind is blowing away from them. Surely there can be no harm; and we have come so far."

"Don't come up those steps," Nurse de Kiriline repeated. Rules were rules. Elzire and Oliva were permitted at any time, but not the cousins. They must wait until the visiting hour and look through the observation window in the office.

The encounter left Elzire stunned and saddened. "I am glad that my babies, my five little ones, are safely at their first birthday, yes," she told a reporter the day her daughters turned one. "But I want them myself, to feel that I am their mother, and have some say about what is done for them. I would keep them in the hospital, certainly, but with people there who would smile at me when I entered, and not turn coldly away, and who would say 'how do you do,' and not act as these people there now do. They won't even look at me. I am treated worse than a stranger."

This "brusque drama" proved the undoing of Nurse de Kiriline. Just one day short of a year as head nurse to the Dionne Quintuplets, the indomitable Louise de Kiriline permanently stepped down from her post. If Oliva and Elzire had taken such a strong dislike to her, she believed, there could be no peace in the nursery unless she left.

Not until years later would Nurse de Kiriline recognize the true blunder at the root of the Dionnes' hostility toward the entire staff. "They felt that they had been ousted and, of course, they were," she admitted. "Mind you, my concern there, of course, was just to keep the babies alive—just to do that. Now, I think, I would take much more time with the parents—realize much more their feelings. . . . I really was quite brusque."

Cécile Lamoureux took over for Nurse de Kiriline on June 1, 1935. "She is very excitable and so excites the babies very easily," Yvonne Leroux noted in her diary. That excitement came with an agreeable trade-off, for head nurse Lamoureux had made a wise move in her opening relations with the Dionne family. "I made a conscious effort to invite, as warmly as possible, Mme. Dionne, so that the overwhelming ostracism that she must have felt would be forgotten."

It worked. Within a matter of days, Elzire and Oliva were visiting the nursery more often and behaving more pleasantly toward the staff. "Mrs. Dionne is a charming woman," Nurse Lamoureux decided. Yet she also recognized that there was more to the shy young farmwife than met the eye. She saw in Mrs. Dionne a woman who knew "how to keep smiling in the face of tomorrow's uncertainty. One who prepares without public display the revenge she will have for her children."

CHAPTER 16

Most Famous of Mothers One of the Unhappiest

ST. LOUIS STAR-TIMES, JUNE 3, 1935

Outside the hospital gates, the world was becoming less and less pleasant for Oliva and Elzire. The Dionnes were being battered by bad publicity. "As a burnt child dreads the fire," Elzire later said of reporters, "we dreaded to see them coming." "They tell lies about us," Oliva said. "Everyone believes the other side." Only the *North Bay Nugget* made a continual effort to give equal weight to the Dionnes' side of the story and present their point of view accurately and respectfully. In return for such courtesy, Oliva Dionne favored the *Nugget* with exclusive interviews.

Beyond North Bay, however, backhanded compliments were the best Oliva and Elzire could hope for as their babies' fame spread through newspapers and magazines around the world. The Dionne family was routinely praised for its ancestral hardiness and "unspoiled, clean-bred stock." If not for these qualities, Dafoe and de Kiriline maintained, no amount of doctoring could have saved the quintuplets. *Pure, simple,* and *strong,* the articles said—all words that should have been complimentary but instead came off as subtly condescending. They might have been describing a particularly fine breed of draft horse rather than human beings.

Oliva and Elzire themselves were most often depicted as rustic peasants. The more charitable writers described them as poor, under-educated, and therefore blameless for their inability to provide scientific hygiene and child care. Other journalists blatantly deemed them shiftless, dirty, and willfully ignorant.

Whether positive or negative, stories about the Dionne family usually emphasized their "primitive" living conditions. Their one-and-a-half-story clapboard farmhouse was called "ramshackle" and "dingy"—"the miserable Dionne shack." Occasionally more tactful descriptions such as "unpretentious" or "modest" turned up, but such sensitivity was not the norm. The Dionne Quintuplets were a rags-to-riches Cinderella story, so the press spotlighted the rags aspect for maximum effect.

Little wonder, then, that Oliva and Elzire found sympathy difficult to come by. If their children were receiving better care than they were able to provide—indeed, better care than virtually any parent in Canada could provide—what right had they to complain? When they baffled the public by failing to take part in the first-birthday festivities for Yvonne, Annette, Cécile, Émilie, and Marie, forsaking even the special Mass celebrated in their children's honor, their image took its sharpest turn for the worse. What kind of parents would refuse even to thank God for their babies' extraordinary survival?

If the Dionnes were to garner any support for reuniting their family, they sorely needed to change the public's perception of them. That spring of 1935, the woman who would help them do it walked past the *No Admittance* sign nailed to the gate and knocked at their back door.

Lillian Barker's first glimpse of Elzire Dionne came through the crack of the kitchen door—a "decidedly handsome" woman with dark hair and eyes in a yellow house dress and matching apron. That apron caught Miss Barker's attention at once. "A kitchen apron, full skirted with five quint heads embroidered in brown across the bottom."

"From the very day the quints were born I've wanted to write your biography," Miss Barker told Elzire in French through the latched screen. Yes, she admitted, she was a reporter, for the *New York Daily News*. That in itself was a strike against her. Reporters, Elzire warily informed Miss Barker, had already made fun of her and Oliva and "printed unkind and untrue things."

Yet everything else about Lillian Barker conspired to keep Elzire talking against her better judgment. Barker was a Catholic, and she spoke French. She was patient, persistent, and above all, considerate. There on the Dionnes' back porch she promised never to write anything about Elzire without her permission. "Whether you let me do your biography or not, I'd like to know the real truth about you," Miss Barker told Elzire. "You can't imagine how much I'd like to know it."

Elzire unlatched the screen door.

Beginning in May, readers the world over became intimately acquainted with Elzire Dionne. First came a two-page interview: *Most Famous of Mothers One of the Unhappiest,* the headline read. A series of biographical articles entitled "My Life and Motherhood" followed, appearing in newspapers from Iowa to Australia that fall and winter.

Free to speak her own language with a reporter she felt safe confiding in, Elzire related columnsful of anecdotes from her childhood, courtship, and early marriage, which Lillian Barker translated into English. Interspersed with those memories was the story of the quintuplets' birth and first year, also told from Elzire's point of view.

Identifying how much of this autobiography came directly from Elzire's memory and how much detoured through Barker's imagination is a dicey proposition, for Barker wrote in a melodramatic "sob sister" style that today might earn her the title of drama queen. Sob sister reporters aimed straight for women's hearts, hoping to sway their opinions by deliberately ratcheting up the emotional stakes in their stories.

For the Dionnes, thirsty for sympathy from the public, that style was an ideal match. The story itself was also tailor-made for Barker, complete with Elzire's brush with death during the miraculous birth, and her anguish at losing custody of her babies not once but twice. The result is something more akin to a soap opera script than a news report.

Nevertheless, it's certain that Oliva and Elzire approved of what Lillian Barker wrote. Had she portrayed them in a way they found objectionable, there is no doubt they would have withdrawn their friendship. After all they had been through with the press, it is impossible to imagine the Dionnes tolerating any further abuse of their trust.

The Elzire Dionne who emerged from Barker's articles was not the bashful, timid farmwife who for the past year had been more likely to beg her husband, "Tell him, tell him," than answer a reporter's questions directly. This Elzire spoke for herself, in an "emphatic way" and with "lightning-quick intelligence."

As Elzire told it, she and her husband had not attended Yvonne, Annette, Cécile, Émilie, and Marie's birthday celebration because the "daily torture" of being separated from them was something she could no longer hide. "Separation by death is one thing, and inevitable, a thing we have to accept, while separation from living babies is something else, entirely different," Elzire said. "I know; I have had both experiences." Living apart from her five daughters was "more and more a crucifixion," she said, harder to accept than the loss of her fourth child, baby Leo, to pneumonia in 1930.

"How could I . . . present myself at the hospital and mingle with guests in festive, gay, chattering mood," she asked, when her grief had become impossible to conceal? Her absence was not a matter of ingratitude, as so many assumed. "To every one who has ever done the least little thing for my five little ones I shall always be grateful," Elzire declared.

"So many people don't understand our position," she explained. "When we first relinquished our parental rights my husband and I—bewildered, distraught and anxious as we were about the babies—felt we were doing the best thing for them. That was why we made the sacrifice—agreed to the separation." All that changed when the government added sixteen years to the guardianship. "Don't, I beg you, talk to me any more about the protection of the government," Elzire said. "What I want is my babies and will never stop fighting until I get them."

Elzire's interviews won her a measure of the sympathy she craved, yet her voice could not dilute the controversy entirely. Instead, debate escalated as mothers of less fortunate quadruplets and quintuplets found themselves compelled to speak out in favor of the Guardianship Act.

To Mrs. Lawrence Wycoff of Sac City, Iowa, the Dionnes' scorn for the government aid their babies were receiving was "perfectly disgusting." The mother of quadruplets born less than two weeks after the Dionnes, Mrs. Wycoff found Oliva and Elzire's attitude toward the Dafoe Hospital "almost unthinkable." It was hardly a surprising reaction, considering that the smallest of her four babies had not survived. "Baby Lorraine might have lived if she could have been in a real incubator," Mrs. Wycoff pointedly informed the *Des Moines Register.*

Another bereaved mother, seventy-eight-year-old Elizabeth Lyon of Mayfield, Kentucky, shared Mrs. Wycoff's sentiment, though she expressed herself far more gently. In 1896, Mrs. Lyon had given birth to five baby boys—Matthew, Mark, Luke, John, and Paul—all of whom starved to death in heartbreaking succession before they were fourteen days old. "I'm sure I could have raised them all if they had had the attention the Dionne children have," Mrs. Lyon told a reporter.

Moving though the Wycoff and Lyon stories were, those tragedies were irrelevant to Oliva and Elzire. All five of their babies were alive and thriving, and the Dionnes wanted nothing more than to be reunited with their little girls.

CHAPTER 17

The Private Life of the Dionne Quints

LIBERTY MAGAZINE, JUNE 1935

As the fight to bring their daughters home lengthened from months into years, Oliva and Elzire overlooked one glaring complication: as far as Yvonne, Annette, Cécile, Émilie, and Marie themselves were aware, they *were* home. For the rest of their lives they would look back on their time in the nursery as "the happiest, least complicated years of our lives."

Sheltered from the controversy between their parents and guardians, the five sisters grew up believing the world revolved around them, for in that small hospital, it did. "We had everything we wanted, everything within the limits of our knowledge and imaginations," they reminisced as adults. "In that house of fives, we were treated like princesses. We were the cause and center of all activity."

The *New York Times* called their nursery "a compendium of Lilliput luxury." All the furniture was specially scaled to their size, from the dinner tables to their five cushioned rocking chairs. Their beds, porridge bowls, hot-water bottles, and everything in between were inscribed with their names. Until they learned to read, small picture-medallions affixed throughout the nursery showed the children which chair, peg, cubbyhole, and toothbrush belonged to each of them. Yvonne's special marker was a bluebird. Annette had a maple leaf, Cécile a turkey, Émilie a tulip, and Marie a puppy. Each also had a color that belonged to her: pink for Yvonne, red for Annette, green for Cécile, white for Émilie, and blue for Marie.

Their closets bulged with dresses and overalls, ruffled sunsuits and posh wool Hudson's Bay Company coats striped in green, red, yellow, and blue. In the playroom were storybooks, toy pianos, trumpets, rattles, drums, building blocks, and balls. One whole corner was devoted to their dolls, complete with beds, cupboards full of clothes, and a china cabinet stocked with miniature dishes. Another room contained easels, paintbrushes, pegboards, plasticine modeling clay, pencils and crayons, scissors, construction paper, and paste. On Wednesdays, Yvonne, Annette, Cécile, Émilie, and Marie reveled in the delights of their own private carpentry shop, where they pounded nails and sawed through soft wood with man-sized tools. Outside were tricycles, wagons, toboggans, hobbyhorses, and kiddie cars.

Admirers showered them with gifts, more gifts than five little girls could possibly make use of. Teddy bears and rag dolls. Handmade dresses and crocheted berets. A one-of-a-kind five-passenger deluxe kiddie car from a fan in California. Patchwork quilts for their dolls. Books. Always, the presents came in multiples of five—except the radio-Victrola. A stack of records, ranging from nursery songs to arias from *La Bohème* and *I Pagliacci* filled the nursery with music that would evoke "a certain gladness" in Yvonne, Annette, Cécile, Émilie, and Marie for decades to come. "The overwhelming memory is of a wonderful, glowing happiness given, received, and shared," they said of those early years.

"Above all else, we had each other," the sisters remembered. The lack of playmates, or of any visitors other than their parents, bothered them not at all. "We were a club, a society, a civilization all our own."

The only thing missing was love. "We had bicycles, we had dolls— everything but family," Annette said. Their nurses adored them, yet were forbidden to indulge in the most basic ways of showing it. "They were not supposed to express their affection," Cécile remembered. "It was very strict on that." Kisses spread germs. Cuddles risked favoritism, or spoiling. "But I do remember that they were very kind to us," Annette added. "They were always smiling."

Mother was not a word the girls fully understood, either literally or figuratively. "We knew that there was one visitor, who came across the road to see us, whom the nurses taught us to call Maman," the sisters remembered. But Maman was only a name. It did not signal love and security the way it did for other children. "A normal child, a mother presses to her breast," Cécile said. "It makes a relationship. We did not know that from a mother." Their first memory of their mother was seeing her through the observation window at the back of the nursery. Because they had known no other way of life, the strangeness of this situation was lost on Yvonne, Annette, Cécile, Émilie, and Marie. "It was not possible for her to be always at our side, mothering us in the true meaning of the word, so how could we miss her on the days she did not arrive, or feel any appreciable sense of loss?"

No matter how much she hugged and kissed her daughters to make up for the time they'd lost together as infants, Elzire's brief visits could not compete with the staff's constant care and attention. "They were always there if we had need of them, to open their arms to us, to join in the laughter and dry the tears," the sisters later said of their nurses. In their memories, the nurses would meld into "a kind of composite mother," who evoked the tender emotions that ought to have belonged to Elzire.

Canada's leading pediatrician, Dr. Alan Brown of Toronto, saw nothing to object to in this arrangement. "To a child, a mother is only somebody who cares for him," he said. According to Brown's way of thinking, round-the-clock attention from a team of devoted nurses compensated for any lack of contact with their own mother. "And a father—Dr. Dafoe is a father to those children."

But the nurses themselves had reason to doubt Brown's convictions. They were there every day to see how the five toddlers reacted when

Elzire and Oliva left the nursery. "Always, those babies clamoured to kiss their parents good night," Nurse Leroux remembered. "When the inevitable moment for departure came, it was always too soon for the little ones. They did not cry. But their mouths drooped, their eyes grew large and puzzled. They shook their heads from side to side, held out their arms, even grabbed at their mother's skirt or their father's trouser-leg as their parents scrambled to get out of the nursery."

Soon enough, the goodbye routine became normal to the children, too. Before they had turned three, Yvonne, Annette, Cécile, Émilie, and Marie no longer made any fuss when Oliva and Elzire left. They had stopped even looking toward the farmhouse or calling for their parents. They were so young when it happened, the sorrowful partings left no imprint on their memories.

Just as *mother* was a foreign concept, the notion of *home* was different for them than for other children. Little in the hospital was especially home-like. "In the nursery itself there was no living room, no family room per se," Nurse Doreen Chaput remembered. Their dining room was plain and serviceable—just small tables and chairs. "I always liked to say that they were the poorest little rich girls I ever knew."

Rather than trying to replicate a homey atmosphere, life in the Dafoe Hospital was structured like a private twenty-four-hour nursery school. In fact, it was modeled after Dr. William Blatz's famous St. George's School for Child Study in Toronto, by none other than Blatz himself. Like the pupils at St. George's, the Dionnes followed a carefully composed timetable that prescribed every aspect of the day, from the 7:20 morning bath to the bedtime drink of water at 6:40. Mornings began at 6:30 with orange juice and cod-liver oil. A set of chimes mounted on the wall rang for mealtimes at 8:00, 11:40, and 6:00. In between came diversions such as "directed play," "relaxation," and "outdoor free play," at intervals running anywhere from five minutes to two hours. Trips to the washroom, dubbed "elimination routine," were scheduled for 6:30, 8:30, 12:15, 2:30, 4:00, and 6:30.

The goal of Blatz's regimen for the girls was twofold: to maximize efficiency and minimize stress for the nurses charged with the daily care of five boisterous toddlers, and also to provide every opportunity to bolster the girls' physical, mental, and emotional growth. Unfamiliar with any other way of life, they adapted readily to this routine. "We didn't know at that time," said Yvonne, "that the whole way of life in which we were raised wasn't good for us." As far as they knew, everything around them—from the nurses and their clipboards to the woven wire fence—was perfectly normal.

CHAPTER 18

Quins Lose Stage Fright, 2500 Gawkers a Day

VARIETY MAGAZINE, JULY 1935

Perhaps the most extraordinary routine in the Dafoe Hospital's tightly structured schedule took place between two and three o'clock each afternoon: visiting hour. As early as the spring of 1935, tourists were being permitted to file past the guard at the gate and the barbed wire on the fences for an inside glimpse at what Dr. Dafoe called "the baby show."

"Visitors still coming by the hundreds," Nurse Leroux wrote on April 2; "they come in and look at the babies through the observation window in the hall and go out by the kitchen door. The babies are beginning to notice them and in spite of our warnings of 'no tapping on windows, no calling, no funny faces,' people forget themselves and scream with joy every time they even move."

Less than a week later, the exposure began taking a visible toll on Yvonne, Annette, Cécile, Émilie, and Marie. "The babes seem to feel the excitement of the visitors and are very agitated after the hour is over," Nurse Leroux observed. "They do so try to be entertaining that it makes them tired." When they began losing weight, Dafoe called off the observation period altogether on April 10.

But the tourists' insistence on seeing the Dionne Quintuplets proved difficult to ignore. "It wasn't a public you wanted to turn away," explained one of Dafoe's colleagues. "They were kindly, they cared about the babies."

A new tactic debuted by mid-June of 1935. "We are showing the babies on the verandah," Nurse Leroux wrote on the fifteenth. "We take them out one at a time and hold them up. The crowd goes wild but we try to make the babes pay very little attention to them." That was next to impossible. Two thousand people routinely pressed against the fence each day. On Sundays in the summer, there might be ten thousand. Suspended in the nurses' arms over a placard proclaiming their names, Yvonne, Annette, Cécile, Émilie, and Marie kicked and waved, played patty-cake, and threw kisses to their audience. "The babes clap and coo and seem to enjoy the whole thing," wrote Nurse Leroux, though she also noticed they were still prone to nervousness if the crowds became too large.

They were shown four times a day—before and after their morning nap, and again before and after their afternoon nap. If one little girl was unwell, the nurses secretly displayed another of her sisters twice, ensuring that everyone left believing they had seen five identical babies.

Oliva Dionne detested every minute of it. His resentment and bitterness "snaps and crackles in his every tone and word," said one New York journalist. The government had seized custody of his daughters to protect them from being exhibited on the American stage, then looked the other way as the hospital's front porch turned into a kind of theater.

Oliva's concerns were not unfounded. His little girls were not old enough to talk or walk, yet all five of them appeared to revel in entertaining the crowds. "Not only did those babies 'play up' like born prima donnas . . . they also displayed all of a prima donna's jealousy," Yvonne Leroux later confessed. "Everybody wanted to be leading lady. No matter which was picked up first . . . the other children's faces drooped in grief."

Dr. Dafoe resented the criticism. "When you know people have driven thousands of miles for a glimpse of them, it is hard to see visitors go away disappointed," he countered. His logic seems off-kilter in retrospect, but then again, Dafoe had learned early on the value of the public's interest. The lifesaving incubators and breast milk would never have come in time if he had squelched the public's curiosity instead of stoking it those first days after Yvonne, Annette, Cécile, Émilie, and Marie's birth. "Sometimes it seems to me that they have been sustained and kept alive by the love and good wishes of the whole world," he said. Dafoe felt he was repaying a debt by indulging the visitors' desire to see the "eighth wonder of the world."

The public's trust in Dr. Dafoe ran so deep that no one seriously questioned his judgment on this issue or any other. Just the sight of his kind, benevolent face "inspired immediate confidence," the *North Bay Nugget* said. That changed in the spring of 1936, when *Cosmopolitan* magazine printed an article on the Dionnes by Dr. Alfred Adler, an eminent psychologist from Vienna.

Dr. Adler took issue with virtually every element of the children's upbringing, and his assessment struck *Cosmopolitan*'s readers like a gut punch. "How will they be prepared for the task of adjusting themselves to life?" Adler asked. "What will be their future?" His predictions were dire. To hear Dr. Adler tell it, the efforts to raise five happy, well-adjusted little girls were backfiring in every way possible.

Keeping them always dressed alike, setting them to play with identical toys, and forbidding contact with other children would hobble their individuality, Adler warned. Living apart from their family also risked consequences no one much wanted to contemplate: "The quintuplets live like the inmates of a model orphanage," Adler wrote, "and a certain emotional starvation is inseparable from institutional life."

He saw no opportunity for Yvonne, Annette, Cécile, Émilie, and Marie to develop independence or initiative. "Everything for which other children must struggle comes easily to the quintuplets," Adler pointed out. Continuing to indulge their every whim would turn them into "self-centered little parasites."

Adler reserved especial disapproval for the way the children were exhibited on the verandah. "Life in a glass house is not conducive to normal human development," he admonished. "Five little guppies living in a fish bowl may not be distracted by constant exposure. But babies are not fishes. Children accustomed to being exhibited are never happy unless they elicit attention." Luckily, Dr. Adler saw no evidence that the publicity and exposure had harmed them—yet. That luck would not hold much longer, though. "There is danger ahead," he cautioned.

All of his points were valid and well reasoned. But then Adler committed a stunning tactical error. His solution—splitting the not-quite-two-year-old sisters apart to be raised "incognito" by five different families, "to destroy the uniqueness of their position, and to make them forget they are quintuplets"—made the public's jaw collectively drop.

"In city after city," the *Toronto Globe* reported, "people jump at him from doorways, wait for him in hotel lobbies and buttonhole him at dinners asking: 'Do you really think that the quintuplets ought to be separated?'"

Humorist Will Cuppy summed up the world's reaction to the article in a single stinging quip: "Why not divide Dr. Adler into five neat parts for his own good and see how he likes it?" All the common sense the psychologist had spoken was drowned in the outcry.

Dr. Dafoe scoffed at Adler's alarm, insinuating that an article published in a fiction magazine should not be taken seriously. What was more, Dafoe said, Adler had been miffed when he found he could not observe the children any more closely than an ordinary tourist. "He was sore when he found the rules were real rules and he couldn't break them no matter who he was."

Nurse de Kiriline, however, spoke out in defense of Dr. Adler's less controversial concerns. Though she no longer had any sway over the happenings at the Dafoe Hospital, she expressed her opinion forcefully, particularly when it came to exhibiting Yvonne, Annette, Cécile, Émilie, and Marie. It was one thing to showcase the children as examples of good care and common sense, she said. "But to use them as a dumping place for indiscriminate curiosity is an abuse of their rights as individuals," she asserted in a national women's magazine. "It can be of no advantage to the babies' mental development to be shown off like baby bears in a zoo."

The controversy did little to dissuade the tourists. They just kept coming—hundreds, if not thousands, by the hour—and the board of guardians showed neither the willingness nor the ability to fend them off. "Whether they like it or not, whether their guardians decree it, whether their parents give their permission, those five famous tots in Callander, Ontario, are the little princesses of the entire world," one journalist decreed. "As such, they are already in and must remain in the public eye as long as the world demands it." The board fell in with this logic, taking the position that gawkers were inevitable, and the more the crowds were thwarted, the more obnoxious they would become. Welfare Minister David Croll reasoned that if the government didn't take the upper hand and find a tasteful way to display the Dionne Quintuplets to their adoring fans, encroachment on the children's privacy would spiral out of control. "We have found that we have to do something to keep hot dog stands and peddlers from our front door. One is so close now that the children smell hot dogs all day long," Croll told the *Toronto Star.* A stairway to the stand's roof invited tourists to climb up and peek into the babies' play yard. That sort of nonsense had to stop.

With the exception of Oliva Dionne, the guardians were not opposed to satisfying the public's curiosity. "These children are the treasures of the world," Judge Valin said. "Why should they not be seen?" The difficulty was keeping Yvonne, Annette, Cécile, Émilie, and Marie from realizing they were being stared at. In that one regard, the board agreed with Dr. Adler: the children were rapidly approaching an age where they could no longer be displayed in front of the crowds like goods in a shop window, and everyone from Oliva Dionne to Dr. Dafoe was adamant that the little girls should not become conscious of their celebrity. "Those babies have a right to some privacy," Dr. Dafoe told the press, "and we are try-ing to work out some plan that will give them more of it."

The board turned the predicament over to Dr. Blatz, who proposed a one-of-a-kind solution: a playground surrounded by a U-shaped observa-tion gallery. This gallery would be an empty, unlit hallway, five feet wide, lined with windows facing the playground. Floor coverings of cork and felt would muffle the sound of any footsteps from within. With screens of fine white mesh covering the glass, the spectators' presence would be obscured from the outside.

To the public, these windows were billed as one-way glass. Hundreds of people would be able to stand inside the dim gallery, gazing through the mesh-covered panes at the frolicking toddlers, who would be con-scious only of "blurred silent shadows." A low fence kept the girls from approaching the windows and discovering their audience. A wading pool, sand pit, swings, and jungle gym filled the grassy space enclosed by the observatory. A concrete path for tricycles and wagons ran around the perimeter of the play area. Twice a day, health and weather permitting, the children would be shepherded into the play yard so the public could ogle them.

"This at first seems like cold-blooded exploitation of these five chil-dren," Dr. Blatz conceded, "in spite of the fact that no admission is charged to the thousands upon thousands of the curious who have trav-elled miles in order to see them." But since a similar arrangement had proven harmless to the children at Blatz's own high-profile St. George's School for Child Study, he argued, it ought to be suitable for the Dionne sisters. "One cannot help but feel that, aside from the fact that these chil-dren must be daily on display, one could ask for no more ideal physical arrangements for bringing up children," Blatz boasted of the hospital-playground complex.

CHAPTER 19

Quintuplet Frolics Play to "Standing Room Only"

PITTSBURGH PRESS, JULY 1936

The observatory opened to the public on July 1, 1936. It was an immediate sensation. By August, three thousand to six thousand people a day were flocking to Corbeil.

"Couldn't even get across the road here for twenty minutes at a time," a gas station attendant remembered later. "Cars all over the place. People used to be lined up three miles out to the highway, right out to Dionne's."

Across the street from the Dafoe Hospital, watchmen with red flags directed the cars to park in rows a quarter mile long, forming acre-sized blocks that eventually overflowed into what had formerly been the Dionne pasture. An hour before "showtime," several hundred cars from over thirty states and provinces routinely accumulated. Excitement and reverence mingled to create an atmosphere somewhere between a circus and a religious shrine as spectators approached the double row of barbed wire–topped fence. A sign proclaimed the rules:

Visitors' Information and Instructions

1. This playground has been erected so you can see the children at play.
2. Visitors will by co-operating and following instructions assist those in charge.

3. Please maintain silence and keep moving.

4. Do not speak to the children.

5. You may enter as often as you wish during the visiting period, but in order to be fair to other visitors you must keep moving toward the exits.

6. If it is stormy the children will not appear.

PLAY GROUND HOURS

9:30–10:30 A.M.

2–3 P.M.

NO PHOTOGRAPHS ALLOWED
TO BE TAKEN OF THE CHILDREN

"A line, orderly and quiet, forms at the entrance gate to the observation gallery," wrote an Ohio reporter who came to record the spectacle. "Before 9:30 more than 1,000 are in line."

Almost everyone pocketed pebbles from a divided wooden trough placed outside the fence while they waited. *Stones from Dafoe Hospital Grounds,* the sign above the bins read. "Already legend has endowed these pebbles with mystic powers—it being suggested that under their powerful magic childless homes are soon blessed with babies." They ranged from coin-sized stones for single births to rocks bigger than softballs for quads and quints. These "passion pebbles" were so prized as good-luck tokens by childless couples that a jewelry firm in New York City offered to make five-stone charm bracelets from them. (In fact, the "magical" pebbles were loads of gravel trucked in from the nearby lakeshore each night.)

"Up and down the restless line dash small boys with shrill, penetrating voices who offer to check your camera for 35 cents," a Baltimore reporter noted. *ANY PERSON IN POSSESSION OF A CAMERA WILL BE REFUSED ADMISSION TO PLAYGROUND BUILDING,* proclaimed a prominent notice. Tourists who risked trying to snap a photo would be stopped by the guards, who seized their film and exposed it to daylight, ruining the entire roll of images. Rumor had it that a Chicago gangster had been arrested—not for toting a gun in a shoulder holster, but for smuggling in his Kodak Brownie camera.

As nine thirty neared, a hush fell over the crowd, "seemingly filled with a common sense of awe, as though they were about to witness a miracle," marveled a journalist for *Woman's World* magazine. Everyone strained on tiptoe, peering toward the hospital until a ripple of murmurs and gasps signaled the first glimpses of the children, "tumbling out on the little porch of their living-quarters as though popped out of a gun."

The children's very ordinariness bowled the audience over. "The effect on the crowd has been instantaneous. The very human children have made them all human and they chuckle with delight. They had half expected to see five little angels float across their visions, or perhaps five tiny molecules of science."

A chain rattled as the guards opened the padlock on the observatory doors and four hundred people at a time passed through turnstiles into the dim observation gallery—half into the left leg of the U-shaped building, half into the right. *PHOTOGRAPHING OF BABIES BY VISITORS NOT ALLOWED,* a final notice at the doorway reminded. *PLEASE CO-OPERATE; SILENCE IS REQUESTED,* said another inside the play yard itself. The rules were to keep moving along the corridor, but everyone wanted a chance to pause at the windows for a good long look.

"It was like viewing a litter of kittens," one Toronto man said; "they were all so cute, you wouldn't know which one to pick." Some spectators burst into tears at the sight of their "breathtaking" beauty.

Clad in bonnets and sunsuits—one each in mauve, pink, blue, orange, and yellow—Yvonne, Annette, Cécile, Émilie, and Marie romped in their wading pool, each pushing and shoving to get the fountain's thin stream of water all to herself. They filled their bonnets with water and drank from them, captivating the crowd and bringing the nurses splashing in ankle-deep to stop them.

"Right along there, ladies, show a little pep," the security guards would admonish from behind. "Keep moving so everyone can see. That's it. A little pep, please."

A few moments and it was over. "Take a last look now, and hop it!" another guard said, coaxing the tourists along to the exits. From door to door, the trip was just over seventy feet long.

Out in the bright sunshine the dazzled spectators exclaimed over what they had just seen. "I thank my Almighty God that I have lived to see this day," a lady from Maryland declared. "We drove 590 miles to see this," one elderly woman said. "But, my gracious! It was worth it!"

None of it—from the parking to the pebbles to the trip through the observation gallery—cost a single cent. Nevertheless, money was pouring into Callander.

Outside the fenced hospital grounds, a carnival-like tourist oasis erupted from the rocky bushland. The papers dubbed it "Quintland," "Dionneville," and "Quintuplet Village." "Long before you cover the 2½ miles to the Dionne home, the sound of hammering and the smell of new lumber are evident," a visiting journalist noted. "Souvenir and hot dog stands, selling everything from postcards to pumpernickel, are rising on every hand."

The first to cash in had been Auntie Legros, who launched her Quintland career—and possibly Quintland itself—by giving lectures and selling souvenirs from a Coney Island–style tent alongside the Dafoe Hospital. The day before her great-nieces' first birthday, she graduated to a wood-frame refreshment stand called "Quinstore," where she and Madame Lebel answered questions and signed their illustrated twenty-two-page memoir of the miraculous birth, *Administering Angels of the Dionne Quintuplets*. When Quinstore had to be torn down to make way for the observatory in the summer of 1936, Auntie Legros simply put

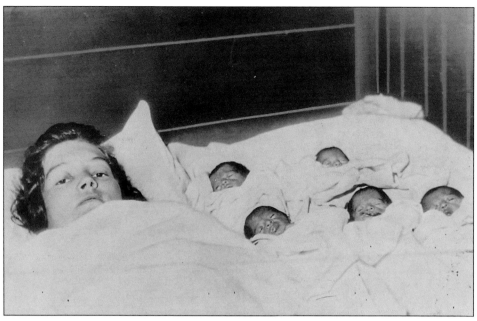

Elzire Dionne and her five newborns, barely six hours after their birth.

Collection of the author

Oliva Dionne and the "old family"—
Daniel, Pauline, Ernest, Thérèse, and
Rose-Marie—on the morning of
May 28, 1934.

Collection of the author

The five elder Dionne children in 1935: Pauline and Ernest stand behind Rose-Marie, Daniel, and Thérèse. (A sixth sibling, Leo, died in infancy.)

Collection of the author

The Little Doc—Dr. Allan Roy Dafoe.

Courtesy of Callander Bay Heritage Museum

Cécile, Émilie, and Marie Dionne in the Chicago incubator.

Courtesy of Callander Bay Heritage Museum

The Dionnes' parlor, transformed into a nursery by Nurse Louise de Kiriline. Incubators line the right-hand wall; above them, a washtub and Kleenex box hang on either side of the makeshift window into Elzire Dionne's bedroom.

Courtesy of Callander Bay Heritage Museum

Nurse Yvonne Leroux placing one of the Dionnes' babies into an incubator.

Collection of the author

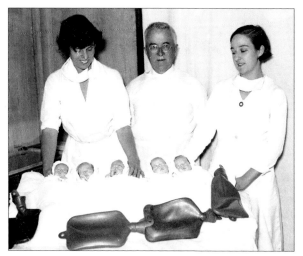

Nurse de Kiriline, Dr. Dafoe, and Nurse Leroux showing off the two-month-old infants.

Courtesy of Callander Bay Heritage Museum

The Dafoe Hospital nearing completion in the late summer of 1934.

Courtesy of Callander Bay Heritage Museum

Ontario Provincial Police standing watch over the Dionnes' prams on the hospital's front verandah.

Courtesy of Callander Bay Heritage Museum

Christmas 1934. One of a scant handful of photographs of Elzire and Oliva Dionne with Dr. Dafoe (center).

Courtesy of Callander Bay Heritage Museum

Yvonne, Annette, Cécile, Émilie, and Marie's "quintessential" baby photo, sold by their father in his souvenir pavilion.

Collection of the author

Émilie, Cécile, Marie, Annette, and Yvonne lolling beneath their sun lamp in February 1935.

Collection of the author

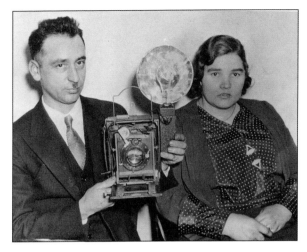

Oliva and Elzire Dionne trying to smile for a comical turn-the-tables-on-the-cameramen pose during their 1935 vaudeville tour.

Collection of the author

Nurses de Kiriline and Leroux watch Marie, Émilie, Cécile, Annette, and Yvonne delight in their first-birthday cakes. None of the babies' first-birthday photos includes a single family member.

Collection of the author

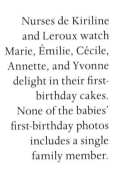

A tourist snapped this photo of the three eldest Dionne children on the front porch in September 1935.

Collection of the author

Thérèse and Rose-Marie mug for a tourist's camera. (The woman on the porch may be Oliva's sister Alma.)

Collection of the author

Auntie Legros's souvenir and refreshment pavilion, complete with rooftop observation deck, in the summer of 1935.

Collection of the author

Tourists make a mad dash toward the hospital's inner fence line in hopes of securing an unobstructed view of the babies on the verandah.

Collection of the author

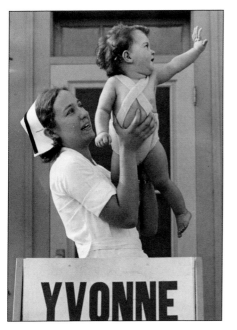

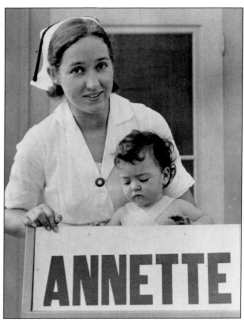

Yvonne waves to quintuplet fans from
Nurse Leroux's arms, September 1935.

Collection of the author

An unusually subdued Annette and Nurse
Leroux on the verandah, September 1935.

Collection of the author

Nurse Cécile Lamoureux with
Cécile, September 1935.

Collection of the author

Nurse Lamoureux and Émilie, September 1935.

Collection of the author

Nurse Leroux coaxes Marie to greet the public, September 1935.

Collection of the author

The babies' twice-daily view of the crowd from the verandah.

Collection of the author

Marie, Yvonne, Annette, Cécile, and Émilie taking the air on the hospital verandah, September 1935.

Collection of the author

The observatory in its final stages of construction, late June 1936.

Collection of the author

The observatory playground, with its tricycle track, wading pool, and sand pit. In bright sunlight, the white mesh screens almost entirely obscure the interior of the observation gallery.

Collection of the author

Panorama of Quintland, circa 1936. Oliva Dionne's souvenir pavilion is on the left, with the Dionne farmhouse just down the road; the staff house is at center; and the hospital and observatory are on the right.

Collection of the author

Madame Lebel and Auntie Legros selling souvenirs, August 1936. Pennants, figurines, plates, and postcards are all visible for sale. Madame Lebel is holding a copy of the midwives' memoir, *Administering Angels of the Dionne Quintuplets*.

Courtesy of Callander Bay Heritage Museum

A woman selects a "fertility stone" from the bins outside the hospital fence.

Collection of the author

The sight that thousands of tourists traveled hundreds of miles to see: Émilie, Marie, Cécile, Yvonne, and Annette romping in their wading pool.

Collection of the author

Marie, Annette, Cécile, Émilie, and Yvonne stacking their building blocks in the playground, 1936. (Tourists complained that the sunbonnets blocked their view of the children they had come so far to see.)

Collection of the author

Actors Rochelle Hudson, Jean Hersholt, and Dorothy Peterson join their pint-sized costars in the playground during the 1936 filming of *Reunion*. (Individual panes are faintly visible in the observatory windows, despite the wire mesh.)

Collection of the author

Aerial view of Quintland, winter 1938. The observatory and hospital occupy the center, with the staff house perched on the hill to the right. Directly across from the staff house sits the Dionne farm. Oliva Dionne's two souvenir pavilions face the hospital, and the clock tower pavilion is just visible at far left.

Collection of the author

The peak of Quintmania. By 1939 at least four pavilions were operating, two of them run by Oliva Dionne.

Image no. x-09293, courtesy of Canada Science and Technology Museum

Tourists lining up to enter the observatory for the three o'clock showing of the Dionne Quintuplets.

Image no. x-09295, courtesy of Canada Science and Technology Museum

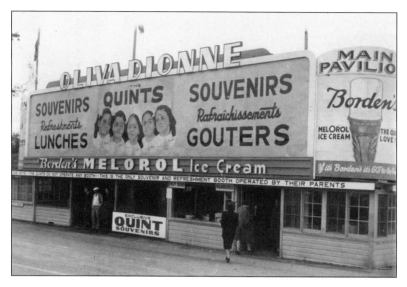

A snapshot of Oliva Dionne's large souvenir and refreshment
pavilion in 1940.

Collection of the author

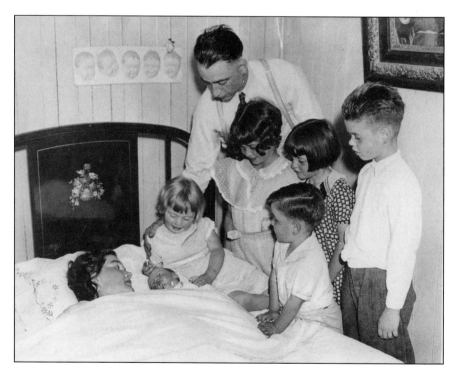

Across the street from the Quintland hubbub, Pauline, Rose-Marie, Daniel,
Thérèse, and Ernest admire their new baby brother, Oliva Jr., born just days after
the opening of the observatory in July 1936.

Collection of the author

up a larger booth across the road. *See Original Basket QUINTUPLETS were placed in after Birth AND use our observation platform—No Charge,* her sign proclaimed. *Personal interviews and autographing free.* In addition to Coca-Cola and Neilson's milk chocolate, Auntie Legros advertised quick lunches, full-course meals, and a "special interview."

Though he deplored the exhibition of his daughters, Oliva Dionne recognized that he could provide a far better living for his family by selling quint souvenirs than by trying to farm his land amid thousands of onlookers. Partnering with a North Bay merchant, he constructed a large booth in the summer of 1936 to sell postcards, photographs, and refreshments. His sign, embellished with giant cut-out silhouettes of his five daughters, proclaimed it *The Only Genuine DIONNE BOOTH.* Locals guessed it raked in $700 a day, with a comfortable profit margin. Knick-knacks and trinkets that cost a nickel or a dime anywhere else in the world sold hand over fist for as much as a dollar in Quintland, with tourists eagerly paying fifteen cents for a pair of penny postcards. At the back of the store, at the end of a "long and patient" line, Oliva Dionne sat at a card table, carefully signing four hundred autographs a day in slow, neat script. At first he left it up to the customers to pay as they liked for this service—until one jokester laid down a single cent. Oliva Dionne was not a man who appreciated pranks at his own expense. "He has been the butt of yokel humor and sophisticated wisecrack until bitterness has etched lines in his face and suspicion darkens his eyes," said the *Baltimore Sun.* After that stunt, Papa Dionne's autograph cost a quarter. Business was so good, Oliva gradually expanded into two stores, branching out into British woolens, English china and toffees, moccasins, religious articles, and round sticks of ice cream called MelOrols.

By 1937 a colossal stand at the corner of the hospital grounds invited visitors to *SEE Babies Picture Gallery upstairs and the Original Basket Babies Were Placed In After Birth.* (That made two "original" baskets. Eventually, there would be three baskets vying for authenticity in Quintland.) A large notice on two sides of the building boasted, *MADAME LEBEL (midwife of the quintuplets) Extends to You a Personal Welcome and Will be Pleased to Answer Questions—Autograph—No Charge.* The two-story pavilion featured a giant clock tower atop one corner of the building. The clock's long red hands did not keep time, but were instead repositioned twice daily to correspond with a sign announcing *Next Showing of the Babies*.

Opportunities to cash in weren't limited to those directly connected with the quintuplets. Nearly anyone in Callander could find a way to make money from Quint-mania. "Leave your car for a minute and you'll return to find two bright-faced urchins scrubbing the windshield and dusting off the fenders," one journalist discovered, "their eyes twinkling with expectation of tourist coins." Kwint Kabins "sprang up like dandelions" along the roadway for tired motorists. Dr. Dafoe's neighbor squeezed three cabins along his lot line, so close that the lodgers could gaze into the Little Doc's windows. Dafoe put up a fence. Other residents threw open their doors to the sightseers. "We had a big house down at the south end of Callander," Jack Adams remembered, "and we slept out on the back porch on a couch or a mattress on the floor while Mother rented rooms to tourists." Uncle Leon Dionne's service station in Callander painted its five gasoline pumps bright red and emblazoned each with a name in gilt: Émilie, Annette, Cécile, Marie, and Yvonne. Those with more limited means peddled peanuts, popcorn, gum, and soda pop outside the hospital gates, hollering out their wares like vendors at a ball game.

To some, Quintland was a thorough delight, an antidote to the grim, gray mood of the Great Depression. "Everything here was new, spic and span, the latest type of modern construction," the *Pittsburgh Press* gushed. Others found it hopelessly tacky. "The Dafoe Hospital, the Dionne homestead, the souvenir stands, are raw looking, despite bright paint and feeble efforts at landscaping," declared the more cynical *Baltimore Sun*. "It is all as incongruous as a gold-rush town and pathetically lacking in charm."

"People are coming in here from all over the world," Dr. Dafoe told newsreel cameras. "We are trying to make their visit as enjoyable as possible, and we hope that you will be able to come up and see these babies."

Tourists took the Little Doc at his word and came flocking like never before. Everyday folks who'd slept in their cars to scrimp on motel fees arrived alongside limousines chauffeuring Hollywood royalty like Jimmy Stewart, Bette Davis, Greta Garbo, and Clark Gable. Child star Shirley Temple, the only little girl as famous as the Dionnes themselves, was begging her parents to take her to Canada to play with them. Celebrated pilot Amelia Earhart visited Callander just ten weeks before she and her plane disappeared forever over the Pacific Ocean. Twenty mailbags of postcards a day left the Callander post office. When the visitors pulled back onto the highway headed south, stickers and pennants bragging *We Have Visited the Dionne Quintuplets* decorated their bumpers and back windows.

By the summer of 1937, Quintland had become a more popular tourist destination than Niagara Falls.

CHAPTER 20

The Threat to the Quints' Happiness

RADIO MIRROR MAGAZINE, NOVEMBER 1936

The success of Quintland hinged on a single principle: no hint of the spectacle could penetrate the walls of the playground and hospital. If the children became aware of their celebrity, the whole experience would be sullied.

From the outside, there seemed no cause for alarm. Visiting reporters always took pains to claim that "the famed quintuplets go about their daily routine of playing and sleeping and eating, utterly unmindful of the hubbub outside the gates of their snug haven."

That was not entirely so. "Of course we knew we were watched every minute that we spent at play there," the sisters said years afterward. The inevitable chuckles and squeals of delight from behind the windows had proven impossible to muffle or disguise. For Yvonne, Annette, Cécile, Émilie, and Marie, the audience's mirth became a kind of reward to seek out. "I remember that we laughed when we heard them," Annette said of the sounds from within the observatory.

Sometimes there were quick glimpses, too. "Those one-way screens were, in truth, two-way screens. We could always see through them, as one can see through frosted glass." A person in white, or a contraband camera lens pressed against the glass, showed up almost clearly through the mesh. Émilie, already aware that photos by anyone other than their official cameraman, Fred Davis, were forbidden, took to covering her face whenever the round eye of a camera appeared.

"Most of the time we yelled and shrieked with the joy of living," the sisters recalled, "and we developed a shrewd idea of what would please the crowds most." They waded into their shallow pool with shoes and socks on, enlisting their invisible audience in the mischief. Émilie's specialty was posing at the tip-top of the jungle gym to tantalize the spectators with the suspense of whether or not she might fall.

Watching what the five toddlers did when the observatory emptied left little doubt of their awareness of what was going on. Scooping up their big hollow building blocks, Dr. Blatz observed, "the children would scamper through the gates in the low fence encircling the playground, place the blocks against the side of the observation building, clamber up, and gleefully wave through the screen to the non-existent spectators."

"They couldn't see them," Nurse Cécile Michaud said, "but they began to realize as they got older that these people had come to see the Quints. They'd say that in French: that people were coming to see the Quints. They knew that they were the Quints. But they weren't excited about it. I don't think they realized how important 'Quints' meant."

"But most of the time," Blatz insisted, "they go about their business without a thought of spectators."

Two nurses, Jacqueline Noël and Claire Tremblay, disagreed vehemently. "To the observer at first glance it seems nothing at all," they said, "but on studying the question in a very critical manner always keeping the children's welfare as the important thing, any person interested in child welfare may see it is very detrimental to the children." The question of when and why the two women decided to challenge Blatz's expertise complicates matters, however.

By October of 1937, Dr. Blatz had become aware that Tremblay and Noël were "uncooperative," especially when it came to teaching the children English. They were also deemed too strict—"almost pathological," Blatz noted—about the children's modesty, and were teaching the little girls to steer clear of all men. Their behavior might have made more sense to Blatz if he had known that Nurse Noël believed Dr. Dafoe was molesting the children. The way Dafoe positioned his hands when they sat on his lap disturbed her so deeply, she called him "the dirty man" in her diary and warned Yvonne, Annette, Cécile, Émilie, and Marie, "If you go near him, Little Jesus will cry." In February of 1938, Tremblay and Noël were dismissed.

The following month the two nurses wrote to the board of guardians, describing their objections to displaying the little girls in Blatz's playground. Their criticisms filled four pages. Regrettably, the timing of their letter made it appear that Noël and Tremblay's claims were a form of retaliation against Blatz and Dafoe for firing them, when perhaps in reality they finally felt free to voice their concerns without jeopardizing their jobs. (Another nurse, Mollie O'Shaughnessy, believed two years of isolation at the hospital had mentally unhinged the two women to the point that they were suffering paranoia and crying jags.) In any case, the picture Tremblay and Noël created of the playground's effect on Yvonne, Annette, Cécile, Émilie, and Marie was darker than any other observer would record.

"Daily the children run to the adult exclaiming about the people viewing them," Noël and Tremblay wrote. "On many, many occasions they were very frightened, hiding themselves and refusing to play." Nightmares often followed these playground upsets, they said.

The two nurses also brought up concerns about the location of the playground. Built on low-lying land that had once been a swamp, it was surrounded on three sides by the observation gallery, and on the fourth by a lattice fence. "The children are therefore forced to remain in this enclosed space, the air of which is filled with the fumes of so many automobiles just a few feet away." What was more, there was no shade apart from what umbrellas could provide. Yet when Yvonne, Annette, Cécile, Émilie, and Marie wore sun hats to protect them from the heat, complaints inevitably followed. People wanted to see their faces, and so to the nurses' dismay, the sun hats were dispensed with.

As the two of them saw it, the public's demands regularly outweighed the children's welfare. If all five sisters did not appear together, the tourists protested. Quintland's policy was that the girls would appear *health and weather permitting,* yet Tremblay and Noël revealed that they were "forced" into the playground "when not feeling well and even with <u>high</u> temperatures in all kinds of weather." And then if the children didn't frolic, the tourists still weren't happy. They had to be cajoled into romping about, regardless of whether they felt like it, "to avoid criticism from the public."

A few perceptive tourists did indeed sense that the whole thing was contrived, lending credibility to Noël and Tremblay's claims—tourists like Gladys Bailey, who was thirteen or fourteen years old when she made the pilgrimage to Quintland. Though she called seeing the quintuplets "the thrill of my childhood," and was "awestruck" by her first glimpse of them, something about it rubbed her the wrong way. The pristine starched dresses, the dainty white shoes and socks, the "stiff, sterile nurses" hovering nearby as the girls pedaled their tricycles endlessly around the small concrete loop. "I had the eerie feeling as I stared and tried to take everything in that it was a fantasy," Gladys said. "It couldn't really be real." The crowd was light that day, so in spite of her "revulsion," Gladys got back into line for a second look. "Again the same scene, small children in an artificial scene created for the masses."

Most extraordinary of all was the rainy-day routine, which blatantly defeated the purpose of the observatory and flaunted the girls' awareness of the crowds that were supposed to be so carefully hidden from them. "As the Venetian blinds are raised promptly at the appointed hour, like the stage curtains at a play," the *New York Times* wrote, "the children, standing on the wide window sills, wave their hands and hold up their dolls to the public."

Yet Dr. Dafoe consistently reassured reporters that the quintuplet exhibitions would continue "only as long as they are unconscious of it." That was obviously not the case. Judge Valin's take on the situation came much closer to the truth than Dafoe's: "The children's health and education come first, but we must keep them before the public if we are to interest advertisers in contracts."

CHAPTER 21

Dionne Endorsements, Incorporated

Canadian Business, May 1937

Anyone with the least bit of sense ought to have seen that it took no effort at all to interest advertisers in contracts. The press dubbed the little girls "human nuggets," for everything Yvonne, Annette, Cécile, Émilie, and Marie touched seemed to turn to gold. Just the sight of their rosy cheeks smiling up from magazine pages prompted consumers to choose Quaker Oats instead of Cream of Wheat, or Karo corn syrup over Bee Hive brand. By their second birthday, the children's bank account had already reached a quarter of a million Canadian dollars—about $3.3 million US today. "The Dionne Quintuplet fund has grown to the point where the income from it will be sufficient for all the normal needs of the Dionne family for the rest of their lives," Welfare Minister David Croll bragged in a radio broadcast.

It was one thing to funnel those advertising contracts into the trust fund for the Dionnes' future. Few could muster any objection to the idea of Canada's princesses growing up to be millionaires, yet even when Yvonne, Annette, Cécile, Émilie, and Marie showed signs of strain—such as in August of 1937, when "a case of jitters and general irritability" brought on by thousands of spectators clamoring to see them prompted the *Pittsburgh Press* to conclude "Life in a 'goldfish bowl' is proving too much for the Dionne quintuplets"—the exhibitions resumed after only a few days. The truth of the matter was that the sisters' trust fund was critical to much more than their future.

Quintuplet dollars paid for everything at the hospital, from Dr. Dafoe's $200-a-month salary to the tins of milk for the guard dog to the electricity and water bills—$1,800 to $2,200 every month. The quint bank account built the observatory and the new staff house where the nurses and guards lived, and paid for renovations to the nursery as the children grew, all to the tune of more than $55,000 (over $750,000 in US currency today). After a good deal of wrangling, Oliva Dionne convinced the board of guardians that it was only fair for the rest of his children to benefit from their five famous sisters' vast income, and so Ernest, Rose-Marie, and Thérèse were granted tuition to be educated at Catholic boarding schools—$1,168.43 in 1938. Oliva himself also received $100 each month from his daughters' bank account, likewise on the principle that half the family should not have to pinch pennies while the other half was virtually showered in riches. (Within two years the family's stipend would triple to $300 a month.)

Anything deemed necessary for the Dionne Quintuplets was fair game for dipping into their trust fund, and *necessary* tended to be interpreted as broadly as possible. The public washrooms in Quintland were built with quintuplet funds. Even the toilet paper in those washrooms was being billed to the girls' fund, along with their own birthday gifts.

To keep the whole system running, to keep cash churning into their bank account faster than it was draining out, the children must be seen—in person, in photographs, and on film. Every birthday, every holiday, and every new advertising contract demanded new quint photographs. Newspapers and theaters expected photos and films in time for each holiday, so weeks or even months before any special event, the world's favorite five sisters dressed up and posed for the cameras.

"We poked our heads through cardboard Valentine hearts, carved pumpkins for Halloween, clambered happily on the knee of a Santa Claus who looked surprisingly like Dr. Dafoe behind the whiskers," the sisters recalled. Their parents and siblings never appeared in these tableaus. The Newspaper Enterprise Association syndicate owned exclusive rights to photograph the Dionne Quintuplets, while Oliva Dionne had sold photo rights for the rest of his family to a competing news syndicate, making it contractually impossible for the two halves of the Dionne family to be photographed together. Consequently, it appeared that Yvonne, Annette, Cécile, Émilie, and Marie had no mother, father, brothers, or sisters. Yet the little girls looked so happy in their photos, no one seems to have noticed what was so obviously missing from their lives—least of all the children themselves. "Picture-taking sessions were as good as parties," they said. "Whatever the season or occasion, we were delighted to join in."

Eventually, though, a sense of artificiality began to color these mock celebrations. "For publicity's sake we were called on to say and do so many things that held no meaning for us," the sisters realized as adults. "Every small event, they needed a picture," Yvonne said. "I couldn't understand why." At the same time, occasions that ought to have had special meaning—such as their birthday celebrations—were stripped of their significance. These "parties" were lavish affairs with frilled gowns, towering cakes five layers high, and heaps of gifts. But nothing was as it appeared to the eager moviegoers who delighted in watching the Dionne Quintuplets receive their presents and blow out their candles. "The gifts were all empty boxes," Cécile remembered. "The cake was a big hole. It was always like that. There was no cake at all when we cut it."

Nevertheless, the girls never failed to do as the photographers requested, regardless of whether any of it made sense to them. As though life were an endless game of dress-up, they donned all manner of costumes from hula skirts to cowboy outfits. "We were obliged to do so many things, so often, that in our head, we didn't feel that we were able to say *No, not this time, another time,*" said Cécile.

Entire magazine articles were devoted to assuring a concerned public that Fred Davis and his newsreel counterpart, Roy Tash, had devised an arsenal of equipment and "fool antics" to photograph five children who were "active as a bunch of crickets" without forcing them to strike or hold a pose. At best, Davis claimed, he had forty-five minutes to an hour to get his shots; if the girls showed any signs of fatigue or agitation, Dr. Dafoe or the nurses called the session to an early halt. "Not even for all the millions who love to see these pictures, will they let me get cranky and say, 'Hey, sit still, will you!'" he complained good-naturedly. Despite such careful procedures, the photo sessions had a noticeable effect on the girls' mood. "We've been having grand days," Nurse Nora Rousselle confided to friends, "except that with the picture taking the babies are a bit cross and irritable and a little harder to handle."

When 20th Century Fox came to film Yvonne, Annette, Cécile, Émilie, and Marie for a series of three Hollywood features, strict precautions were taken for the sake of the girls' physical well-being. Only five people were permitted in the room with the children, and each one had their nose and throat sprayed with disinfectant first. The director, cameraman, and sound engineer all wore sterile surgical gowns and slippers. The actors' shoes were not allowed outside the nursery. Every bulb in the floodlights was diffused with blue glass and a silk screen to prevent any glare from damaging the toddlers' eyes.

"Moving picture staff most cooperative and willing to adjust," one nursery insider noted, but despite the camera crew's best efforts, the five little starlets proved neither oblivious nor immune to the inevitable commotion. Time and again, Marie stood frozen when the girls were supposed to run across the playground together, appearing entirely bewildered by all the people shouting instructions at her. Émilie spent one whole morning crying and screaming, preferring to cling to the nearest grown-up rather than be shepherded onto the jungle gym with her sisters. After more than a month of "amusing, coaxing, directing and interfering," the moviemaking experience had completely derailed the children's daily routine, created a fierce craving for constant attention, and left them all "overstimulated, and in consequence, emotionally unstable."

All the while, nearly every newspaper and magazine story about the

Dionne Quintuplets emphasized the care that was being taken to keep the exposure and publicity from interfering with their health and happiness. Yet between Dr. Adler's *Cosmopolitan* article, the rise of Quintland, and the children's Hollywood debut, it was becoming harder and harder to pretend that this sort of childhood qualified as any kind of normal. By 1937, Dr. Dafoe had abandoned the charade.

"They can't live the normal life of ordinary individuals so there isn't any point in bringing them up as normal children," he admitted. "They must have the training of Royalty, to give them reserve and stamina and calm acceptance of the interest and curiosity of the multitude. They must learn to be looked at, talked about, written to and studied, without losing their sense of proportion or their ability to enjoy life. And because they will always have to buy their privacy and pay dearly for it, as all people in the glare of publicity must do, we are trying to build up sufficient funds to make it possible for them to have peace and freedom as the years go by."

The government had taken custody of the quintuplets to save them from being exploited—to keep crowds from gawking at them, and to prevent promoters from using them to line their pockets with cash. Now thousands of people stared at the children twice a day, while Karo, Palmolive, Lysol, and dozens of other companies enjoyed unprecedented profits. What made this different from what Ivan Spear had proposed to do in Chicago?

Granted, no one was charging admission. It would never cost a cent to enjoy the sight of the five little girls splashing in their pool or scaling their jungle gym. And no one could use Yvonne, Annette, Cécile, Émilie, and Marie's likeness without making a hefty contribution to their bank account. Indeed, the sisters' earning power was so closely guarded that the Ontario Legislature passed an act trademarking the words *quintuplet, quints, quins,* and *cinq jumelles (five twins)*. It was for their protection, the lawmakers said—to ensure that no one in Canada but the Dionne girls could use those words to turn a profit without the written consent of the board of guardians. Nor would there be any knockoff products, like generic quintuplet baby dolls, to divert profits from the Madame Alexander company's phenomenally popular Dionne Quintuplet Dolls, for example.

To the children themselves, such niceties made no difference. "There was a terrible tendency on the part of some people to think of us in terms of property and scarcely ever in human terms," they reflected. "We were an object of curiosity, and therefore we could be used to make money." The curiosity that compelled quintuplet fans to visit Corbeil felt to the sisters themselves like "a tidal wave."

"It is not possible to imagine its force until you have felt it personally," they said. "It is mighty enough, unless your parents are very watchful, to contort your lives so that you will not be thought of as human beings with hearts and minds and souls, but as a tourist attraction like Niagara Falls or the Empire State Building." In August of 1936, it was also mighty enough to cause a five-thousand-person stampede that trampled several women and children waiting outside the nursery gates.

The more people streamed north, the clearer it became that the whole of Ontario stood to benefit from exhibiting Yvonne, Annette, Cécile, Émilie, and Marie. As one newspaper report bluntly put it, the children were "the Province's national resource and the community's gold mine." The five little girls locked behind the fence in Quintland were every bit as valuable as $500 million locked in a bank vault. By one accounting, the Dionne Quintuplets were bringing $25 million tourist dollars (about $326 million US today) into Ontario each year.

CHAPTER 22

Dr. Dafoe Himself

The Parents' Magazine, February 1937

Dr. Dafoe's bank account was swelling just as handsomely, though it was impossible to tell by looking at him. He lived in the same brick house, wore the same rumpled suit and otter fur winter coat, and often contented himself with suppers of baloney, cheese, and crackers. New books were about the only thing he treated himself to.

These simple habits endeared him to the public. He appeared to be a man impervious to fame, devoted solely to the welfare of Yvonne, Annette, Cécile, Émilie, and Marie. So if Dr. Dafoe proclaimed that *"Only Palmolive!"* was gentle and pure enough for the Dionnes' skin, mothers the world over rushed to buy Palmolive soap for their babies.

"Government bulletins and other authorities on child rearing tell parents many of the same things I do," Dr. Dafoe admitted. "But they won't listen as they will to anything that comes directly from experience with the quintuplets."

"My mother fed me the same food they ate," Connie Vachon, a contemporary of the Dionnes, confessed with a laugh. "If they switched to Carnation milk I had to have that as well." As a child, Connie was aware that she was eating certain foods and playing with certain toys because they were Dionne-endorsed. "I guess my mother just felt that what was good for them was good for her child—because they were given the very best."

The idea that Dr. Dafoe was being *paid* to endorse everything from

Colgate toothpaste to Baby Ruth candy bars seemed never to enter the public's mind. That was the way Dafoe wanted it. He wasn't the sort to brag about such things, nor the $30,000 he received from 20th Century Fox for serving as a "technical adviser," nor the $1,000 he could command for a single radio appearance.

The Little Doc had become nearly as beloved as the girls themselves, for as far as the public could see, without Dr. Dafoe, there would be no quintuplets. Figures from Toronto's Burnside Hospital showed that more than 80 percent of premature babies who weighed under three pounds at birth died, yet in the words of one admirer, this unsophisticated backwoods doctor had "made super-babies out of those five bruised-bodied midgets so sure to die."

From the first, Dafoe brushed off attempts to paint him as the hero of the story. "Rubbish," he'd say. "I did what any other country doctor would have done in a premature birth—one or five. Is there anything remarkable about that?" Compared to the night-and-day duties he'd been carrying out alone, acting as doctor, dentist, and veterinarian for the isolated and impoverished people of the district for the past twenty-six years, Dafoe said, "This was nothing. It was over in two hours, and afterward there was the world to help me."

Such comments exuded modesty, and the public loved him all the more for it. Because he refused to be a hero, Dafoe's admirers compromised by viewing him as a saint. "Anyone who ever spent more than seventeen seconds with that grand country doctor up in Callander, Ontario, would have to come out with some kind of inspiration," Charlie Blake of the *Chicago American* said. "He radiates everything everybody is searching for in the way of human beings and humanity." In 1934, Dafoe was nominated for a Nobel Prize. The following year, King George V awarded the Order of the British Empire to the Little Doc.

Dafoe's initial indifference toward his own celebrity may well have been genuine. There was no question that he recognized his limits as a physician. "I wasn't especially bright at school," he admitted. "I just

nd protect
speaking

e had little
d his posi-
pected he
te, Cécile,
d to would

/hen Marie contracted a painful ear infec-
ble to relieve on his own in April of 1935,
on his brother and Dr. Alan Brown from
God he is not so small that professional
Leroux wrote that day.

ël joined the hospital staff, however, an-
ling itself to close observers. He had been
credit for Yvonne, Annette, Cécile, Émilie,
vas due—to the midwives and nurses, the
rs, and especially to his brother. As the
ever, Dafoe's praise for others tapered off.
rivately confided her belief that the Dr.
care for the children . . . as long as he has
Noël's dislike for Dafoe ran deep—so deep
ed the pleasure he took from hobnobbing
act the loneliest man I have ever met in my
led decades later. "It was startling. I don't
casion having happened—a friend dropping
happening. Dafoe sitting down and having a
did happen."

tive novels, the children appear to have been
njoyment. "He may unconsciously have come
ng akin to his own children," the sisters acknowl-
that Dafoe had a son of his own. Looking at his
tom-made with die-cut fronts that open to reveal
raphs of himself with Yvonne, Annette, Cécile,
t's hard to think otherwise.

vas mutual. To most young children, da-da means
ive little girls who lived in the Dafoe Hospital, da-da
know his car when it comes & flock to the window
it appears," wrote Nurse Leroux. "They love having

daddy
was do
screechi
his visits.

"I remember Dr. Dafoe as a good man, wanting to save us a[
us," Annette said. "And I always disagreed when I heard peopl[
against him. I never liked that."

Whatever his true feelings about his worldwide fame, Dafo[
choice but to project an image of nonchalance. His job an[
tion on the board of guardians depended on it. If anyone su[
was acting in his own best interests instead of Yvonne, Anne[
Émilie, and Marie's, the new life he had become accustome[
evaporate in a heartbeat.

CHAPTER 23

Science Designs a Life for the Dionnes

New York Times Magazine, October 1937

The Dionne Quintuplets were irresistible. To fans, to tourists, to advertisers—and to science. Yvonne, Annette, Cécile, Émilie, and Marie represented an unprecedented opportunity that doctors, geneticists, and child psychologists had only dreamed of: the chance to guide and study the development of five apparently identical children in a completely controlled environment.

"One of the supreme satisfactions I have found in my association with the case of the Dionne quintuplets is something which every physician will understand," Dr. Dafoe wrote. "All his life he will have seen little children weakened and warped because he could not tell their mothers what to do, or the mothers, if told, would not obey." Prescribing the best care and watching dutiful nurses carry it out to the letter was something Dafoe deemed "worth any amount of personal sacrifice."

There could be no better circumstances to put the most up-to-date child-rearing methods to the test. "If ever the question, 'How to raise a child to be a genius,' is to be answered, it will be done by the Dionne Quintuplets," a journalist confidently predicted. Or as one expert put it, "If, at the end of eighteen years, we can't inculcate in these children integrity, good judgement and a sense of values, what good is education?"

The scientists had to tread lightly, though. Neither the fans nor the guardians would tolerate the idea of Yvonne, Annette, Cécile, Émilie, and Marie being experimented upon. "They should never become 'guinea pigs' of science," Dr. Dafoe assured the public. However, he also believed it was possible to study the children safely, so long as it was done "with appropriate dignity and efficiency."

Dr. Blatz was the obvious choice to head the research. His team's first step was to determine whether the children were truly identical. Anyone looking at the five sisters in person or in photos was invariably dazzled by their exceptional similarity, but as yet there was no scientific proof that they were single-egg quintuplets. Without DNA technology, Blatz's team had to rely on a battery of minute biological observations.

"We were weighed, measured, tested, studied, and examined to the heart's content of doctors and scientists," the sisters remembered. "In the gentlest possible fashion, we were peered at, pricked and prodded for years." The researchers mapped the shapes of their ears; the ridges on their fingertips, their palms, and the soles of their feet; the flecks of color in their irises; and the color and texture of their hair.

Even without DNA tests, Blatz's team concluded definitively that the five girls had indeed descended from a single egg cell. Any two of them—Annette and Marie, or Cécile and Yvonne, for example—were as similar as a set of identical twins. All had the same blood type. Their eye color, hair color, and skin tone were deemed "nearly indistinguishable." The shapes formed by the crinkles and folds of their ears—a feature used for identification before the discovery of fingerprints—looked as though they had all been cast from the same mold.

All five of their left handprints were remarkably similar, as were their right handprints. In fact, the resemblance was so great that the print of Émilie's left hand, for example, was a closer match to her four sisters' left handprints than to her own right handprint. (The opposite was true of their siblings. The print from Ernest's left hand was more similar to that from his right hand than to any of his brothers' or sisters'.)

Yvonne, Annette, Cécile, Émilie, and Marie shared more unusual characteristics, too. All five sisters' eyelids folded in an uncommon way at the inner corners. The flesh between their second and third toes extended a quarter inch beyond the joint, an observation that spawned a rumor that the Dionnes were web-footed but in reality only gave those toes a slightly stubby look. And they all had whorls—spiral patterns—on the palms between their third and fourth fingers, a trait usually seen in only one or two of every two hundred people.

Gauging the intensity of these similarities from one sister to the next eventually allowed the scientists to construct a theory of exactly when and how a single egg had divided itself into the makings of five children. Yvonne and Annette were most alike. They were also the largest, signaling that they were probably the first to separate. Émilie and Marie were mirror twins—reverse images of each other. (Émilie was left-handed, Marie right-handed. Marie's hair whorl turned clockwise, Émilie's counterclockwise.) Being the smallest, they were likely the last to separate. Cécile shared characteristics of both sets, making her a sort of bridge between the two pairs. Thus, the "blueprint" for the Dionne Quintuplets went like this: First, a single egg split into two masses of cells. Then one of those halves split again, forming Yvonne and Annette. The remaining half split twice—once to create Cécile, and then finally the last unnamed mass of cells divided itself into Émilie and Marie.

Satisfied that they had documented every possible physical similarity, Blatz's team next set out to scrutinize the girls' personalities. Month after month for two years the researchers traveled from Toronto to Callander to watch the sisters interact—first in pairs in playpens, then all together in the playroom.

With clipboards in hand, Blatz's team recorded "any physical or other contact between children, other than of a casual nature, which implies social awareness." Pushing counted. Shoving back counted. Talking, laughing, and crying counted. Offering a sister a toy counted, as did stealing a toy. Getting attention counted as much as giving attention.

For instance, if Cécile approached Annette and attempted to capture her attention "by gesture, touch, or word," that counted as initiating contact. Any sort of reply, verbal or nonverbal, would be credited to Annette as a response. A single interaction quickly racked up multiple "points" for each child: if Annette snatched Yvonne's hair ribbon, making Yvonne cry, and then gave it back, prompting Yvonne to stop crying, the researcher noted four social contacts: one initiation (grabbing) and one response (returning) by Annette, and two responses by Yvonne (crying and then stopping).

After analyzing 1,367 contacts, the researchers determined that Annette was the most outgoing, because she initiated the most interactions. Yvonne was in a sense the most popular, but also the most passive. She did not have to bother with attracting attention because her sisters sought her out more often than anyone else. Cécile, "whose unpredictable behavior delights her sisters," came in at second most popular. Émilie was something of a loner, the least likely to either seek out or respond to her sisters' attention. Though Marie was very much interested in engaging with her sisters, she attracted the least amount of attention—largely because she was usually the last to learn a new game or skill, making her less interesting to the other four.

What did it all mean? According to Blatz, these differences proved that the girls' individual personalities were already unique. Yvonne, he said, was the matriarch of the group. Little Marie fit the role of the baby, always tagging along behind her bigger, faster sisters. Annette was labeled aggressive, though not in the sense that she was quarrelsome. ("Annette seeks an audience" was how he put it.) Émilie won the title of "happy-go-lucky," for her willingness "to give and take on a fifty-fifty basis." Cécile apparently stumped Blatz's team, her behavior defying a simple label. They dubbed her "the unknown quantity."

"One thing is certain and that is, that these children do not fit into a similar mould of personality development," Blatz wrote. Their five personalities, he believed, were not innate, but sprang from the children's individual responses to the "social environment."

Quint fans reveled in this information. A series of newspaper stories spread Blatz's conclusions across the continent. *Life* magazine published a six-page article, complete with charts and over three dozen photographs. Yet some more critical readers, like twin expert Horatio Newman, dismissed Blatz's conclusions as "artificial."

According to Newman, the researchers had come up with these "personalities" only after hours of hovering over the children with charts and clipboards, noting infinitesimal differences between them. "Anyone watching them play together would be at a loss to pick out the 'matriarch' from the 'baby' or the 'aggressive member' from the 'happy-go-lucky' one," Newman argued, and a writer for *Better Homes and Gardens* confirmed his theory.

"I was sure I would be able to spot Yvonne and Annette by their leadership, Émilie by her independence, Marie because she is the littlest," the magazine's child care and training director boasted after attending the conference where Dr. Blatz presented his results. But seeing the children in person the very next day confounded her. "Tell them apart? Just try it yourself sometime!" she exclaimed. "The one who played so long in the sandpile by herself proved to be Yvonne, not Émilie, and Marie turned out to be Cécile."

The setup for such studies, Newman pointed out, "is about as poor as it could possibly be made." How were the researchers supposed to find authentic differences in five identical children living in an identical environment? "Indeed, a wider variety of experience seems to be exactly what they need and should have from now on."

Little proved Newman's point better than their language skills—or rather, their lack of language skills. At nearly two, they did not say *mama* or *papa*. Instead, they called both of their parents "Ah." At age three, when most toddlers know 200 to 450 words, Yvonne, Annette, Cécile, Émilie, and Marie's vocabulary hovered around 75. The unofficial language of the nursery was "Quintalk," a French baby talk understood only by their nurses. Blatz and his researchers had no choice but to note the "apparent retardation" of the girls' language skills.

"It's the most natural thing in the world that the quints don't talk more," Dr. Blatz assured the public. "Language is a tool used when needed. The Quints haven't needed this tool." The sisters never left the nursery grounds. Everything was familiar, giving them no reason to ask "What's that?" all day long like other youngsters. Their routine was so predictable and their nurses knew them so well that they rarely needed to ask for anything at all before it was handed to them.

Still, the report quickly gave rise to the notion that the Dionnes were "backward." The results of their mental tests didn't help dispel that impression.

"The quintuplets already provide perhaps the clearest test we have ever had of our modern educational skills and theories," said the *New York Times*, yet according to the data Blatz's team gathered, those skills and theories were doing nothing to boost the sisters' mental growth. Yvonne, rated the brightest of the five, was behind on nearly every score—by some measures, almost a year behind.

Blatz's routine and disciplinary methods weren't producing extraordinary results, either. The girls were, in fact, as trying and as difficult to control as any other toddlers. They sucked their thumbs, fought, and sometimes bit one another. They delighted in banging their wooden building blocks against the nursery windows until the glass shattered.

When it was time to be bathed or dressed, the five sisters mobbed the washroom door, erupting into a frenzy as they all vied to be first. They were still being spoon-fed at age two, and hated every minute of it. After a few bites the toddlers darted out of reach, flung their food across the nursery, and threw tantrums.

More tantrums came at playtime. The nurses had been so attentive for so long—literally doing everything for them since the day they were born—that the little girls did not even know how to use their toys without help. If an adult did not sit down and amuse them, they quickly screamed with boredom or frustration.

At bedtime they could be so unruly and reluctant to lie down that getting the five of them to stay under the covers was "in actual fact . . . the equivalent of tucking seventy-one children into bed." To top it off, toilet training was not progressing by the usual timetable, in part because the girls had discovered that demanding a diaper change was a foolproof method of winning a few coveted minutes of individual attention.

By the standards of the day, discipline was lax. Dr. Blatz believed that obedience should not grow out of fear, nagging, or dread of punishment. He advocated teaching children that every behavior has consequences— some pleasant and some unpleasant—and leaving it up to the child to choose. So there were no threats, spankings, or angry reprimands for the Dionnes. Instead, "the machinery of their pleasantly ordered lives stops when they don't obey." The only punishment for stubborn or unruly episodes of "non-compliance" was a time-out in a small sunny room with a table and chair and a few playthings. It was officially known as the isolation room, but the press preferred to call it "Dionne jail."

"It was in no sense uncomfortable," the sisters remembered, "but the four who were left behind when the offender had been marched off always felt that they were suffering as much as the prisoner. Punishment for one was punishment for all."

Blatz's techniques succeeded in halting the washroom stampedes and the mealtime woes. The graphs and tables that charted "emotional episodes" and "non-compliance behavior" proved that the girls were beginning to master self-control—as most children do as they approach age three. Even so, any one of them could rack up at least a dozen noncompliance episodes in a single day. And when Yvonne, Annette, Cécile, Émilie, and Marie took it into their heads to misbehave as a group, they were almost impossible to dissuade. The only way to keep them all in bed was to pin the legs of their pajamas together. Nothing, not even shatterproof glass, could compel them to stop banging the windows to smithereens.

CHAPTER 24

Home or Science? The Dionnes' Case Debated

NEW YORK TIMES MAGAZINE, OCTOBER 1937

Dr. Blatz's dominion over the nursery meant that Oliva and Elzire had virtually no say in how their daughters were fed, educated, disciplined, or even toilet trained. Though the staff theoretically sympathized, it was not a situation they showed much willingness to change. "When [Mrs. Dionne] came over," one of Blatz's colleagues remembered, "the nurses had instructions to let her be in charge. Dr. Blatz told them to be sure to let her do things for the quints—to feel that she was their mother. But the nurses had difficulty letting her do it."

Oliva and Elzire's resentment and frustration were so palpable, it made their visits unpleasant for everyone. "The mother and father felt that the doctor was stealing the children's love, and vice versa," Nurse Mollie O'Shaughnessy reflected. That sense of rivalry between the Dionnes and the staff grew until they regarded each other as opponents. As Oliva and Elzire snatched desperately at any illusion of control, the two sides found themselves engaged in an ongoing series of spats.

Oliva tended to direct his ire at Dr. Dafoe, challenging the hospital's rules and procedures in ways that undermined the doctor's authority. When Yvonne, Annette, Cécile, Émilie, and Marie came down with head colds, Oliva told the press he was being kept in the dark about their true condition and demanded a second opinion. (The outside doctor confirmed Dafoe's diagnosis.) On another occasion, when he was turned away at the gate because the children in the farmhouse were recovering from measles, Oliva defied the quarantine and crawled under the hospital fence through a drainpipe. (The guards permitted him to look through a window at his daughters, then sent him home.) He was not above making cutting remarks about his rival, either. "If they look like anybody, it must be Dr. Dafoe," a bitter Oliva replied when a reporter remarked on the girls' striking resemblance to Elzire.

While Oliva tussled with the doctor, Elzire butted heads with the nurses—so much so that the girls came to remember their mother primarily as a source of distress. When Elzire was in the nursery, Cécile said, "there was always some dispute." She interfered with the tricycle processions the nurses arranged for the tourists in the observation playground. Her temper could flare at the way the staff spoke to her children, spurring Elzire to give the offending nurse a shove or a slap while the girls watched. "You will listen to me, not to her," she told her daughters when a nurse tried to discipline Yvonne. Accustomed to serving her elder children hearty meat soup, mashed potatoes and gravy, crusty brown bread, and all the milk they could drink, Elzire protested in the *North Bay Nugget* about the "greenish mush" (strained fruit blended with oatmeal) the nurses fed Yvonne, Annette, Cécile, Émilie, and Marie. Her little girls were restless from hunger, she said, and bruised easily. Her concerns appeared in newspapers across the continent.

"The Dionne family," Dr. Dafoe countered, "are accustomed to lumberjack meals." Such hearty fare was more than the children's digestive systems could handle, he claimed, adding that "the Dionne quintuplets are today the happiest and healthiest bunch of little crickets I have ever seen." What Elzire termed restlessness was in Dafoe's eyes "vitality and pep." He shrugged off her accusation that Yvonne, Annette, Cécile, Émilie, and Marie received only a third of a cup of milk at lunch, saying he was ordering at least five quarts a day to keep up with them. "That just shows how much the parents actually know about their own children," the doctor remarked.

Even the girls' long brown sausage curls caused an uproar. To keep the famous Dionne ringlets looking fresh for each observatory show, they had to be curled twice a day. "Their hair was so long and so heavy that you know, it just didn't stay up," Nurse Doreen Chaput explained. Cutting their hair would save the nurses time and effort, but Elzire would not consent. "So finally one day we just decided we'd thin it out," Nurse Chaput remembered with a rueful grimace. When Elzire learned how the nurses had evaded her wishes, more trouble erupted. The next thing Nurse Chaput knew, the board of guardians received a letter from the Dionnes' lawyer, threatening a lawsuit over the children's hair. "They thought we were going to sell it for our personal gain. We had simply thrown it in the garbage."

Powerless in the nursery, the Dionnes took their campaign outside the hospital gates, with Elzire narrating heart-tugging magazine articles with titles such as "I Am the Most Unhappy Mother in the World" and "Don't My Babies Need Me?" Oliva could be just as plaintive as his wife. "This being cut off from my baby girls for so long a time has cut me to the heart," he told *Liberty* magazine. "For the Dionne quins, for all their world fame, are still to me just my babies."

Their anger showed as plainly as their grief, for both Elzire and Oliva had a knack for making piercing remarks about the Guardianship Act—remarks that lingered in the public mind and rubbed many quintuplet fans the wrong way. "Even pigs are allowed to bring up their own young," Oliva told *Maclean's* magazine. He often pointed to his singly born children as proof that their home was just as fit for youngsters as anyone else's. "This baby is fine, without the government's help," he said of his youngest son in 1936. "Why should I cooperate with them in the kidnapping of my children?" Asked in 1935 if she planned to have more children, Elzire had famously answered with a rueful laugh and a twinkle in her brown eyes, "Not for the government."

◆ ◆ ◆

Though the disputes and name-calling appeared petty, public sympathy for Oliva and Elzire's situation was slowly beginning to gather. Anyone could see that Yvonne, Annette, Cécile, Émilie, and Marie were physically normal. Dr. Dafoe had been saying it since they were five months old. Their upbringing wasn't making them any smarter or better behaved than any other children. Why, then, were they living in a hospital instead of with the family who so desperately wanted them back?

Major news outlets weighed the pros and cons, gathering opinions from experts and fans alike. "Does or does not the best interest of these children include a life in their normal home?" wondered the *New York Times*. "Is there anything after all peculiarly precious and necessary in the homely joys—in family sharing and hoping, in coming home and confiding in mother, in dabbling in the home kitchen, and playing tag with the neighbors' children?"

For Elzire Dionne, the answer was a resounding yes. An institutional upbringing left a visible mark on children who grew up without the instinctive love of a father and mother, she argued. "Just visit any orphanage, no matter how fine and clean and well kept," she told *Liberty* magazine, "and see the heart-hungry, home-hungry looks on the faces of the children there!"

A number of child specialists agreed, pointing to "a kind of emotional vitamin" found only in a warm and loving home life. Without it, children stood no chance of thriving.

Even David Croll, Ontario's welfare minister and the Dionnes' special guardian, had come around to this point of view. "They have wealth, they have money," he told legislators upon his resignation from the board of guardians in 1937. "What they need now most of all is a normal domestic life, association with their brothers and sisters, the love and discipline which their parents alone can completely provide. There is no substitute for a mother."

Dr. Charles Gilmore Kerley, president of the American Pediatric Society, disagreed. "It is obvious that the quintuplets have been getting exquisite maternal care from their nurses," he said, ". . . or they would not have flourished as they have." However, Dr. Kerley's opinion overlooked the fact that hospital life came with steep tolls for the nurses, which in turn impacted Yvonne, Annette, Cécile, Émilie, and Marie.

Though the nurses rarely expressed anything but sheer delight at working with the world's sweethearts, the rate of turnover at the Dafoe Hospital spoke for itself. Shouldering twenty-four-hour responsibility for the most famous children on earth was a strenuous job that exacted a deep emotional investment. "They are so sweet and they need to be loved so much," Nurse Jacqueline Noël wrote. "I would stay for their sweet little smiles." Yet withstanding the intense public scrutiny while simultaneously navigating ongoing squabbles with Oliva and Elzire required an almost superhuman resilience. Privately, Nurse Noël vented to her diary about her isolation, her mediocre pay, and the frustration of watching someone else take all the glory while she did all the work of maintaining the girls' health, as well as keeping the peace with the Dionnes. Her jumbled feelings were not unique. "It was too much," another of her colleagues echoed. "The fight was always going on." Despite their genuine affection for the children, not a single nurse lasted more than three years at the Dafoe Hospital. By the time they were nine, Yvonne, Annette, Cécile, Émilie, and Marie would tearfully kiss well over a dozen nurses goodbye. "We could not help weeping," they recalled, "because we loved them all."

The nurses were just as devastated. "I left a piece of myself there. Yes, it was like dying a little," said Cécile Lamoureux of her departure. "One cannot leave them without terrible suffering." And yet they did go, one after another after another.

Patricia Mullins left in the spring of 1935, shortly after the Dionnes lost custody of their children. Louise de Kiriline stepped down after clashing with Elzire in May of 1935. Her replacement, Cécile Lamoureaux, departed to be married eight months later. Yvonne Leroux, aware that she was growing too fond of the children, tore herself away in December of 1936. Claire Tremblay and Jacqueline Noël were dismissed simultaneously in February of 1938. Fed up with hospital power struggles, Nora Rousselle "just resigned and walked out" that same July. In 1939, three more nurses left to be married—Louise Corriveau, Cécile Michaud, and Mollie O'Shaughnessy—two of whom simply slunk away without any kind of farewell. Almost a year and half passed before tuberculosis forced Leona Dubeau's 1941 departure. ("I feel certain," she wrote, "that conditions at the nursery contributed to my illness.") Doreen Chaput and Gertrude Provencher retired in 1943.

For Yvonne, Annette, Cécile, Émilie, and Marie, who were more attached to these women than to their mother and father, each departure was akin to losing a parent. A new nurse always came to fill the empty place, but whether this new mother figure would remain for months or years was anybody's guess. To make matters worse, the sisters' grief at losing a beloved caretaker widened the gap between them and Elzire. "Mom could not understand why we wept when a nurse departed. It was still another cause of bewilderment and pain for her. It made her angry, and we in turn did not understand the reason for that."

The sisters' only chance to form permanent bonds was with one another, a reality that went hand in hand with Oliva and Elzire Dionne's most deep-seated fear. "The babies will grow away from us," Oliva predicted. "They will think they are better and will turn from their natural brothers and sisters as though they were strangers."

The distance between the two halves of the family was indeed broader than the width of the road that separated the farmhouse from the hospital. Ernest, Rose-Marie, Thérèse, Daniel, and Pauline were seeing the world in an entirely different light than their five famous sisters. Unless something changed drastically, it seemed likely that the distance between them could only grow. "Will the five ordinary Dionne children find themselves shoved more and more rudely into the background?"

asked *Pictorial Review* magazine. "Will jealousy and other bitter emotions create lifelong dislike of their five younger sisters . . . ?"

Kathleen Norris, a prominent author and newspaper columnist of the era, scoffed at the idea. "To have glory somewhere in the family ought to be a matter of glory all around," she wrote. "Jealous? Healthy youngsters whose parents love them and are presumably teaching them some of the fundamental principles of their Faith—charity, joy, peace, patience and the rest, are not much in danger of growing up twisted and embittered and crushed because the miracle of achieving five delicious little sisters at one blow has been vouchsafed them." Norris's was a fine sentiment, but it bore little resemblance to the realities of life in the Dionne household after May 28, 1934.

CHAPTER 25

Just One Big Unhappy Family

TORONTO TELEGRAM, MAY 29, 1937

The moment their five baby sisters were born, the uncomplicated childhood Ernest, Rose-Marie, Thérèse, Daniel, and Pauline had known shattered. "We had a normal family life, then everything changed," Ernest remembered.

Their parents were consumed by the quintuplets—first with anxiety over the babies' survival, then with the grief of losing custody, followed by the crusade to win their daughters back. "My youth ended because there was so much suffering," Thérèse said.

The struggles fundamentally changed Oliva and Elzire. Ernest, Rose-Marie, Thérèse, Daniel, and Pauline watched as their parents were shamed and humiliated from all sides. Papa Dionne jokes were all the rage. Childless women tried to touch him, as if their father were a fertility charm more powerful than the bins of passion pebbles outside the hospital gates. At the grocery store in town, people talked openly about their father and his "litter" of babies. Others asked, "Don't you think it would be a good idea to sew the mother up so she cannot have more children?" If they went to the movies to see their baby sisters' Hollywood debut, the older siblings also had to endure seeing their father portrayed as a bumbling hick and their mother as a silent simpleton. "They took my father's pride," Ernest said through tears decades later; "he never had a chance."

Through it all, Oliva and Elzire remained devoted to the principle of functioning as a united family. Ironically, their insistence on treating all their children equally sometimes resulted in the exclusion of Yvonne, Annette, Cécile, Émilie, and Marie from family occasions. When Oliva and Elzire arrived at the hospital on Christmas Day of 1935, Nurse Cécile Lamoureux recalled, everything started off "All well and good." That is, until the older brothers and sisters were barred from entering the nursery, owing to their ever-present colds. "No amount of pleading moved the hospital officials. M and Mme Dionne refused to see the quints unless the whole family could share in the occasion. They left without seeing them."

Such scenes left a lingering impression on the elder Dionne children. The following year, Rose-Marie asked Santa Claus to bring her five baby sisters home instead of presents, while three-year-old Pauline insisted on "buying back Marie" with the five dollars she'd received for Christmas.

"Nobody would believe what we suffered," Thérèse recalled. "Half the people had no clue there was anyone else in the family. We were second-class citizens." It was a state of affairs Elzire Dionne deplored. All of her children should benefit from the "intelligent culture" and "scientific training" the five youngest were receiving, she told the vice president of the Ontario Liberal Women's Association.

In July of 1936, "the forgotten five" quickly became "the forgotten six" when Elzire gave birth to a son, Oliva Jr. The newspapers had been so eager to see whether the "Callander madonna" might produce another set of quintuplets that Elzire was forced to spend the last suspenseful week of her pregnancy with the doors locked and the shades pulled in hundred-degree heat. When only one baby arrived, the disappointed reporters cleared out as quickly as they had come.

The Dionnes, on the other hand, delighted in their new son. "This one will never go away," Elzire said.

CHAPTER 26

Guardians of Dionnes Seek Better Relations with Tots' Parents

INDIANAPOLIS STAR, MAY 22, 1938

In 1938, Oliva Dionne landed his first punch in the fight to unite his family under a single roof. Concerned that his daughters' trust fund was being "dissipated" by "extravagance," he requested that the attorney general open a judicial inquiry into the children's finances. He charged that Dafoe was engaged in "schemes to divorce the affections of the quintuplets from their parents," and that the doctor habitually jeopardized Yvonne, Annette, Cécile, Émilie, and Marie's health to please the public.

Oliva also wanted some say in the hiring and firing of the nurses who cared for his children, and he was adamant that his four-year-olds ought to master French before anyone attempted to teach them English. They ought to be raised "as Catholic and French children should be brought up" and not trained to be pint-sized Hollywood starlets.

Perhaps the threat of financial investigation spooked the board of guardians. No probe into the $600,000 trust fund ever materialized, and for the first time, Oliva Dionne was granted some control over his daughters' upbringing. Not only would he enjoy the authority to reject or confirm new nurses and teachers, but the board had also promised to hire an architect to design a new "dream home" for the entire Dionne family—a home that could be divided in half to quarantine the family in case of infection.

"Well," Oliva said, "that's the first time I was given any satisfaction."

The press hailed "a new spirit of cooperation" between the girls' parents and guardians, but quint fans were not so keen on the changes. Because Oliva had used the quintuplet trust fund as his leverage, Dr. Dafoe believed the Dionnes had become the puppets of "outside interests" trying to get control of the girls' wealth. "That $600,000 bank account is a pretty juicy plum, you know," he said with a grin.

"When the children were poor and had no money, there wasn't so much interest shown in them," Dafoe told the *Nugget,* and the public was more than willing to believe that Oliva and Elzire were only after their children's trust fund. "We, the people, are with you!" a Cleveland admirer wrote to Dr. Dafoe. "If it were not for you, Dionne would be glad to get potato parings. What's wrong with that damned frog?"

In reality, though, nothing had significantly changed for anyone. Yvonne, Annette, Cécile, Émilie, and Marie remained in the hospital, where Dr. Dafoe retained his sole authority over their health. Oliva and Elzire still hoped for the day when their family would be united. Talk in the papers had been that the Dionne dream home might be ready as soon as September, yet September came and went and the house remained on the architect's drawing table. Meanwhile, their latest attempt to wrest their children out from under the government's protection had given rise to a fresh wave of anti-Dionne sentiment.

"As with most primitive people, emotion has triumphed over reason with the Dionnes," one especially blunt journalist remarked. "Consciously or unconsciously they cannot bear the prospect of their famous children acquiring a culture superior to the six little Dionnes at home. Already they see signs of what highly intelligent twig-bending does to children, for the quints are infinitely prettier and more attractive looking than the other children, and that would still be true if the quints were put into the same clothes as the six at home wear. They have acquired a certain graciousness and charm as a result of superior association and training."

It was true that Yvonne, Annette, Cécile, Émilie, and Marie quarreled "surprisingly little." They also did better at sleeping, washing, dressing, undressing, and putting away toys than a group of similarly aged children at St. George's School for Child Study. Those results were enough for the editor of the *Parents' Magazine* to gush that "the five little sisters stand as the most remarkable demonstration that has ever been made of the value of scientific methods in child care."

There was no doubt that the example set by the Dionne Quintuplets was doing good in the greater world. When Dr. Dafoe credited pasteurized milk for their health, for example, it led parents to trust the pasteurization process, which meant that fewer children suffered milk-borne illnesses such as tuberculosis, salmonella, listeria, and E. coli. Photos of Marie and Yvonne Dionne tearlessly receiving a diphtheria vaccination likewise prompted apprehensive parents to have their own babies inoculated against "that deadliest scourge of childhood."

Yet as the children continued to thrive, some wondered whether guarding Yvonne, Annette, Cécile, Émilie, and Marie's health so intensively was doing *them* more harm than good. "Today they are five splendid physical specimens," *Chatelaine* magazine explained. "But take them away from their special environment . . . leave them open to infection, exposed to disease, and Dr. Dafoe doesn't believe they could stand up to it." (A suspiciously convenient problem for the Province of Ontario, considering that Quintland had become "the greatest tourist attraction Canada has ever known.") According to *Chatelaine,* Dr. Dafoe was of the opinion that "the quintuplets haven't the stamina yet to face the rough and tumble of daily living." That was the logic behind keeping their brothers and sisters out of the nursery until the girls were two years old. Cats and dogs were likewise forbidden, as were woolly toys, all for fear of spreading infection.

The situation led Sidonie Matsner Gruenberg, director of the Child Study Association of America, to envision an eerie glassed-in future for Yvonne, Annette, Cécile, Émilie, and Marie—a future in which their suitors would be fumigated, immunized, doused with microbe killer, and garbed in sterile white gowns before entering their home for a date. "The excessive care to protect them from infection may save their bodies but chains them to the necessity of living permanently in the shelter of a hospitalized incubator," she predicted in an article entitled "Will 'Hothouse' Life Weaken Dionne Quins?" Even if the Dionnes' care proved that total isolation could guarantee a disease-free childhood, what practical use was that to anyone else? Every youngster in the world could not be sealed into an air-conditioned chamber for eighteen years.

Despite all the worthwhile knowledge the Dionne case had provided, Gruenberg cautioned, "we may reach a point beyond which we can continue to learn only the wrong things." To fully flourish in both body and mind, Yvonne, Annette, Cécile, Émilie, and Marie needed a chance to experience the world outside the nursery gates. "Those poor quintuplets," Helen Watson of the Child Education Foundation agreed, "have not had as much experience of reality as my dog."

CHAPTER 27

"Felt Right at Home with King and Queen"

TORONTO STAR, MAY 23, 1939

When it finally came, their first taste of the world outside the nursery bore more resemblance to a fairy tale than to reality. In May of 1939, the Dionne Quintuplets were invited to meet King George VI and Queen Elizabeth during the royal couple's visit to Toronto.

Not once had the five almost-five-year-old girls set foot outside the barbed wire–topped fences that surrounded the Dafoe Hospital. Their lifetime of travel amounted to crossing the Corbeil road at the age of four months, and looping their playground on wagons and tricycles. A week before their fifth birthday, Yvonne, Annette, Cécile, Émilie, and Marie piled into a waiting automobile, together with two nurses and a teacher. Their parents, three brothers, and three sisters followed in another car. A police cruiser led the way.

As the cars motored down the road and the wide world began to flash by the windows, the girls could not contain their delight. "Cow!" Marie shouted. "Sheep! Horse!" Émilie chimed in. Until this moment, the animals had existed only in their storybooks.

"Faster!" they all cried, eager to overtake the police cruiser at the head of the procession. "Pass them, pass them!" they begged their driver.

The sun was beginning to set as the cavalcade reached the Fisher Street crossing a mile north of North Bay. Only about forty or fifty people stood waiting. (Eleven miles away in Callander, a crowd of three thousand was beginning to realize they were the victims of a "dirty rotten trick." By order of the commissioner of the Ontario provincial police, the location of the departure had been switched at the last minute for the Dionnes' safety.) A gleaming crimson-and-gold seven-car Temiskaming and Northern Ontario Railway train stood puffing at the crossing. Dubbed the "Quintland Special," it consisted of a customized nursery car, a combination dining and parlor car, two sleeping cars, a business car for the guardians and railroad officials, a baggage car, and a day coach for the police guards and reporters.

On the back platform of the nursery car waited Judge Valin, one of the children's guardians. "Hello, Monsieur le Judge," Marie said.

"Bonsoir, mes chéries," the old gentleman replied. *Good evening, my dears.*

To Yvonne, Annette, Cécile, Émilie, and Marie, who had been practicing their curtseys in front of a photograph of George VI and Queen Elizabeth, and "playing 'King and Queen'" for days, it apparently seemed a perfect opportunity to display their new skill. "As though the judge were the King himself, the little girls curtseyed," the *Toronto Star* reported. "Yvonne bowed so low, she nearly fell in the dust."

In contrast to their nurses, the girls appeared "neither nervous nor worried" as one by one they were lifted from the car to the train by officers of the provincial police. Once on board, however, their excitement ran riot as they began to understand all that "going to meet the king and queen" meant.

Five small steel cots decorated with ducks had been installed in the nursery car. As a special surprise, a pair of new scarlet slippers dangled from each one. In the dining car, Yvonne, Annette, Cécile, Émilie, and Marie "bounced up and down with shrieks of delight" on the full-sized leather chairs. The bathroom, however, proved a disappointment. "Such great big sighs they gave when they saw it," said the *Globe and Mail*. A chuckling Nurse O'Shaughnessy explained, "They hoped there would not be one so that they would not have to take their baths."

Soon all five of them were bundled into their pink woolen pajamas, ready for what, to them, may have been the most suspenseful moment of the evening. For the first time in their lives, the sisters would sleep divided. Their nursery car contained three bedrooms, each with two cots. Two sisters would share the first bedroom, two more the second, and in the last, a lone quintuplet would have Nurse O'Shaughnessy for her bunkmate.

Anyone who worried that the girls might be distressed by the unfamiliar sleeping arrangements was entirely mistaken. "The quints regard sharing a room with the nurse as a great privilege," explained the *Globe and Mail.* "As soon as they were in their pyjamas and their new red bedroom slippers, they solemnly drew straws to determine where each would sleep. Émilie won." Then they said their prayers, asking a special blessing for the king and queen, and none other than Mama and Papa Dionne tucked them in and kissed them good night. That, too, was a rare enough occurrence to make the papers the next day.

"But to sleep?" the *Globe and Mail* mused. "Well, would you—if you were their age and were on the train for the first time in your life . . . and if you were going to wear beautiful new long white organdy dresses . . . and be presented to the King and Queen?" One reporter imagined them "saucer-eyed and excited—and perhaps a little frightened" in their cots, each cuddled up with a favorite plaything. "Little Émilie lies there in the berth beyond us, hugging her three-year-old toy monkey. She hasn't yet given up the idea that she might be allowed to sleep with the Queen."

As usual, it was Dr. Dafoe who indulged the reporters with choice tidbits about the happenings in the nursery car. The whistle and swaying of the train kept the girls awake. They wanted glasses of milk and water. Nurse O'Shaughnessy listened at their bedroom doors until their chattering died down, and, the *Star* reported, "the Dionne daughters spent their first night away from home in tearless and sleep-filled wonder" as the crimson-and-gold train "trundled south through a rainy spring night to the serenade of croaking frogs."

The children were not the only ones who were reluctant to settle down. "I don't know whether the newspaper people will go to bed," the *Globe and Mail*'s reporter confided. The press car rattled with the sounds of typewriters, and of playing cards snapping onto the tables. The reporters were as excited as the five little girls, and as preoccupied with the youngsters' safety as the police. One American journalist was biting his nails so nervously, someone asked if he thought there was a bomb on the train tracks.

Émilie and Marie were up first the next morning, clapping their hands at the sight of the Toronto Irish Regiment's pipe band swinging by the siding where the train had halted. "Now we are in Toronto. Now we can see princesses!" they chanted.

After a familiar breakfast of soft-boiled eggs, bacon, and brown toast, Nurse O'Shaughnessy and Nurse Corriveau dressed the girls in their traveling clothes: double-breasted blue flannel coats over pale blue silk broadcloth dresses. The "sweet little dresses" boasted puffed sleeves and white collars trimmed with dark blue stitching. Three inches of "delightful" dark blue and pink smocking bordered two rows of pearl buttons. Fine white straw poke bonnets woven through with pink ribbon and blue forget-me-nots framed Yvonne, Annette, Cécile, Émilie, and Marie's dark curls. White buckskin slippers and little white "chamo-suede" gloves completed the dainty ensemble. Once again, the nurses came across as more excited than the children. Unnoticed by almost everyone, "the other Dionne children, looking on with grave, wondering expressions, roved restlessly here and there . . . as a couple of police were set to guard the box of clothes which will be worn by the girls for their presentation."

At nine-thirty, Nurse O'Shaughnessy and Nurse Corriveau led the girls off the train.

"Les journalistes!" Mrs. Dionne sighed as reporters pressed close.

Her daughters did not share her dismay. "The Quints blew kisses to the crowds as they left the train and broke into a hearty laugh as Dr. Dafoe approached them from another coach," Nurse Corriveau recalled. Dr. Dafoe, decked out in a formal morning suit complete with a silk top hat and tails and a pink flower in his buttonhole, struck the children as absurd. "It's crazy, the doctor's hat. It's crazy!" Émilie said, rolling her eyes and pointing.

At the sight of the seven-passenger automobile that would carry them to the Parliament building, Yvonne, Annette, Cécile, Émilie, and Marie "began dancing and yelling 'Voiture, voiture!'" *Carriage, carriage!* The motorcycle escort that whisked them through the cheering streets of Toronto was just as dazzling, and as they had done the night before, "the children shrieked for more speed and clapped their hands."

"The girls were especially entranced by the kilties and the bagpipe band," Nurse Corriveau remembered, "and asked why the people were laughing and yelling so much." Nurse Corriveau answered as simply as she could: "The people are happy to see you." (The children were not quite as innocent of their fame as the nurses wanted to believe, however. Years later the sisters would reflect, "Now we had a much better idea of what went on behind the screens at the observatory, what those dim shapes really looked like when the camouflage was removed. They waved to us all along the route, and we waved back and threw kisses, just as if this was one more observatory show.")

Although Yvonne, Annette, Cécile, Émilie, and Marie were doing a remarkable job of taking all the fanfare in stride, there were moments that betrayed what a sheltered existence they were accustomed to. "On their way to the legislative building the Dionnes passed a bugle and drum band which was playing at full blast," the *Toronto Star* noticed. "The noise seemed to frighten the children and they ducked their heads until the car passed the band."

The *Star* also observed that "the happiest in the entire group seemed to be Mrs. Dionne"—perhaps because unbeknownst to almost every-one, Elzire carried a letter addressed to Queen Elizabeth in her purse. It began:

> *Your Majesty:*
>
> *Is it permitted for a mother who is very unhappy to solicit your kindly intervention to the end that her family be united? You are a mother and consequently in a position to realize the sadness that wrings our hearts when we are separated from our five little girls.*

It was Elzire's hope that her heartfelt plea for help—bolstered in no small part by witnessing her daughters' irresistible charm firsthand—would move Queen Elizabeth to intervene to reunite the entire Dionne family. Only "a word of astonishment at this separation" would be enough, Elzire asserted.

With this mission in mind, Elzire mounted the steps of the Parlia-ment building, clutching the arm of her confidante, Lillian Barker of the *New York Daily News*. Elzire's grip was so insistent, Barker was ushered past the police guard preventing reporters and photographers from en-tering the building. "Don't go away," Elzire whispered. "You're not just a reporter. You're my friend."

Barker made it as far as the anteroom where Nurse Corriveau and Nurse O'Shaughnessy were helping the girls change into the court dresses they would wear to greet George VI and Queen Elizabeth. Dubbed by one reporter "the last word in little-girl loveliness," the ankle-length gowns were confections of white organza, complete with cape collars, puffed sleeves, and wide taffeta sashes. Black patent-leather slip-pers peeked from beneath the ruffled hemline, and for a finishing touch, the girls wore old-fashioned white lace mittens. "As the children walk," Dr. Dafoe promised the press, "the skirt will move gracefully like a cloud of mist about them." To help distinguish the five sisters from one another, a different flower was nestled into the dark brown curls under each bonnet brim: a sprig of heather for Yvonne, a spray of green for Annette, Scottish bluebells for Cécile, pink rosebuds for Émilie, and yellow rosebuds for Marie.

At the door to the chamber where the royal audience would take place, an official in a coat trimmed with gold braid informed Elzire that six of her children would not be admitted—only the quintuplets and their caregivers. Ernest, Rose-Marie, Thérèse, Daniel, Pauline, and Oliva Jr. would have to sit and wait while their parents and their five identical sisters were presented to King George and Queen Elizabeth.

For weeks, the six of them had dreamed of nothing else. "We're going to meet the King—the King," Ernest had proudly crowed as the family inspected the Quintland Special just days before. In truth, no one was certain whether they would be formally presented to George VI and Queen Elizabeth, but, the *North Bay Nugget* reported, "they had been told that they would be granted the great privilege of at least seeing the Royal couple." Ernest, Rose-Marie, Thérèse, Daniel, Pauline, and Oliva Jr. had no reason to doubt this promise. Their parents had taken them out of school and bought new Eton jackets for the boys and organdy dresses for the girls especially for the momentous occasion. The disappointment of their last-minute exclusion would ache for years to come.

With her letter to the queen, Elzire Dionne intended to put an end to such divisions between her children. "Keep your fingers crossed," Elzire told Lillian Barker before they were parted. "I just hope I can give it to her."

Seven members of the Dionne family, Dr. Dafoe, and the children's attendants were ushered into the lieutenant governor's music room. Its high ceiling, sparkling chandeliers, and lush draperies reminded Oliva and Elzire of a movie set. Their five daughters climbed up onto a lounge and sat kicking their feet as they awaited the royal couple.

In strode King George VI and Queen Elizabeth, accompanied by

Prime Minister Hepburn and Mrs. Hepburn. The girls were entranced. Annette could not take her eyes from the woman in the powder-blue dress and hat. "La belle Reine," she said. *The beautiful Queen.*

Prime Minister Hepburn grandly presented Dr. Dafoe to Their Majesties: "This is Canada's most famous doctor."

Dr. Dafoe started to bow. "But I was only halfway down when the King held out his hand, and I shook it. You couldn't help feeling perfectly at ease with him."

Then the doctor introduced the nurses, and Mr. and Mrs. Dionne. Finally, it was the children's turn. Dafoe, the newspapers claimed, "came to the royal audience in fear and trepidation, for he thought at least one of the famous little girls would stand on her head, grab the King's gloves or otherwise behave as five-year-old children often do."

The five sisters known as Canada's princesses stepped forward as, one by one, Dr. Dafoe introduced them. They curtseyed, just as they had practiced, and called out their names for the king and queen. A pause followed. No one had told them what to do after that. The king and queen smiled. Some spontaneous signal passed from Cécile to her sisters. They looked at one another "and then took a headlong rush toward the royal pair."

With Cécile in the lead, the children "kicked up their heels to court etiquette," put their arms around Queen Elizabeth's neck, and kissed her. Annette, still captivated by "the beautiful lady," presented her small bouquet to the queen. One nosegay, and another and another followed. "Wherever will I put them all," Queen Elizabeth asked with a laugh.

Yvonne took it into her head that the king was not receiving his share of attention, and ran to his side to put her hand in his. "His Majesty stooped over and whispered something to her," the *Star* recounted, and the two shared a hearty private laugh. "Marie then decided that her sister was having too much fun with the tall man in the blue sailor suit, so she ambled over and handed the King her bouquet."

Émilie, ever fascinated by "mechanics or gadgets," touched the brass buckle on the king's belt. "Just like Mr. Ouellette's buckle!" she told Nurse Corriveau.

"What did she say?" asked King George.

"The buckle on your belt is like the one Mr. Ouellette has on his belt," Nurse Corriveau answered. "He is one of our police guards." The king smiled broadly and knelt down to explain each of the bright decorations on his uniform. Enchanted, Émilie stretched out her arms and puckered her lips. The king blushed like a schoolboy. "Kisses are for the Queen," he protested, but Émilie would not budge until His Majesty King George VI had kissed her upturned face.

"There was no majesty stuff in that room," Dafoe boasted to the press when it was all over. "I think for a few minutes the king and queen forgot all pomp and ceremony and were just loving parents."

Even Nurse Corriveau was not immune to the peculiar magic the Dionne Quintuplets seemed to work upon the emotions. "What a scene it was; I had a lump in my throat!"

"You must be proud of your little daughters," Queen Elizabeth said to Elzire as the visit was drawing to a close. Elzire Dionne could not have contrived a more perfect opening for her letter. But she did not act upon it. Her nerve failed, or the opportunity was too fleeting. As they were escorted out, her plea to the queen remained hidden in her purse.

CHAPTER 28

Dionne Suing Dafoe for Libel;
New York Photo Basis of Action

NORTH BAY NUGGET, MAY 24, 1939

When Dr. Dafoe returned to Callander, triumphant over his brush with royalty, a lawsuit greeted him like a slap in the face. *Dionne Accuses Dafoe of Libel,* the papers announced. The doctor, Oliva Dionne charged, had insulted him in the press.

The grounds were a charity luncheon in honor of Dr. Dafoe, given the month before in New York City by the Circus Saints and Sinners Club of America. There Dafoe took part in a skit that was equal parts sketch comedy and celebrity roast. He arrived onstage in a horse-drawn buggy labeled *Rural Free Delivery,* carrying a black doctor's bag marked *Dr. A. R. Dafoe—Mass Deliveries.* A paper cutout stork swooped overhead holding a sign proclaiming *Dr. Dafoe unfair to organized storks. No mass production of babies.*

One of the players—a slim fellow clad in lumberjack plaid with wildly unkempt hair and a narrow mustache like Oliva Dionne's—put a coin into a machine labeled *Matrimonial Slot Machine Co.* When "Papa Dionne" pulled the lever, out tumbled five grown men in baby bonnets and nighties. "Yvonne! Marie! Émilie! Annette! Cécile!" they shouted one by one before bursting into song:

There are men who just love babies and it really is a shame,
Night after night they labor with an acquiescent dame!

By the time it was over, Dafoe was decked out like a graduate in a pink-and-white bathrobe and a mortarboard with a baby rattle dangling from one corner, the proud recipient of the degree of "Doctor of Litters." Photos of the Little Doc sporting his newfound honor made the papers coast to coast.

To Oliva Dionne, it was all a colossal insult. Though meant in fun, the skit salted a wound that had been throbbing from the moment the first newspaper reporter had asked him, *"Well, do you feel proud of yourself?"* Papa Dionne had been the butt of lewd jokes and crass innuendo about his "litter" of babies ever since. "And any man can get pretty sick of kidding in four years," one of the clerks at his souvenir shop told a reporter the year before. Even Dr. Dafoe had once admitted that the "nasty remarks" Oliva endured were enough "to break one's spirit."

Anyone else might have laughed off the skit, or simply ignored it. But for Oliva Dionne, a man whose life had been turned so thoroughly upside down that he'd barely managed to keep a grasp on his dignity, watching Dafoe poke fun at his daughters' birth was intolerable. "We are insulted by the affiliation to pigs and rabbits," Oliva's lawyer wrote to the attorney general. "Is it fair that Mr. Dionne should be compelled to keep this clown as guardian of his five children?"

Oliva struck another blow to his rival in July with a second lawsuit. This one demanded that the doctor produce all the advertising contracts that tied his name with the quintuplets. (That was virtually every one of them; advertisers knew that in the popular mind, Dr. Dafoe was "the sixth quintuplet.") Oliva believed any money Dafoe had made on commercial endorsements belonged to his daughters, and called for the doctor's profits to be deposited in their trust fund.

Dionne Suit May Bring Showdown, the *Toronto Globe* predicted. *Guardians' Patience over Interference Reported Exhausted.* For five years, the board of guardians had been untouchable. Even the king and the pope had declined Oliva's petitions to intercede and reunite the Dionne family. Suddenly, however, the board seemed to cower under Oliva's demands. The threat of exposing Dafoe's financial gain proved to be the critical bull's-eye. Rather than reveal the tens of thousands of dollars he had made from the Dionne Quintuplets, Dr. Dafoe chose to resign as guardian.

In exchange, Oliva dropped the two legal complaints against his rival. Both sides agreed no more lawsuits would follow. Though Dafoe would remain Yvonne, Annette, Cécile, Émilie, and Marie's personal physician, "in sole charge of their health and hygiene," as of January 15, 1940, he would no longer have any say in their upbringing. "The physical, intellectual, moral, and religious education and social training of the quintuplets will be under the sole jurisdiction of the Dionnes," the agreement read. If the children became seriously ill, Oliva would have the right to call in another doctor of his choosing.

That in itself was a tremendous victory for Oliva Dionne, but it was not all. Over a year and a half had passed since the board had mollified him with the prospect of building a single home for his entire family. Now Dafoe himself publicly conceded that the time to reunite the Dionne family was at hand. "The doctor declares that the quintuplets' education would remain incomplete unless they are soon restored to family life and atmosphere," read the agreement. "For that purpose he strongly advocates the erection during the summer of 1940 a common dwelling house for them and their family."

"This is the best New Year's news any family ever has received," Oliva said.

The Dionnes' new home—the Big House, as they would call it—was not completed by the summer of 1940. Nor was it finished in 1941, or even 1942. Nearly three full years would pass before the board of guardians and the Province of Ontario fulfilled their promise to unite Yvonne, Annette, Cécile, Émilie, and Marie with their family.

"A curious lack of reality flavors those years in memory," the sisters recalled. "We were told nothing of the tumult outside, and we would have had no means of understanding it, no frame of reference, anyway. But the spirit of uneasy compromise that ruled our lives, the need to shield us from the facts, became reflected in a peculiar, unpleasant way. We were brought up, in short, to practice deceit and accept it as a normal part of the pattern."

At one extreme, they indulged the cameras by posing as happy little girls leading a normal life—donning uniforms for a Girl Guide initiation ceremony, for instance, despite never being permitted to leave the nursery to attend a single Brownie troop meeting afterward. At the same time, Yvonne, Annette, Cécile, Émilie, and Marie were helping spread the notion that they were secretly miserable in their nursery and wanted nothing more than to live with their parents and siblings. It wasn't true. It was just another kind of performance, though these were orchestrated by Elzire Dionne instead of a photographer or a newsreel man.

With the smallest of rewards—one Life Savers candy apiece—Elzire could entice her daughters to put on a show of unhappiness. Candy and sweets were a treat rarer than hugs and kisses in the nursery. The sisters had not even tasted ice cream until their fourth birthday. "So we were only too happy to say or do anything if Mom promised us a taste of forbidden delight in assorted flavors," the girls later explained. "More than anything else, she desired us to say, and if possible to believe, that we longed to go home to her. The words had no significance for us, and we were pleased to oblige."

The girls played their parts to perfection when reporters and priests visited, sometimes bringing clergymen to tears. Father Francis Talbot recalled being beckoned by Yvonne during a 1941 visit. "She put her hand close to my ear and whispered in French. I did not fully comprehend at first, and asked her to repeat. What she said has haunted me ever since."

"Father, will you pray for the Quints, so that very soon they may go to live with Mamma and Papa? Will you please pray?"

Later he heard Émilie or Marie, he was not sure which, beg, "Father, bring us to our home right away, to where our Mamma and Papa live. . . . Will you please help us? Will you please pray for us?"

Father Talbot was so moved by their pleas, he wrote a four-page article for a Catholic weekly magazine, urging that the five little girls be returned to their family, "and thus save them from the danger of becoming neurotic and psychopathic."

But the fraud itself was having more immediate effects on the girls than the separation from their parents. Now, for the first time, they distinctly felt the two sides pulling at them. For the five sisters who knew themselves to be "eager to please anybody and everybody," it was an excruciating position.

"They were fine until the parents came," Nurse Doreen Chaput remembered, "or someone from the family and you could just feel that sort of . . . tension." As long as their parents remained in the nursery, the girls deliberately distanced themselves from the nurses they dearly loved.

According to Elzire Dionne, Nurse Chaput retaliated by poisoning her daughters' minds behind her back. "Yvonne and Émilie whispered to me that she had told them they mustn't love their family," Elzire confided to Lillian Barker. "She said, 'Your people are dirty, jumelles—all of them, Papa, Mama, and the brothers and sisters. You don't want to love dirty people, do you? You want to love Dr. Dafoe.'"

Yvonne, Annette, Cécile, Émilie, and Marie were seeing more of their family now than they ever had before. Daniel, Pauline, and Oliva Jr. were coming to the Dafoe Hospital—rechristened Pouponnière des Jumelles Dionnes, *Nursery of the Dionne Quintuplets*—to have lessons in their sisters' private schoolroom, and every Sunday the five girls dutifully crossed the road to have dinner around the big kitchen table in the farmhouse where they were born.

If the nurses did indeed worry that these Sunday reunions would divert the girls' affection, their fears were entirely misplaced. "It would be fitting to say that we delighted in these visits and spent the week looking forward to them," the sisters said. "That was the impression that was created, but it was entirely untrue. The five of us sat through the meals like strangers."

They *were* strangers. Ernest, Rose-Marie, Thérèse, Daniel, and Pauline had spent the first two years of their sisters' lives looking at them through a pane of glass instead of playing with them. The first time Rose-Marie had held Yvonne's hand, it was through a gap in the fence. In the meantime, new babies had arrived in the Dionne home, patching up the hole the quintuplets had left behind—Oliva Jr. and then Victor, born in 1938. "Émigrées from our home but never from our hearts," Oliva had called his five daughters, but the girls themselves were unable to summon the same depth of feeling in return.

"We knew instinctively the emotions of joy and contentment that Mom and Dad wanted us to feel every time we walked through their weather-beaten front door. But no matter how hard we tried to behave as we were expected to and to feel in our hearts what we were supposed to feel, it was no use. It did not work. We preferred the nursery, familiar, safe, and dear as it was to us."

The best Yvonne, Annette, Cécile, Émilie, and Marie could do to please their parents was to substitute obedience for love. The five of them obeyed unquestioningly, without any understanding of the consequences they were capable of setting in motion. At six years old, how could they? All that mattered to them were their parents' smiles, and the taste of candy.

And so on Mother's Day of 1941, the sisters startled the continent when they deliberately spoiled a radio broadcast aimed at American tourists. They had two lines to say. First Yvonne was to ask, *Won't you come up and see us this summer?* And then Marie would add, *We hope that all mothers are very happy today.* As a finale they would all sing "There'll Always Be an England."

"People on the program drilled us in our lines all day before the show was to go on the air. But we had held a private rehearsal of our own under Yvonne's direction before that," the sisters later revealed. "Mom had chosen her to be the ringleader."

On the morning of the broadcast Yvonne told her astonished nurses, "I don't want to speak English." Coaxes and threats would not sway her into giving up the candy she had been secretly promised as a reward.

Cécile was called upon to substitute. Midafternoon, she and Marie both mutinied. "Five little chins became stubborn," the *Nugget* reported as Annette and Émilie followed suit. "Five little mouths became fixed in obstinate lines." The panicked adults had no choice but to give in and allow the girls to speak the two lines in unison, in French. They did not sing.

From the way the public reacted, Canada's five sweethearts might as well have shouted obscenities over the airwaves. Four thousand angry letters arrived at the Provincial Tourist and Travel Bureau in the space of three days. Complaints jammed the director's phone lines. "We, the English-speaking peoples of Canada, have not the slightest objection to the 'quints' speaking in French, but insist that they also give it to us in English. If that is refused they should not be heard at all," one listener informed the editor of the *Toronto Star*. "If the quints won't speak English, they might, in deference to the visitors from across the line who have contributed so much to their fortune, at least speak American," griped another.

The "insurrection" was only half over. Two weeks later, on their seventh birthday, Yvonne, Annette, Cécile, Émilie, and Marie again stood before a radio microphone. This time, the script was in French to avert another last-minute standoff. All they had to do was say *Oui, oui, Monsieur Thomas* to the show's host, and then send a get-well message to Dr. Dafoe, who was recuperating from a major operation in Toronto. (Unbeknownst to the public, he was being treated for colon cancer.)

As the broadcast began, the *Nugget* reporter noticed Cécile steal a glance at her mother and indulge in "a private little chuckle." Their cue came . . . and the airwaves crackled with silence. Host Lowell Thomas asked again if the girls would help him. No response. Perhaps the message for Dr. Dafoe? he suggested. Nothing. The only sound the sisters conceded to make came from Annette, who plunked out two verses of "Frère Jacques" on her miniature organ.

"I do not know what got into them," guardian Judge Valin said of the incident. "It may be that someone has been making suggestions to them that should not have been made."

Blame for the two fiascos immediately fell on Oliva and Elzire. Though Oliva insisted—"in excellent English"—that he was as puzzled over his daughters' behavior as the rest of the world, the denial rang hollow in the public's ears. Everyone knew how the Dionnes felt about Dr. Dafoe, and if Yvonne, Annette, Cécile, Émilie, and Marie refused to speak English, it meant they could no longer communicate with their parents' rival. Their refusal even to wish him well in French certainly did nothing to quell such suspicions.

When Dafoe returned from his long convalescence in Toronto, he witnessed for himself how the girls' allegiance had shifted in his absence. Photographers were on hand to capture what they expected would be a gleeful reunion: the Dionne Quintuplets, welcoming home their beloved Dr. Dafoe after months apart. The girls' subdued reaction was impossible to overlook. "They just wouldn't go near him," Nurse Chaput recalled, shaking her head. "We literally had to push them."

"He looked much older and very frail," the sisters themselves remembered. "We politely wished him health as a kind of goodbye, but we showed him none of the old warm affection, and we did not hug him as before. We were old enough to know that Mom and Dad did not want us to do that. We were anxious to please. The little doctor did not allow the hurt to show on his face or in his manner."

In the privacy of his home, however, Dafoe made no attempt to hide the bitterness of his disappointment over being ousted from the girls' affections. "Do you think," an acquaintance asked him, "that there was a better way to have handled this business? Perhaps a greater understanding of the parents' point of view?"

"Maybe," the doctor conceded. "I don't know. My job was to keep the babies alive."

"But maybe if someone had taken the time to explain things to Oliva . . ."

"Impossible," Dafoe said, jabbing at the air with his pipe. The doctor claimed that Oliva could not comprehend the necessity of sterilizing diapers and bottles, apparently confident that the public would believe that a northern Ontario farmer could be so ignorant as to deny the existence of microscopic organisms. "His babies were dying of dysentery and he wouldn't believe it because I couldn't show him the germs. How could anybody talk sense to a man like that?"

The following February, Dr. Dafoe resigned from his position as Yvonne, Annette, Cécile, Émilie, and Marie's personal physician. "I feel that my usefulness for the five lovely girls has come to an end," he told the press. "They were sweet children," he added with a glance at the office wall where their photo hung.

CHAPTER 29

Dionne Wins Control over His Five Girls

AMERICA MAGAZINE, OCTOBER 25, 1941

Two weeks before Dafoe's resignation, Yvonne, Annette, Cécile, Émilie, and Marie attended a groundbreaking ceremony for the new nineteen-room home they would share with their family.

Anyone could see that the guardianship was on its last legs. Tourist traffic was tapering off, and it wasn't solely due to the radio debacles. The United States had joined World War II, shifting Americans' attention from the petty skirmishes in Callander, Ontario, to the literal battlefields of Europe and the Pacific. Gasoline and tire rubber were rationed, curtailing long-distance road trips. And Nurse Louise de Kiriline, with her character-istic brusqueness, voiced something everyone else was too tactful to say. "I was disappointed in them," she told a reporter after visiting Quintland that spring of 1942. "I thought they were not as pretty." Five ordinary-looking seven-year-olds simply did not have the same pull on emotions or pocket-books as a quintet of rosy-cheeked toddlers with bouncing ringlets.

For the first time, the press's sympathy was firmly with the Dionne family. *Liberty* magazine, which in 1935 had praised the Dafoe Hospital as "exactly the sort of place you'd want your own baby to be," had done an about-face. Since the miraculous quintuple birth, *Liberty* had published a stack of at least ten articles wooing the public over to Dafoe's side, com-pared to only two favoring the Dionnes' point of view. In 1940, *Liberty* printed a scathing indictment of the children's upbringing, secretly writ-ten by none other than Nurse Yvonne Leroux. "I wouldn't want children of my own kept permanently in cotton wool or in velvet-lined cases as a sort of museum piece," she said of the hospital. "If you knew them as well as I do . . . you would be sorry for the quintuplets."

Nurse de Kiriline's sympathies had likewise shifted. During her 1942 visit, the lock on the front gate affected her in a way it never had before. "The guards wouldn't let me in the enclosure until they got permission," she told a reporter. "I saw in a flash how Mrs. Dionne must have felt all those years—waiting to have a locked gate opened so she could see her own children."

As the guardianship fractured, more and more people began to give serious thought to the lingering effects that eight years of controversy might have on the children themselves. They debated over the quins, fretted about the quints. No one seemed to take into account that "the quints" were five separate people, each of whom might react in her own way. Their fans knew them only through photographs and newsreels, where the seven-year-old sisters appeared so very much alike that it was almost impossible for anyone who did not know them personally to fully appreciate their differences.

Yvonne, Annette, Cécile, Émilie, and Marie themselves felt the oversight. "Among ourselves, there was obviously never any question about who was whom from the moment that we could sense ourselves to be individuals," they said. "We could not understand how anyone could be so foolish as to mistake one for another."

For those who took the time to study the girls closely, there were ample physical cues to distinguish them from one another, like the singular symmetry of Cécile's face, or the way Yvonne's cheeks scrunched her eyes into something almost like a squint when she smiled. Annette had an uneven tooth, and dimples. Marie's forehead was the narrowest, giving her face a diamond-like shape, while her subtly drooping eyelids sometimes made her appear drowsy. Émilie had the broadest smile and the lushest eyebrows. She also lacked her sisters' chubby cheeks, rendering her face more elfin than babyish.

Even in still photographs, sparks of personality announced the girls' individuality more and more strongly as they grew. Careful observation revealed that Marie often tilted her head and shot a wry half smile at the camera. From the time she was an infant, Yvonne had a way of looking up through her extra-dark eyelashes that suggested a hint of concern, or wariness. A certain lift of the eyebrows marked Annette's expression, as though the camera always managed to snap just as a delightful surprise had popped into her view, lending her face a particular sparkle and vivacity. Even with the corners of her mouth turned down, she might appear to be on the verge of giggling. Cécile, on the other hand, exuded serenity with her steady gaze and soft smile. The most outgoing of all, Émilie had a habit of looking the camera straight in the eye, sometimes with her lips pressed into a flat, sly grin that seemed to warn of impending mischief.

But the public's fascination with the Dionne Quintuplets was not with their differences. In newspaper and magazine articles, the subtleties of their five distinct personalities were reduced to single characteristics: the leader, the coquette, the thoughtful one, the prankster, the baby. "We were treated as five who really amounted to one, five of a kind so close to each other and alike in every respect that we were virtually indistinguishable. We could not possibly have separate identities or desires." When they appeared in the observatory playground or before the cameras, they were always dressed alike. Wearing identical clothing looked like great fun to their fans, but for the sisters themselves, it felt like wearing uniforms.

"I suffered a lot when young," Cécile said. "We were all always together and people were there looking at us and I knew all the time that nobody was going to say, *Hey, hello, Cécile!* No. It was only, *Hey, the quints!* And that was very difficult to accept."

Yet in their sisterhood was a unique strength and comfort. Nothing in their lives provided such love, trust, and constancy. More than anything else, Yvonne, Annette, Cécile, Émilie, and Marie would rely on their indelible bond to see them through the tumultuous years to come.

PART THREE

FINDING HOME

June 1943–May 1998

CHAPTER 30

Quints Will Soon Move to New Home

Ottawa Journal, November 6, 1943

Only days after they turned nine in 1943, the most fundamental aspects of the life Yvonne, Annette, Cécile, Émilie, and Marie had known began a dizzying reversal.

Dr. Dafoe was dead. He had survived colon cancer and a long-neglected case of diabetes only to be felled by a sudden bout of pneumonia on June 2. The Little Doc had just celebrated his sixtieth birthday. The press reported that Émilie said, "We will ask God to take care of his soul," but in truth, the news of Dafoe's death was kept from the sisters for six months. The doctor had been a more prominent father figure to the girls than their own father, but when Oliva finally told them Dafoe was gone, they concealed their sadness, "because we knew, without being told, what Dad wanted us to feel."

One hundred yards to the west of the nursery, a Georgian mansion of yellow bricks neared completion. The opposite of the farmhouse in every way, it boasted nineteen rooms, nine bathrooms, bedrooms for maids and a nurse, a two-car garage, and a fully modern sparkling-white kitchen with a walk-in refrigerator. A large oil painting of Yvonne, Annette, Cécile, Émilie, and Marie—artwork from a 1940 calendar—hung over the mantel at one end of the thirty-foot living room. There was a music room, and a library paneled in knotty pine for Oliva, with a crystal chandelier, black marble fireplace, and leather couches. Beneath the foyer's lantern-shaped light fixtures, a dark walnut stairway curved past a statue of the Madonna set into a window niche. Upstairs were two bedrooms for the boys and four for the girls, with a bathroom connecting each pair. Each of the girls' rooms was done up in morning glory chintz—one in pink, one pale turquoise, one canary yellow, and one dark blue. Bellpulls in each bedroom rang in the nurses' room. The basement, with its Ping-Pong table, fireplace, and second kitchen, belonged entirely to the children.

"It cost me $75,000, not including the furniture," Oliva liked to say (over $800,000 in US currency today). In fact, it had likely cost him nothing. Funds for the Big House came out of his daughters' trust. Unaware that they themselves were paying for a home they did not desire from a bank account they did not know they possessed, Yvonne, Annette, Cécile, Émilie, and Marie watched the construction with trepidation.

"The fable was that we had always felt, up to this moment, like institutional children, separated by cruel law from the rest of the family," the sisters recalled. Nothing could have been further from the truth. Never in their lives had they wished to leave the nursery. "It was a haven to us, not a prison. It was familiar and friendly, the place where we had laughed so much more often than cried." It was not a house, yet it was home. Only one thing about the Big House mirrored the nursery: its locked gate and barbed wire–topped fence.

Almost twenty-two months passed between the February 1942 groundbreaking and the day the Dionnes moved in—November 17, 1943. War shortages had made building materials hard to come by, delaying construction again and again. Oliva had waited to move his family in until every last detail was in place, as though something as trifling as an unpainted doorjamb or an out-of-place ashtray might jeopardize the success of the reunion he had battled so long and hard for. Yet to Yvonne,

Annette, Cécile, Émilie, and Marie, the move to the Big House seemed to occur in a heartbeat. "Like that," Cécile said as Yvonne snapped her fingers at the memory. "Without being prepared."

Determined to integrate the two halves of his family, Oliva Dionne immediately introduced new patterns to keep "the little girls" from forming a separate cluster within the household. No longer would they sleep all together in a single room. Annette and Cécile were given the yellow bedroom, Yvonne and Émilie the turquoise one. That left Marie to share the pink room with ten-year-old Pauline. They were not to sit next to one another at the table, either. That first night when the two dining room tables were pushed together, each of the five girls found herself positioned between two unfamiliar siblings.

"Now, we're one big family," Oliva announced at dinner. "No more divisions. You little girls, you have to stop seeing yourselves as quintuplets. Look how we've seated you at the table: here, each of you is one child among twelve. Not one among five, one among twelve. I've always wanted all my children to be treated the same."

However well-intentioned Oliva's efforts might have been, they backfired. Yvonne, Annette, Cécile, Émilie, and Marie were too disoriented by so many sudden, drastic changes to open their tight circle. "Every instinct urged us to keep to ourselves, to shy away from these brothers and sisters whom we did not know very well," they said. Communication was difficult, for the younger girls had been taught French almost exclusively, while their father and siblings favored English. (Though Elzire understood enough English to enjoy American radio programs, she did not speak it.) "We clearly seemed as strange to the family as they did to us. Some of them seemed to go out of their way to say wounding things about us, about how they all had been happier before we came into their lives."

"These were very hurt people," a friend explained of the family's strained relationship. "On both sides. . . . There was resentment all the way around. There had to be some love as well. But the resentment, I think, sort of overshadowed that."

Nothing in the Big House was turning out as Oliva Dionne had pictured it. Instead of healing his family, the longed-for, dreamed-of reunion was opening fresh wounds—on both sides of the divide. Yvonne, Annette, Cécile, Émilie, and Marie had moved only a hundred yards, yet in a very real sense they were experiencing a rude dose of culture shock. Not only the language, but the atmosphere, the routine, and the expectations in the Dionne household all were miles apart from what the girls had known in the Dafoe Hospital.

For the first time in their lives, Canada's princesses had responsibilities beyond hanging up their washcloths and clearing their plates from the table. Now they were expected to pitch in with everything from washing dishes and scrubbing toilets to milking cows and shearing sheep. If they did not obey, or if their work did not meet the family's standards, there were consequences that contrasted bluntly with the toy-stocked isolation room at the nursery.

In the Big House, discipline could be accompanied by sharp words, or a swat. Spanking and verbal reprimands were very much the norm in the world beyond the Dafoe Hospital, but these tactics were entirely foreign to Yvonne, Annette, Cécile, Émilie, and Marie. For almost a decade they had been surrounded by soft-spoken nurses who weren't allowed to kiss them, much less paddle them. "If we spanked one of those kids the whole world would yell at us," Dr. Dafoe had said years earlier.

Now that Oliva and Elzire finally had control of their daughters, they exerted it in full measure. "In each other's presence, they competed to see who could treat us more strictly," the sisters remembered. "There was no end to their instructions to do this or not do that."

A side of their mother that had scarcely been glimpsed before surfaced as nine years of stifled pain, resentment, and frustration bubbled up from behind Elzire's sweet-faced exterior. "For sure, the grief ruined her health, not to mention her character," the girls remembered one of their brothers saying. "She has no patience left." Everything Yvonne, Annette, Cécile, Émilie, and Marie did wrong, or perhaps only differently, was a reminder to Elzire that her daughters had been raised by strangers. "Did a nurse tell you to do that?" she might reproach them. When irritation ignited something deeper, a swift backhand from Elzire could send one of her daughters reeling to the floor, as Yvonne learned when she tried to intervene to protect Émilie and Marie from their mother's temper. "I think sometimes she didn't realize what she was doing," Yvonne said later. "She had to take it out on somebody." The words their parents used in anger were as painful as the blows. *Brat. Stupid. Crazy. Dirty pig.* "If I'd raised you, you'd be normal, like the others," Yvonne remembered her mother saying.

Beneath their own throbbing emotional wounds, Oliva and Elzire still desperately craved their daughters' love. "The most important lesson, to be learned immediately now that we were all together away from outsiders' eyes, was to show beyond doubting that we truly loved our parents," the sisters recalled. "Somehow it had to be proved to them that the years of turmoil and struggle had been worth the cost." At Oliva and Elzire's insistence, Yvonne, Annette, Cécile, Émilie, and Marie dutifully kissed their parents good night each evening. If they forgot, they were marched downstairs to line up and complete the ritual. For the girls, it was as mechanical as shaking hands with a visiting dignitary, or kissing a bishop's ring.

Guilt permeated the girls' every memory of life in the Big House. "We were convinced that we had brought misery and nothing else upon people whom we ought to love," they remembered. They sensed it in their parents, too, who "behaved toward each other as though they had been partners in some unspoken misdeed in bringing us into the world."

The sisters' unhappiness in their new home was so profound, it spawned an almost unspeakable desire. "If only I could have been a sin-gle child," Yvonne, Annette, Cécile, Émilie, and Marie each whispered before falling asleep.

Their brothers and sisters remembered the reunion entirely differently. "Their return was a true celebration," Thérèse said. For Thérèse, memo-ries of life in the Big House were infused with music. "At our home, for example, we sang almost all the time while working or simply for the pleasure of singing. . . ." After chores, there were evening card tourna-ments, dances, games, and more songs. Thérèse also had fond memories of Elzire, whom she always counted on for a sympathetic ear and good advice. "My mother didn't have a lot of education, but she had a wisdom that was instinctive," Thérèse said. "Beat us? Throw us to the ground? I never saw her do such things!" The very idea that Elzire could be physi-cally violent toward her own children disturbed Thérèse deeply. "Despite all that she had to endure, she could still smile through the tears."

Like Thérèse, Victor could remember his five sisters joining in on parties he had at home, if only to tease his friends from the sidelines. Their brother Daniel's wife, Audrey, also recalled noticing that Yvonne, Annette, Cécile, Émilie, and Marie kept their distance from the rest of the family. "Yet there was lots of joy in that house," Audrey Dionne added. "Christmas—that was real family life, something like I had never seen before. It was a beautiful time of the year, and I always looked for-ward to Christmas with them. . . . And in the summertime—we used to play baseball and take long walks and pick berries, and there were always sing-alongs and home movies. And at night we would get together and pray in front of the big statue. It was a good life."

The Dionne children's memories are so at odds, they might have been living with two different sets of parents, in two different houses. In a sense, they were. Ernest, Rose-Marie, Thérèse, Daniel, Pauline, Oliva Jr., and Victor had entirely different feelings toward one another, and toward their parents, than their little sisters did. The girls themselves knew it. "We had been ordered to mix with our brothers and sisters as if we were ordinary members of the family, but neither they nor we believed this to be true. There was a difference in us, no matter how we regretted it." On this point, at least, all of Oliva and Elzire's children could agree. "We were raised to live a normal life," Thérèse said. "For them, there were five nurses and five children. We just didn't have the same background."

Dr. Dafoe and the Province of Ontario had begun with the purest of intentions. A germ-free cocoon to fend off potentially deadly infection. A guardianship arrangement to thwart those who would jeopardize the babies' health for the sake of profit. A hospital to provide the fragile infants with the very best care science could offer. Yet everything they did to protect Yvonne, Annette, Cécile, Émilie, and Marie's lives had simultaneously widened the breach between the girls and their family until it was too broad to bridge. The Dionnes had ceased to be a single family from the moment Nurse de Kiriline hung the white sheets and mosquito netting across the parlor doorway. "The girls grew up in captivity," Elzire's cousin said. "If only the government had not shown up. The whole family would be happy today."

One morning before seven o'clock a cry from Émilie's side of the room woke Yvonne.

Émilie lay in her bed. Her face was pale, her eyes wide open. Yvonne touched Émilie's arm. Stiff. The muscles were clenched, as though Émilie were exerting an extreme effort instead of lying in bed. Yvonne tried to slap her sister awake, calling her name. No response. Yvonne ran for Annette, Cécile, and Marie.

"Our first instinct was that we should treat Émilie ourselves," the four remembered. "We thought we could nurse her as we had looked after dolls when we played doctor and nurse, which was one of our favorite games. . . . But the color of her face and the ceaseless twitch of her muscles terrified us. We realized within seconds that the situation was beyond us."

It was a seizure—a sort of short circuit in Émilie's brain that commanded all her muscles to contract tightly enough to make her back arch and her eyes roll back, so tightly she could hardly breathe. Her cheeks were turning blue.

By the time the four girls fetched Oliva and Elzire, Émilie's body was convulsing as her muscles tensed and relaxed in a rapid, violent rhythm. Pink-tinged foam bubbled from her mouth.

"My god!" Elzire exclaimed when she saw her daughter. "The grand mal!"

Rose-Marie ran to phone the doctor. Oliva shouted for a spoon. He pried open Émilie's jaw and forced the handle between her teeth, for fear she might sever her tongue. Slowly, her tremors calmed. Within minutes Émilie was breathing heavily, as though asleep.

Elzire gathered up the blankets that had fallen to the floor and tucked her daughter in. "Now, no one will know anything happened," she said. "Leave her to rest."

It was epilepsy, Elzire explained as they all waited down in the kitchen for the doctor to arrive—an incurable neurological condition whose alarming symptoms carried a centuries-old stigma. "If anyone found out about this I would be so ashamed!" Elzire said. "A sickness like this hurts a family's reputation. We've drawn enough attention already." They were not to breathe a word of Émilie's seizure to anyone, Oliva instructed. Not even to the priest, or the doctor himself. As long as they gave her room to move and kept her safe from choking during her convulsions, he said, there was nothing to fear.

Dr. Joyal came and went. Told only that Émilie had fainted, he attributed the incident to her first menstrual period. Yvonne, Annette, Cécile, and Marie waited by Émilie's bedside for her to awaken.

"How do you feel?" Yvonne asked when Émilie opened her eyes.

Émilie was as puzzled by their presence as the lingering sensations in her body. "I ache all over—my back, my arms, my legs—as if I'd been working hard." She had no memory of the seizure or the commotion it had caused.

With a single shared glance, Yvonne, Annette, Cécile, and Marie decided they would not keep the secret from Émilie. They did not know much, but they told her all of it. The news thoroughly unsettled Émilie. Even her sisters' solemn promise to take care of her could not erase the feeling that she had been invaded by something that could take control of her anytime it pleased.

Yet Émilie decided to be braver than she felt. "As long as you're with me, I won't be scared," she said. "I know nothing will happen to me."

Émilie's seizures struck several times a week. An argument, or "any stormy scene from which she could not escape," might trigger one. Even when things were pleasant she could count on at least one seizure a month, coinciding with her menstrual period. Yvonne took responsibility for watching over her sister, keeping a spoon in the drawer of the nightstand the two shared.

"The cry coming from her bedroom, then Yvonne hurrying in to wake the rest of us—this was an accustomed part of life, too," the others remembered.

From the outside, everything looked fine. There were photos of a happy, united family to prove it. Yvonne, Annette, Cécile, Émilie, and Marie themselves told the press exactly what everyone wanted to hear. "It is lovely to have mama and daddy always near," Yvonne said to the *Toronto Star*. "I am so happy. It is just like the picture books, our new house is so nice." But the reports from the Big House, the sisters later confessed, contained "truth and falsehood almost inextricably blended."

Double standards ruled their lives now more than ever. Unlike their brothers and sisters, the girls were obligated to do their homework under their father's supervision in the living room to ensure that they wouldn't congregate privately together upstairs, away from their siblings. Anytime there was an audience, though, they were still required to be the Dionne Quintuplets. Oliva Dionne, who had spent six years watching with disgust from the upstairs window of the farmhouse as his daughters were driven "like sheep" into the observatory's playground twice a day, suddenly took inexplicable pride in showing them off himself. For a year after their move from the nursery, tourists could watch the famed sisters—along with Daniel and Pauline—in the playground during recess hours. Their father accepted invitations for them to perform at public Victory Bond rallies to support the war effort, launch a quintet of battleships, crown the queen of North Bay's winter carnival, and participate in the centennial celebration of the Ottawa diocese. He even allowed TV cameras into his home to film his daughters saying the rosary for a special Easter Sunday broadcast. Birthdays—including their own—and Mother's Day were occasions for the Dionne Quintuplets to perform private concerts for their father's guests in the basement playroom. Other times, he let the visitors peep into the girls' bedrooms while they feigned sleep to avoid being put on display.

As Yvonne, Annette, Cécile, Émilie, and Marie matured into teenagers, their hunger to be recognized as five separate people intensified. "We were caught, it seemed, between two fires—wanting to be treated as individuals, which was not allowed, and wanting to keep together as a group united by a special bond of sympathy and understanding, one for the others."

Yvonne was "the strong one, the decisive one." Though she was the most fearful, protecting her sisters would always be Yvonne's overriding instinct. When all five of their Shirley Temple dolls disappeared soon after moving to the Big House, it was Yvonne who took it upon herself to confront Elzire. Yet Yvonne was also acutely sensitive; she had formed a deep bond with her doll and felt the loss more keenly than anyone when Elzire informed her, "You are no longer children. Those dolls are not for girls of your age." Despite her courage, Yvonne was not one to press matters—she understood that in the Big House, peace was more valuable than victory.

Obedience and an eager desire for her mother's approval character-ized Annette's teenage years. Singing and dancing were her respite from the troubles in the Big House, and her innate humor and optimism gave Annette additional weapons against despair. "I would like to put light in the darkness of everybody," she said. "I work very hard to be positive, to see beauty in a grey sky." To sustain herself, Annette nurtured a dream of starting a family of her own. "During difficult moments, I said to myself: *Endure, Annette. One day you'll have your family. You will have them, your children.*"

Cécile's outgoing personality masked a constant uneasiness, for she carried the weight of everyone's troubles as though they were her own. Her resemblance to her grandmother Legros became a shield against Elzire's anger—a shield Cécile shared with her sisters. "My mother said that I had the same eyes as her mother," she recalled. "I used that to pre-vent Émilie and Marie from bad treatment. I could soften Mom, change her mind. I mostly protected them." Her selflessness took its own toll. "I think Cécile, in the Big House, put too much on her shoulders," Annette reflected. "She felt responsible for everything." Even when her parents quarreled, Cécile blamed herself.

Émilie was the most changed. In the nursery she had been an irre-sistible combination of mischief and piety, "the one quickest to show kindness and understanding." As a little girl, she would climb from her crib in the wee hours of the night to soothe Yvonne and Cécile from their nightmares. Émilie was also the one who famously took pity on

Mother Hubbard's hungry dog, laying a piece of her bacon next to his picture in the nursery rhyme book. After her illness set in, Émilie's sisters remembered, "her nature seemed to turn in on itself," and the effort of hiding her seizures from the public transformed her from a happy-go-lucky child into "the most sober-minded" of the five.

Marie combined the mildest exterior with the fiercest streak of rebellion. She alone dared to ride her bicycle down the road and over the hill, out of sight of the front windows, or to talk back to Oliva. She took after her mother in the kitchen, producing butterscotch cakes Elzire could be proud of. "Most of whatever happiness she knew came from Mom's praise of her skill," her sisters recalled. Marie never let her diminutive size hold her back and often doubled her load of chores to spare Émilie as much physical strain as possible.

On top of the unique troubles of being a quintuplet, Yvonne, Annette, Cécile, Émilie, and Marie were plagued by insecurities familiar to any teenage girl. The chubbiness that had made them such adorable toddlers now embarrassed them, especially when the *Toronto Star* printed their weights for the world to see on the occasion of their fourteenth birthday. Their mother made or chose all their clothing—all of it identical, usually in the big flower prints Elzire liked best, and always about twice as large as it needed to be. "And we were already short and big," Cécile lamented. "We saw it in the papers, that we looked clumsy and awkward, and it was very difficult to accept."

They simultaneously craved and dreaded the "rare adventure" of a trip into North Bay. When they went to town to see a movie, a police escort roared up the highway along with Oliva's car. The attention their father so enjoyed "never failed to dampen the pleasure of being allowed out of the house." (The police dreaded it, too, and called it "Petticoat Patrol.") Shopping was just as fraught. Five identical brunettes stood no chance of strolling North Bay's streets unnoticed. As their father had done years before, they kept their eyes down, pretending not to notice the stares as their cheeks burned with self-consciousness. "I wouldn't be my sisters for anything," Pauline said of their burdensome fame.

It was not long before the teenagers wearied of pretending everything was fine. "The old newspapers contain many a story deploring the fact that the Quintuplets grew into sullen, sad-looking girls," they observed. "We could not entirely disguise our feelings. They showed on our faces."

CHAPTER 31

Dionne Quints Get Schoolmates, Nine Specially Selected Girls

Toronto Globe, September 27, 1947

Yvonne, Annette, Cécile, Émilie, and Marie had one haven: school.

Rather than send them off to boarding schools like their elder siblings, Oliva Dionne decided to turn the former Dafoe Hospital into a private school of his own. "It was impossible to enroll the Quintuplets in a regular school," he told the press. "This way they can continue their education as far as they wish. They will have normal companionship of girls their own age without being deprived of the home atmosphere and home protection." And so in 1947 a dormitory was added to the girls' beloved nursery, rechristened Villa Notre Dame.

Though they had hoped to leave Corbeil—had even dared to imagine attending five different boarding schools—the girls thrilled at the prospect of spending five days and nights away from the place they were supposed to call home. "At the start of the school year, we left the Big House behind us and took ourselves back to the old, familiar building which, transformed as it was, represented hope and happiness."

Five Sisters of the Assumption were brought on as teachers, and they in turn carefully selected a class of Roman Catholic girls to become the Dionnes' schoolmates. Connie Vachon was one of them. Her first impression of Villa Notre Dame: "Barbed wire. And a long, low building. I thought, *Gosh, it looks lonely, and it looks very big.*"

At first the two groups of girls were tentative with one another.

"They kept to themselves," Connie remembered; "they were still frightened, even of us. They wouldn't confide in us for a long, long time. We would ask them a question and they would barely answer with a yes or a no, to begin with. You had to really, really work on gaining their confidence and their trust before they would open up to you." She did not know that Oliva had cautioned his daughters about their teachers and schoolmates the morning they left for Villa Notre Dame: "You're smart enough to size things up. Don't believe everything they tell you. They might try to influence you in the wrong way, turn you against your parents, try to divide our family again. If that happens, I want you to tell me right away. I'll take care of it fast."

The other girls had their own adjustments to make to life at Villa Notre Dame. They didn't know how to tell their five identical schoolmates apart, and worried about mixing them up. Jacqueline Giroux was so homesick, she cried before she even set foot on the porch steps. All the other girls seemed sad at bedtime, too. "I remember being very surprised to see girls like us who seemed to be very happy with their families," Cécile said. "It was not like that for us."

Émilie took special care to ease the other girls' homesickness, treating them to chocolates and going out of her way to make sure none of them felt inferior because of her sisters' fame. Her epilepsy came as a particular shock to her new schoolmates. "It surprised me at first because I was not told that she had seizures," remembered Simone Boileau. "No one was," said Connie Vachon. "And we weren't to tell anyone, either."

Once the ice was broken, Yvonne, Annette, Cécile, Émilie, and Marie reveled in their new companions. Hearing the ordinary details of other girls' everyday lives felt as fascinating and exotic as encountering an undiscovered civilization. "They would ask us questions like, *Do you have dates? Do you have a boyfriend? What do you mean, 'go and have a soda'?* So we had to explain everything you do, as a teenager," said Connie Vachon, still wide-eyed at the memory. Something as simple as going to a movie with friends was almost beyond their ability to imagine.

"We hung on every word they said," the sisters recalled, "storing it away like five goblins hoarding gold."

The other girls had questions for them, too. "Didn't it bother you that people were watching you?" Jacqueline Giroux asked Annette one day when they wandered into the old observation gallery. Jacqueline had visited Quintland when she was six years old. At the time, she had envied the five little girls in their identical yellow dresses. They looked so happy, she had wanted to play with them. Now, standing inside the enclosure herself, it seemed to Jacqueline that they must have felt like prisoners.

It wasn't like that at all, Annette tried to explain. They had grown up being looked at; if you didn't know any different, the spectators were perfectly natural. "We were happy," she said.

To their unending delight, the Mother Superior endowed Yvonne, Annette, Cécile, Émilie, and Marie with nicknames they would use among themselves for the rest of their lives as "a kind of bond, a badge of the 'club,' and a token of individuality, if that is possible." Marie, always the smallest, was dubbed "Peewee." Émilie was shortened to "Em" and Cécile to "Cis." Yvonne became "Ivy" and Annette "Netta." For once, the five sisters felt as though they belonged.

"It was a state of affairs Dad could not allow to continue," they soberly observed.

Watching his daughters give the affection he and Elzire craved to teachers and schoolmates could only have pained Oliva. "Morally, those people are taking you farther and farther from your parents," he told his daughters at the end of their first year at Villa Notre Dame. "They are there to divide our family once again." His solution was for Yvonne, Annette, Cécile, Émilie, and Marie to return to the Big House for their meals, and at bedtime. "For the second time, we were bundled off to the Big House, reluctantly, with heavy hearts," the girls recalled. Cécile enlisted Pauline to convince their father to make one concession: Émilie, whose epilepsy was exacerbated by the tension at home, would be allowed to spend her nights at Villa Notre Dame.

All five of them knew it was best for Émilie, yet the nightly separation tested the very limits of their tolerance for being apart. For as long as they could remember, they had seen the world and everyone in it as if through a five-sided prism, uniting every perception into a single shared experience. Being apart, even briefly, required that they "learn a new way to live."

Little though they spoke of life at home, Yvonne, Annette, Cécile, Émilie, and Marie's unhappiness was apparent to the residents at Villa Notre Dame. Teachers and pupils alike had had glimpses that hinted of something amiss behind the Big House gate. The nuns had experienced Oliva's suspicion for themselves, and saw the way Elzire's mood could pivot in an instant. Occasionally their classmates pitched in to help with the chores on weekends, experiencing the sisters' workload firsthand.

Some of the other girls sensed there was more to the sisters' gloom than housework or the loneliness of sleeping and eating apart. From time to time, Jacqueline Giroux remembered, one of the Dionne girls appeared troubled by something, and the five of them would silently unite, bolstering one another. "But what the problem was I never knew," Jacqueline said. "I never knew. I couldn't guess, and I never asked any questions."

"Many times I felt there was a subtle strangeness," Connie Vachon reflected, "but I didn't know what it was."

Strangeness was a word far too mild for what was happening behind the Big House gate. As Yvonne, Annette, Cécile, Émilie, and Marie remembered it, their unspoken distress had an innocent beginning. Elzire was away, attending a Mother of the Year ceremony in Ottawa. All five of the girls were ill with whooping cough—one of the many childhood illnesses they suffered as teenagers as a consequence of a germ-free upbringing—so their mother had taken Thérèse and Pauline instead. In Elzire's absence, Oliva seemed "more relaxed, not as strict, and a little less distant," the girls recalled. When he came upon them gathered all in one room, he did not scold.

"How are my little girls?" he asked instead. "Have you taken your syrup?" The five of them detected an unaccustomed note of gentleness in his voice. "I have a surprise for you," he added, and drew a box of chocolates from behind his back. None of them could remember their father ever giving them a treat without a photographer on hand to record it. "Keep them for yourselves," he said. "And don't tell anyone, especially your mother. Make sure she doesn't find the box when she gets back from Ottawa."

For that one moment, sharing a secret with their father was as sweet as the candy itself.

Later that evening, Yvonne remembered, Oliva knocked at the door of the bedroom she shared with Émilie. "Why didn't you answer right away when I knocked?" he asked.

Yvonne laughed. "I was swallowing my chocolate," she said.

Émilie offered the box to Oliva, and he ate one with a smile. "You're still coughing," he said. "I heard it when I was at the door." He sat down on the edge of Yvonne's bed. A brown bottle was in his hand. Liniment—"excellent for chest colds," he said.

When Yvonne reached for the bottle, Oliva said, "I'll rub you down myself."

Yvonne's cheeks flamed. She was thirteen years old. She did not want to unbutton her pajama top with her father looking on. Something in her told her to resist—something more instinctive than modesty. "Are you shy in front of your own father?" Oliva asked. "Come on, now! I only want to see you healthy."

Yvonne could not meet her father's gaze as she disobeyed her instinct and did as she was told. She was as ashamed of her nakedness as of her anxiety. He didn't realize that she was modest, Yvonne told herself. What did it say about her, she wondered, if she interpreted a gesture of good-will and compassion as something sinister? Oliva rubbed the liniment on her neck and shoulders, then across her sternum and ribs. *Let it be over quickly!* Yvonne thought. Oliva poured more liniment from the bottle and moved his palms lower.

"Feels good, eh?" he said.

Yvonne did not answer. Émilie's gaze met hers over Oliva's shoulder and Yvonne closed her eyes. Oliva's back was to Émilie; Yvonne knew her sister could not see the way their father's hands moved farther down Yvonne's torso and lingered where they had no need or right to be.

"I'm getting cold," Yvonne said, and crossed the sleeves of her pa-jama top over her chest.

"Your turn, Émilie," Oliva said.

That was not the sisters' only memory of Oliva violating them. Yvonne, Annette, Cécile, Émilie, and Marie soon came to dread riding in the car with their father. The back seat of the Cadillac had been removed for repairs, forcing Oliva's passengers to squeeze into the front and putting the girls in easy reach.

"Who wants to go with Dad for a drive?" Elzire would call outside after supper. Cécile knew what would happen to Émilie and Marie if they went with him. Her father had taken her by surprise with a French kiss during one of those rides. "I was afraid for them. I said, 'I'll go.'"

It happened to Annette, too, during a driving lesson. "He put his fin-ger into my blouse. I was thirteen; it was 1947. I froze, unable to speak.

He said, 'You don't like that, eh?'" For two years after that, Annette hid herself beneath turtlenecks, no matter the season or the weather.

When Oliva drove fifteen-year-old Yvonne to the family's cottage on Trout Lake and instructed her to do something unthinkable, Yvonne had the courage to refuse. Ever after, Yvonne managed to dodge her father's advances. "I always saw when something was coming," she said.

Émilie was not so lucky. Cécile recalled coming across her sister huddled in a corner of the basement, hugging her knees to her chest with a Chopin record muffling the sounds of her sobs. Émilie would not say what was wrong, but when Cécile asked, *Dad?* Émilie sobbed harder. "It's over, Émilie, it's past," Cécile soothed.

Silently, Cécile vowed that it would not happen again. Ever. "We must never leave Em all alone when we are here," she told Yvonne, Annette, and Marie later. "One of us must keep an eye on her twenty-four hours a day. Understood?"

"Me neither," Marie implored; "don't leave me all alone."

Before falling asleep each night, Annette imagined "going downstairs at night, without making a sound. I take the key in the kitchen and I go outside. I talk softly to the dogs so they won't bark. I go to the fence, open the lock, and there I am, on the road." She did not share this fantasy with her sisters. "Oh, no," she said with a rueful laugh. "That was private."

Decades later, when the others learned of Annette's urge to flee, they expressed a touching mixture of support and concern for her safety. "It would have been very difficult because we were closely watched," Yvonne said. "I don't know how she could have made it."

"I think I would tell her not to try it because I was already so afraid," Cécile reflected of her younger self. "But now, at my age I would say, *Yes—go on!*"

All of them recognized that it had been an impossible daydream.

"First of all, I didn't know where to go," Annette said. "And the fence was very high."

"And sharp," Cécile added.

Instead, Annette summoned the fortitude to confide in the chaplain of Villa Notre Dame, Father Bélanger. He listened with his "customary calm," hands clasped behind his back, shaking his head and keeping his eyes lowered as they walked across the school grounds. Yet Annette's relief at unburdening herself was quickly smothered by the realization that the priest had no solution to offer.

Nor would Father Bélanger intervene, even when Annette asked him outright to speak with Oliva. Annette had no way of knowing that her secret was not entirely a surprise to the priest, or that the clergy at Villa Notre Dame already felt trapped in an impossible position. "These sisters, the nuns, lived through hell in there," Sister Tremblay, a fellow member of the Sisters of the Assumption, said later. "They saw what the family did to the quints and couldn't do anything about it." Émilie had already confided in one of her teachers that Elzire did not love her. The same woman had also heard from Yvonne that "her father loved her only 'when interested for other reasons.'" As much as this knowledge disturbed them, the nuns did not dare put the girls' only safe haven at risk by telling what they knew. "They would have been fired, and it would be worse at home for the girls," Sister Tremblay concluded after speaking with the staff of Villa Notre Dame.

Father Bélanger wrestled with the same dilemma. "Even if we are not in the confessional, I must keep your secret," he told Annette. "What you tell me, I don't have the right to repeat."

When she asked what they should do, he replied, "Continue to respect your father. 'Thou shalt honor thy father and mother . . .' It's a commandment. Pray and have faith in divine providence."

"But the car trips?"

"Wear thick coats," Father Bélanger advised. "I'll pray for you."

It would be decades before Annette and her sisters risked speaking out again.

They did not tell their mother, or their siblings. When news of their allegations broke some fifty years later, Rose-Marie, Thérèse, Pauline, Oliva Jr., Victor, and Claude (the youngest Dionne child, born in 1946) were thunderstruck. "We assert that we had good parents," Thérèse said on behalf of herself and her surviving siblings, "and that to our knowledge our father was certainly not a sexual abuser." Victor termed his sisters' claims "a lot of trash," adding, "There is no way we agree with what they've said."

Although Thérèse, like most of her siblings, had spent months at a time away from home at boarding schools in Ottawa and Quebec, it still struck her as unimaginable that her five youngest sisters could have hidden such a monumental secret for decades. "How could it happen if no one else in the family was aware of it?" she asked. Nothing remotely similar had happened to her, to Rose-Marie, or to Pauline. "Never," Thérèse declared.

Yvonne, Annette, Cécile, Émilie, and Marie did not confide in their schoolmates, either. Yet when Connie Vachon read the experiences her girlhood friends divulged about their father, it was as though feelings that had been too vague to call suspicions began to come into focus. "Is this why I was uncomfortable?" she asked herself. "Is this why I felt the tension?" Suddenly, Connie could imagine motivations behind the sisters' behavior that had puzzled her as a teenager. "Is this why they didn't want to be the one that went to the movies?" she wondered. None of them ever looked forward to their turn for a trip to the theater in North Bay with their father. "And I thought, you know, at the time, *Gee, I would want to go to the movies, get out of the compound.*" Time and again, their recollections stirred "many thoughts about those years."

"I do believe in the quints," Connie decided.

CHAPTER 32

Dionne Quints 16 Now, But No Dates, Says Stern Papa

BERKELEY DAILY GAZETTE, MAY 27, 1950

As the years passed, the pretty paintings that graced Brown & Bigelow's popular Dionne Quintuplet calendars showed five carefree, indistinguishable brunettes sailing, camping, horseback riding, even telephoning boyfriends for dates. Little in the images bore any resemblance to Yvonne, Annette, Cécile, Émilie, and Marie's lives. Aside from a brief trip to New York City in 1950—their view hampered by an ever-present wall of police escorts, reporters, photographers, and gawkers—and an appearance at a winter carnival in Minnesota, the world beyond the gates of the Big House and Villa Notre Dame was still largely a blank to them.

Books and movies gave the girls fleeting glimmers of how other people lived. Yvonne, a Bing Crosby fan, favored history books and wanted to visit Rome. "I like Shirley Temple best of all," Annette told a reporter. She enjoyed reading novels and imagined visiting France one day. Cécile, too, liked the thought of seeing France. She was drawn to travel books and Deanna Durbin films. Émilie preferred movie star Gloria Jean and "found much satisfaction" in the lives of the saints. Her first choice would be to visit the Holy Land. Marie, like Yvonne, dreamed of a trip to Rome. Short stories and Ingrid Bergman movies were her favorites.

Newsreels showed the five girls in white caps and gowns smiling shyly as they stepped forward to receive their high school diplomas alongside their schoolmates in the spring of 1952. What Yvonne, Annette, Cécile,

Émilie, and Marie would do with those diplomas, however, was anybody's guess. "I don't remember the girls ever saying anything about what they would like to do," said Connie Vachon. "I think they just wanted out of the compound."

Graduation itself did not reward the five sisters with any particular sense of accomplishment. "We had our new names as a private legacy to take away with us," they said of their treasured nicknames, "but little more than that. As scholars, we had not distinguished ourselves. Five places near the bottom of the class were our usual achievement when examinations came around." What they knew best was how to sing and perform skits, to make collages of religious images, and to embroider.

"In that time," Cécile explained, "there was only two choices: to be a nun or to get married." Yet Cécile felt a pull toward nursing—a topic almost impossible to broach with her parents, who still harbored an intense mistrust of nurses and doctors. Nursing attracted Yvonne, too, though not as strongly. Annette's love of music made her wonder if she could be a music teacher. Émilie knew only that she wanted to help people somehow. While her sisters flirted with the possibility of stretching their boundaries, Marie secretly contemplated a life of faith.

Before any of them could decide which paths to choose, Oliva decided for them. He enrolled his five daughters at the Institut Familial, a small Catholic women's college in Nicolet, Quebec.

"When Dad told us that we had been enrolled at the Institut for the new school year, beginning in September, our spirits soared," they remembered. "At long, long last we should be set free from seclusion and confinement. We five were going to be by ourselves again, happy in the company of each other, without the stresses and strains that family living seemed constantly to impose."

Fear tinged their excitement. The thought of being on their own in the world was wholly new and overwhelming. At night Yvonne, Annette, Cécile, Émilie, and Marie lay awake wondering whether they would feel safe without fences, dogs, and police guards to protect them. What would happen if they were recognized on the streets of Nicolet? Could they possibly walk out together without causing a stir? Should they use different names? Cécile and Annette took it into their heads to dye their hair and ended up staining only their hands.

When they arrived in Nicolet, the sisters immediately realized that the time they had spent worrying about such things had gone to waste. "Half pleased, half disappointed, we found that the pattern had changed only little," they said.

The Institut was run by the Sisters of the Assumption—the same order that staffed Villa Notre Dame. The Dionnes lived in a dorm with twenty other girls, much as they had that first year at Villa Notre Dame. The bulk of their classes mirrored what they had studied in high school: home economics, languages, music, elocution, literature, dietetics, and decorative arts. Cécile was relieved to be enrolled in a chemistry course she needed to enter nursing school, but the absence of any math classes troubled her. Physics, psychology, diction, and typing rounded out their academic schedule, but Yvonne, Annette, Cécile, Émilie, and Marie found themselves spending most of their time refining skills like drawing, knitting, weaving, and singing. Just as at the Big House, a birthday or a visit from an honored guest was an excuse to pull them from classes to perform, or sing at funeral Masses for the clergy. The frequency of Émilie's seizures made it doubly difficult for her to attend classes regularly.

The feeling of being watched had followed them as well. "There was still that finger in the back to say 'Sit up straight' and 'Behave yourselves.'" Any misstep, they sensed, could be reported to Oliva, who had left special instructions that hampered his daughters' first chance at freedom. On Sunday, when the other girls went into town or welcomed visitors, the Dionne sisters were shut into a classroom, writing letters to their parents. This was their most taxing assignment of the week. "Dad was a great one for reading between the lines. The letters could not be too short, or he would feel slighted, nor too glib, or he would suspect we were keeping things from him, nor too gay, because he did not regard life as a matter for jokes." ("Pat him on the back," an acquaintance used to say of the girls' notoriously hard-to-please father. "Never step on his toes.") Each letter needed to contain precisely the right combination of love, gratitude, and homesickness. Appearing too happy to be away might wound their parents; too much pining for home risked bringing Oliva and Elzire to whisk them back to the Big House.

There were unexpected liberties, too. Yvonne exulted in the feeling of finally letting down her guard for the first time in nine years. "I felt free like a bird," Annette echoed. "That's a part of my life I enjoyed and won't forget. Never, never." With no one to scold them for spending "too much" time together, Yvonne, Annette, Cécile, Émilie, and Marie reveled in one another's company in a way they had not enjoyed since their nursery days. Secure in their sisterhood, each began to feel the freedom—and the desire—to express the individuality that had so long eluded them. "They saved us," Yvonne said of the nuns at the Institut. "They were so good to us."

Yvonne and Cécile made a bold move late in the fall, daring to ask the nuns' permission to go into town on Saturday afternoon rather than the forbidden Sunday. Remarkably, the answer was yes. The two did not go far, but the taste of the open world, free of photographers and fences, proved intoxicating.

Visiting the local shops also alerted the sisters to the fact that compared with their schoolmates, their monthly allowance of $2 apiece was pathetic—enough to cover notebooks and pencils and nothing else. Too timid to ask Oliva for more, they brought up the problem with the Mother Superior. "The interview had us all trembling at the prospect of the trouble we feared we might be causing," they said. "But the Mother Superior did what we dared not do. On our behalf, she asked Dad for more money. We were overjoyed to have our allowances raised to five dollars."

"You are rich enough to buy the entire college if you cared to," she told them. The remark baffled Yvonne, Annette, Cécile, Émilie, and Marie. As far as they knew, every dime they spent came straight from their father's pocket.

CHAPTER 33

Famous Dionne Quintuplets to Be Separated for First Time This Fall

Eau Claire Daily Telegram, September 4, 1953

"I have an announcement to make," Marie told her parents and sisters on her nineteenth birthday. "I am going to enter a convent and serve God," she said. "I have thought of it for a long time. I have prayed, and I have decided. I care nothing for the things of the world. I feel I belong in a convent. It is the only place where I can be happy."

Marie's calm resolve astounded Yvonne, Annette, Cécile, and Émilie as much as the news itself. The frailest one among them, the sister they all called Peewee, was the first to take charge of her own life. She had not hinted or requested. She had not asked permission at all. With just two words—*I am*—Marie had informed her parents that the decision was already made.

Does that mean I might be able to do what I want the most? Yvonne wondered.

Marie's chosen order was Les Servantes du Très Saint Sacrement—*the Servants of the Blessed Sacrament*—an order that brought to mind words such as *strict, austere,* and *sheltered.* Its members did not teach or minister to the poor. They devoted themselves to perpetual adoration of the Eucharist—praying for three-hour stretches in groups of two or three, twenty-four hours a day. When they were not praying, they sewed altar cloths and vestments for priests and made Communion bread. "I have chosen this particular order because it responds to my desire of loving God more intensely," Marie told the press.

To Yvonne, Annette, Cécile, and Émilie's dismay, it was a cloistered order; once Marie professed her perpetual vows, she could not set foot outside the convent for any reason for the rest of her life. Visitors were permitted for just one hour each month, with a grille of thick wooden lattice separating Marie from her guests. When she died, Marie would be buried in the convent cemetery.

"I am very grateful to all the people all over the world who prayed for my sisters and me when we were babies," she explained to the press. "I want to return this faith from which we benefitted. From now on, all my prayers will be for them." Marie did not mention that more than any of her sisters, she recoiled from the feel of strangers' eyes upon her. In the convent, she would never again have to bear the scrutiny of the public.

"How do you feel about being separated from your sisters?" a reporter wanted to know.

"I will suffer greatly, but I will offer this sacrifice to God," Marie replied.

For her sisters, relinquishing Marie to the cloister was akin to a death among them. Émilie took it hardest of all. She would not ruin Marie's happiness with her grief, but privately Émilie's emotions ran so high at the very thought of parting with her mirror twin that Yvonne, Annette, and Cécile feared that her sorrow and anger would trigger a seizure. It was one thing for Marie to turn her back on the material world—a world none of them had experienced enough to truly miss. "But she's letting go of us!" Émilie protested.

Émilie did not even have a proper goodbye. On the November day when Marie entered the convent, Émilie remained in Nicolet at the Institut. Elzire had refused to bring her to Quebec City. "It will be too emotional for you," Yvonne, Annette, and Cécile remembered their mother telling Émilie. "You'll get sick." Among themselves, the sisters believed that Elzire's real concern was not for Émilie's health, but fear that her daughter would have a seizure in front of the reporters.

Émilie's grief preyed on Yvonne's conscience, for Marie's bravery had spurred Yvonne to seek a path of her own. That fall, Yvonne had not returned to the Institut Familial with Annette, Cécile, and Émilie. Instead, she went to Montreal, to study art at Collège Marguerite-Bourgeois. She had also enrolled in courses that would prepare her for nursing school—without her father's knowledge. "It was a big shock," she said of living apart from her sisters for the first time, "but I had to do it." Though Yvonne consoled herself with the thought that she had not been the one to break up their "family" of five, leaving Émilie behind so quickly after Marie's departure troubled Yvonne down to her soul.

"Are you taking good care of her?" Yvonne asked Annette and Cécile as they approached the yellow stone convent in Quebec City where they had gathered to bid Marie goodbye.

"It's all right, Ivy," Annette soothed. "We're looking out for her." Cécile had shouldered Yvonne's protective role, bringing Émilie her supper every night, and even crawling under the locked stall door when Émilie had a seizure in the students' bathroom. With a sympathetic look, Annette made Yvonne understand that it was all right to leave them. *Do what you must, and we'll take care of Émilie,* Annette's face said. *Later, when you can, it will be your turn.*

With Elzire, Pauline, and Rose-Marie, they waited in the visitors' parlor while Marie exchanged her gray coat and blue hat for the black cotton caped dress, white veil, and thick-soled shoes that would designate her as a postulant for the next six months. If, after her testing and self-examination, Marie met with the nuns' approval, she would be promoted to novice. Another two years and she could profess herself as a permanent member of the order.

When the black wooden grille rose to reveal Marie, now garbed as a postulant, Annette saw "a new serenity that had transfigured her sister's face." Smiles dissolved into tears as one by one the sisters whispered their goodbyes.

In some ways, the convent was not so very different from the life Marie had known in the nursery. Walls and gates isolated her from the world. Once again, she was one of a group of identically dressed sisters. The sound of the bells dictated how she spent her time, just as the ringing of chimes had signaled when to rise, eat, and sleep throughout early childhood.

In other ways, though, living among the Servants of the Blessed Sacrament was more restrictive than life in the Big House. The nuns slept under rough sheets on straw mattresses laid over planks, and spoke to one another only during two thirty-minute periods each day. All their personal property was surrendered to the church. Marie did not have a room to call her own. The dormitory was composed of tiny cubicles separated by cotton curtains. Sentimental attachments, even to a particular cubicle, were to be avoided, compelling the postulants to switch cubicles regularly. Heads were to be lowered, hands concealed. Marie could not look through a window at the sky without permission. Like all postulants, she kept a notebook listing each and every one of her weaknesses, down to "the slightest hesitation in obeying the calls of the bells." Though her immediate family alone numbered fourteen, Marie was permitted to write just two letters a month.

"It was very severe," Cécile reflected, "too severe for Marie. Given Marie's emotional nature, it was too hard for her."

"She was too young to choose that way," Annette agreed.

Practicing poverty, chastity, and obedience came easily for Marie, but detachment from the world and her loved ones "hurt her as if she were cutting into her own flesh." Separation from her sisters caused a pain she could subdue only with "superhuman effort," and every letter she received from Yvonne, Annette, Cécile, or Émilie reawakened it. Her little notebook revealed that thoughts of the sky and the grass, the songs of birds, and the scents of flowers interrupted her devotions. Nevertheless, Marie remained committed to her vocation. "It touched the other sisters to see how hard Marie tried to do her duties," the Mother Superior wrote, all the while suspecting that Marie was "a little too delicate to endure the vigorous requirements of the order."

While Marie struggled to find the inner silence that would bring her peace, Émilie embarked on her own path of faith. She, too, had long felt a yearning to offer her life to the service of God. "As time slipped by, she had grown less and less communicative, more and more engrossed with an internal life of her own," her sisters remembered. "She was a soul apart," they said, "who cared nothing whatever for clothes or make-up or money, while we at least liked to talk about such things." Romance and marriage did not intrigue Émilie, either, even in the fairy-tale sense the others enjoyed contemplating. (None of them had been encouraged to marry, but Émilie may have felt herself especially excluded due to the stigma of her epilepsy.)

For Émilie, stepping away from the outside world meant releasing herself of her past. In a convent, she hoped, she could find it in herself to forgive the harm she had suffered. Yet Émilie knew she could not renounce the world entirely, as Marie had. "I prefer to remain a child in the woods and unattached," Émilie had written as a schoolgirl. "Nature means so much to me."

Émilie set her sights on L'Hospice de L'Accueil Gai—*the Warm Welcome Hospice*—in Sainte-Agathe-des-Monts, Quebec, a pious society of seven Oblate nuns who cared for aged priests in a rest home nestled in the Laurentian Mountains. As an Oblate Sister of Mary Immaculate, Émilie would not be required to wear a habit, take perpetual vows, or permanently wall herself off from her sisters as Marie had done. L'Accueil Gai welcomed, but did not demand, a lifetime commitment to God's service. Each year, Émilie would have the opportunity to renew her vows, or choose to move on. It seemed the best of both worlds.

Only Émilie's physical condition stood in the way. The second-smallest of the five sisters at birth, Émilie had always been considered somewhat delicate, and the convent required "robust health" of its members. Her epilepsy also remained a closely guarded secret. But Émilie would not be thwarted. Shortly after watching her beloved Marie be promoted to novice in late May of 1954, Émilie set off for Sainte-Agathe, telling her parents she intended to spend several weeks at the hospice to build up her strength and contemplate whether L'Accueil Gai was where she belonged.

Émilie "took to it heartily," the Mother Superior noted. The twenty-year-old was not there to convalesce, but to begin a new life. Though "so quiet we could not tell whether she was happy or not," no one could deny Émilie's willingness to be of use. "She wanted to work, to do too much," one of the residents said. She could hardly bring herself to follow the Oblates' wishes that she rest. "She wanted to help people."

Less than two months after receiving the white tunic and scapular of a novice, Marie—now Sister Marie-Rachel—found herself exhausted by the rigors of cloistered life. Her appetite was suffering. Loneliness refused to loosen its grip on her. "I decided the only intelligent thing I could do was to come home," Marie said.

What she wanted most of all was Émilie. Father Parent, the founder of L'Accueil Gai, fetched Marie from Quebec City and brought her to his Oblate convent in Richelieu, just across the river from Montreal. Then he arranged for Émilie to catch a bus to Richelieu so that she could comfort her sister. Someone would be waiting at the Richelieu station to meet her, the priest assured Émilie.

When the bus stopped, Émilie rushed off, anxious to get to Marie as quickly as possible. No one greeted her. The crowed dwindled, and Émilie decided that rather than wait, she would ask directions and walk to the convent. No one knew where it was. Many had never heard of it. Finally, Émilie realized her mistake—"I was very confused, and I got out too soon—in Montreal, not Richelieu." As Émilie walked up and down the streets, unable to retrace her steps to the bus station, the crowds and the noise and the traffic overwhelmed her. She had no money, no identification, and her bus ticket had vanished. Fatigue and shame at her ignorance brought Émilie to the verge of tears as night fell and the neon signs began to blare their brightly colored messages at her.

According to the Montreal police, this was when Émilie approached a traffic constable, identified herself, and asked for directions. She "appeared dazed and ill," so the police drove her to the chancery of Cardinal Léger, Archbishop of Montreal, whose secretary escorted Émilie back to the bus station the next morning and ensured that she boarded the correct bus to Richelieu.

Émilie remembered the encounter entirely differently—she was walking down Pine Street in a daze when a patrol car stopped to see if she was all right. Émilie knew what kind of feeding frenzy the press would have if word got out that a Dionne Quintuplet had been found wandering the city, so she resisted revealing who she was or where she lived. The officers took Émilie to Station 10 to question her further, keeping her there overnight before delivering her to the archbishop.

"They thought I was stupid," Émilie told Cécile the next day. "I made them promise first that they would not let anyone know if I told them I was a Quintuplet, but they broke their promise. They were not polite."

One of the policemen leaked the story. Just as Émilie had feared, "all kinds of rumors" were in the Montreal papers the next morning. Among them was the report that reached Oliva Dionne before Émilie could contact her father herself: Émilie Dionne had been picked up by police and spent the night in prison. Oliva was furious—even more so when Émilie refused to return to Corbeil with Marie to join their sisters for the remainder of the summer.

"I do not intend to go back home," Émilie told Oliva. "I am going into the convent, and I shall spend the rest of my life there."

Émilie did exactly that.

CHAPTER 34

Four Quints Dry-Eyed and Close to Shock

LOWELL TIMES, AUGUST 7, 1954

Less than three weeks after Émilie returned to L'Accueil Gai, on the afternoon of August 6, the telephone rang at the Big House. Yvonne, Annette, Cécile, and Marie were finishing lunch with Oliva Jr. and Victor, dousing bowls of fresh blueberries with cream and sprinkling them with sugar, when their mother came into the room. For a moment Elzire stood without speaking. Oliva Jr. got up and turned off the radio. The look on Elzire's face was all the warning Yvonne, Annette, Cécile, and Marie had.

"Take hold of yourselves," their mother said. "The nuns telephoned. Émilie has died."

The news reports at first were garbled. *QUINT DIES OF STROKE,* said the *Toronto Globe*'s front-page headline. Heart disease, said the *Toronto Star.* There was speculation that a childhood attack of polio had played a role. Émilie's epilepsy had been so carefully guarded that even Mort Fellman, editor of the *North Bay Nugget* and one of Oliva Dionne's few friends, had no idea it was at the root of Émilie's death.

Around four o'clock the afternoon before, the Sainte-Agathe postmaster noticed the residents of L'Accueil Gai heading toward the edge of the woods for a picnic. "They were all talking and laughing," he said. "I noticed Émilie when she left and when she returned with them. She seemed to be enjoying herself." Émilie was so adept at hiding her condition, the postmaster could not have guessed that a seizure had struck her during the excursion. There had been another earlier that day, in the kitchen, that left her with a bruised ankle. Expecting more attacks, Émilie asked one of the Oblates to sleep in her little gray-walled cell—to keep an eye on her. Three more seizures came during the night. In the morning Émilie told the others she still felt unwell and wanted no breakfast. She was sent back to bed while the rest of the Oblates went to Mass as always. "I looked in on her before we went, and she was sleeping peacefully," one of them said afterward. "I thought she was all right." The Oblates did not understand the true nature of Émilie's condition, apparently attributing her "frequent weak spells" to feebleness in her legs and heart.

Sometime between 9:15 and 10:00 that morning, yet another seizure struck. This time the spasms caused Émilie to vomit. No one was there to reposition her or clear her airway. Unable to breathe, Émilie suffocated.

Mother Superior Anne-Marie Tardif told the papers, "We had no idea she was so ill. When we did realize it, there wasn't time to get the doctor."

Émilie was twenty years old.

"Cécile, you will never feel so bad again in your whole life," Cécile told herself as she watched the hearse approach the Big House late the following night. Losing Émilie made Cécile and her sisters feel "like widows and orphans at the same time." The pain was not only in their hearts and minds, but in their flesh. Once, for a brief flicker of time before they were born, they had all been one. One single being. Though they were no longer joined, that physical bond still lingered deep within their separate bodies. The very fact that the rest of their hearts could continue to beat without Émilie's was more than Yvonne, Annette, Cécile, and Marie could comprehend. "It was like a nightmare," Cécile said later. "Because knowing that the birth was a miracle, as people said, I thought we would never die."

For Yvonne, the sensation was as though a light had gone out inside her—"a flame that would never again be revived." If she had been there, watching over Émilie as she had always done, Yvonne knew her sister would still be alive.

When Annette found no comfort in the prayers she had been taught to recite, her grief flared into rebellion toward God for stealing Émilie away.

Guilt weighted Cécile's grief. "Inside, there's a voice that said, 'You should have done this or that,'" as though one tiny change might have prevented her sister's death. That voice would echo in Cécile's mind for years to come.

Marie made a double-layered cocoon of her pain, sealing herself off from both her own grief and those around her. All she allowed to exist inside her was a scream, reverberating between the shells she had built within and around herself. Marie was certain she belonged in the casket instead of Émilie—or at least laid out beside her mirror twin.

Their legs trembled as they descended the stairs to see Émilie's body. Marie held Yvonne's arm to keep from fainting. Annette clasped her own hands while Cécile bit her lips; both feared their emotions would break loose if they did not keep tight hold of themselves.

Émilie's gray steel casket filled the big bay window of the living room. She had been laid out in a powder-blue voile dress with a white lace collar. A white rosary twined between her fingers. Trucks of flowers arrived every hour, until the arrangements banked around the casket touched the ceiling. Thousands of sympathy cards accumulated across the floor in stacks of fifty.

Together the four sisters took their turns touching Émilie's cheek, holding her hands, kissing her forehead, and speaking silently to her. They sat next to her casket until the wee hours of the morning, then tried to sleep. It was no use. Before dawn, Yvonne, Annette, Cécile, and Marie were at Émilie's side once more.

Only the arrival of photographer Arthur Sasse "broke the spell" the sisters had cast over themselves that morning. He had come to capture the final picture of the Dionne Quintuplets together—Émilie in her casket, with Yvonne, Annette, Cécile, and Marie gazing down at her face one last time. Cécile balked. But Mr. Sasse reminded them they were still under contract for newspaper photographs. "Just one, then," Cécile said.

"Émilie is still playing the part of a quintuplet for the camera," Yvonne thought as they dutifully posed, "even though she's dead."

When Mr. Sasse had finished, the four sisters retreated upstairs. For the first time in eleven years, Oliva Dionne was unlocking the gate and opening the doors to the Big House, welcoming "persons genuine in their grief" into his home to view his daughter's body. Yvonne, Annette, Cécile, and Marie wanted no part of this last quintuplet show.

Five thousand people filed past Émilie's casket that day, admitted in groups of twenty, every one of them quiet and orderly. Outside, the line stretched a third of a mile in spite of a light rain. Six police constables managed the traffic as cars from as far away as California, Florida, and British Columbia came up the Corbeil road.

Inside, Oliva stood beside the bier, accepting handshakes and words of comfort from the mourners. "The way everyone has been so kind to us is more than we can express," Oliva said. "We are very, very grateful." Elzire sat near the doors to the verandah. Now and then a pang of emotion twisted her face as she silently received whispered condolences, but her eyes remained dry. "She is stronger than I am at a time like this," Oliva said of his wife. "We have come through a lot during the past twenty years and she has always been wonderful."

◆　◆　◆

Elzire's grief spilled free at the funeral service the next day. As reporters looked on and movie cameras whirred in the balcony above, the shy farmwife who had spent two decades spurning the limelight wept openly through the solemn requiem.

Yvonne, Annette, Cécile, and Marie hardly noticed the onlookers. "It was very dark in the church," Cécile recalled. "I found it awful. I didn't see them at the time but after it I saw pictures and I knew there was a lot of people." The four of them sat in two tight pairs: Yvonne and Marie, Annette and Cécile. They craved one another's touch, so that they might cling to the conviction "that they were still part of a single living body, to believe that Émilie would always be with them, not in a coffin at the foot of the altar." Even to strangers, Marie was the most visibly stricken. She alone of her sisters cried throughout the Mass, her sobs taking control of her when the priest sprinkled Émilie's casket with holy water. The sight of the black-draped casket passing down the aisle at the close of the service affected Marie so profoundly that her mother and sister Rose-Marie supported her as she left the church.

The press had been waiting outside the fence at the tiny Sacred Heart Cemetery for nearly two hours by the time the mourners arrived. Dressed in gray suits with gray gloves, Émilie's four brothers and two brothers-in-law carried her casket to the edge of the freshly cut earth. Behind them came Oliva, "face haggard with grief," holding tight to the hand of his youngest child, seven-year-old Claude. Elzire appeared to be "almost in a state of collapse."

Over two dozen photographers and newsreel and TV cameramen assembled on the far side of the grave, facing the family. As they confronted the flashbulbs, Yvonne, Annette, Cécile, and Marie felt entirely detached from the ceremony; it might as well have been happening to someone else. The four of them clustered together, white-faced and sobbing "bitterly" as the priest intoned the committal service. To Cécile, standing in the cemetery was "senseless"; she did not want to bury her sister, but "to keep Émilie alive within her soul." Once again the bluntness of Marie's pain singled her out from her sisters; the depth of her shock was so visible on her face, she looked as though she were in a trance.

As the Dionne family filed away at the end of the graveside rites, the spectators, many of them American, breached the police guard at the cemetery gate. "We are not lowering the body until every last one of you leaves," Father LaFrance informed them. It was the custom in the district to wait until the cemetery was empty before lowering the casket.

One of Émilie's schoolmates plucked a red rose from an arrangement on the casket before turning to go. Three more followed suit. Then strangers began stepping forward to claim blossoms. "Have you no respect for the dead?" Father LaFrance asked them. His rebuke shamed the souvenir hunters into leaving, but there was nothing to keep them from returning to Émilie's grave after the burial was complete. At ten-thirty that evening, they were still coming. The flowers lasted an hour, Leo Voyer of Callander remembered. "All gone. And the grass—they even picked up the grass around the grave."

CHAPTER 35

Four Dionne Sisters Start Life Anew

San Rafael Independent Journal, September 16, 1954

The cage is open and the birds are flying away, Annette thought as she watched the farmhouse, the nursery, and the observatory disappear from view. The last thing Émilie had done was show her sisters that it was possible to disobey, to follow their own desires. Now that she was gone, they adopted her courage as their own. Just as Émilie had insisted on returning to Sainte-Agathe, Yvonne, Annette, Cécile, and Marie defied their parents' wishes and set out for a new life in Montreal that autumn of 1954. Yvonne and Cécile would study nursing. Annette intended to take up music, and Marie would try turning her attention to literature.

Beneath the ever-present weight of their grief, there was a strange new lightness. "I remember feeling that it was a sort of release, being that one was dead," Cécile confessed. "For all of us."

If only being a quint was a secret one carried inside oneself, Yvonne had wished only the month before when people stopped to stare at her. Now that there were just four living Dionne sisters, that wish had begun to materialize. Yvonne, Annette, Cécile, Émilie, and Marie's private bond remained indelible. Yet in the public's eyes, the set had been irreparably broken. Émilie's death scattered the magic that made the Dionne Quintuplets irresistible to the public.

"I knew it was better like that," Cécile said. "Although it was very painful. I think it was the start of finding our individuality."

◆ ◆ ◆

Yvonne and Cécile entered Hôpital Notre-Dame de l'Espérance as student nurses and shared a room in the nurses' quarters. The smells of antiseptics and anesthetics, so uninviting to others, became to them the scent of freedom. "I like everything about nursing," Yvonne said; "taking care of people, getting them to bed, working on case histories." For the first time in their lives, they were encouraged to wear makeup—"a touch of lipstick to brighten up the patients' spirits." No milestone was too tiny to revel in.

Marie and Annette enrolled at Collège Marguerite-Bourgeois, taking rooms next to each other. Their studies were not driven by the same focus and ambition that Yvonne and Cécile enjoyed. Without a clear vision for the years ahead, the two of them were a little bit at sea—Marie more than Annette. "An inexplicable weariness and undefined anxiety formed a screen between her and the world, preventing her from enjoying her new life," her sisters noticed. Annette was hesitant about engaging with the world, too. "I think she wants to be friendly but she's afraid," a nun at the college reckoned. In the back of her mind, Annette always wondered who was truly interested in getting to know her—Annette Dionne—and who sought out her company solely for the prestige of befriending a Dionne Quintuplet.

Living separately, even "two by two," was difficult to tolerate. As little as a day or two apart rarely failed to trigger a fundamental loneliness in either pair of sisters. "The feeling is as deep as thirst or hunger," they tried to explain, "but it is difficult to put into words. Possibly a bird experiences the same sensation before it migrates, or an animal when it sniffs water in the distance somewhere. Each of us has it, though not in exactly the same degree at the same time. It is a kind of pull, an attraction that obliterates distance or immediate circumstances." The need to be together was so strong, taxi fares between the college and the hospital ate up most of their pocket money and forced the sisters to scrimp on other expenses.

There were practical challenges as well. Everyday tasks that any other young woman would navigate without a second thought baffled and intimidated the Dionne sisters. "Nobody had thought fit to show us how to walk into a store, go up to the counter, and exercise a modicum of judgment by choosing a dress," the four sisters reflected. They did not know what sizes they wore, and if not for the dollar sign on the tag, might not have known how to tell the price from the size in the first place. The same went for buying groceries or cooking a meal. As children they'd had an elaborate play set complete with shelves of real food, a scale, shopping bags, and a cash register, but never in their lives had they set foot in an actual grocery store.

The problem ran deeper than simple ignorance. "We had been raised without a shred of independence or mental muscle," Yvonne, Annette, Cécile, and Marie realized, echoing the very concerns Dr. Alfred Adler had voiced while they were still toddlers. "We were introverts through and through, imbued with the conviction that we were not capable of making up our own minds about anything or of doing anything without seeking somebody's permission."

Meeting and befriending young men "represented a riddle that left the mind reeling."

Cécile became the first to risk making a date, almost by accident. All she did was return a telephone message with a number she did not recognize. A man's voice answered—Philippe Langlois, a CBC technician who had been intrigued by her face at a Montreal Symphony Orchestra concert, then recognized her picture in an article about Cécile and her sisters. The paper said they were "sequestered" in Montreal.

"That is absolutely false," Cécile told him a little hotly. They could come and go as they pleased, just like any other students.

"Oh," Philippe said. "And I had hoped to come to your rescue, even though I don't have a white horse or a suit of armor." Cécile laughed in spite of herself, and Philippe invited her out for a cup of coffee.

She agreed, largely to prove to herself that she could do such a thing, and regretted her decision the instant she hung up the phone. But Philippe Langlois turned out to be tall and thin, with "sparkling eyes and an attractive smile." He shook Cécile's hand and presented her with a red carnation, charming her with his gentle manners and easygoing confidence.

For their first date she wore a black coat, two sizes too big, that reached her ankles. Yet Philippe did not hesitate to ask Cécile for a second date. "The first few times I met her," Philippe remembered, "I sensed that in her childhood she must have missed love. It was revealed in many ways—although I can't explain exactly how. But I knew." Movies, walks through the city, concerts, and plays followed that first cup of coffee, excursions that allowed Cécile to experience life in a way she never had before.

"From the smile on her face and the happiness in her eyes," her sisters said, "we judged it was good for her and wondered if the same, inexplicable thing might happen to another of us one day."

The Dionnes' next suitor came by way of a case of appendicitis. When Germain Allard—Gerry to his friends—came to visit his brother in Hôpital Notre-Dame de l'Espérance, Cécile recognized an opportunity to play Cupid for Annette. Annette and Gerry had been exchanging occasional letters for years, but the two had never met. Gerry's sister had attended Villa Notre Dame, and had read his playful letters aloud so Annette could enjoy his sense of humor, too. One day Annette told Gerry's sister to write, "Annette says good-bye," at the end of one of her replies.

"So in my next letter I put down, 'Good-bye, Annette!'" Gerry remembered. "That's how it all started."

When Cécile realized who he was, she told Gerry he ought to get to know Annette in person. He agreed. Ten days later, a "spic and span" Gerry arrived at the college. Cécile had not told Annette a thing. All she said to her sister was "Someone is expecting you."

That was how Annette, who was shy enough to burst into tears and flee if a reporter approached asking questions, found herself face to face with a young man she had never laid eyes on. She stood stranded in the doorway as Cécile introduced them, unwilling to enter the room.

"Finally Cécile walked out," Gerry recalled, "and there we were, just the two of us." The memory made him smile. "Are you afraid to be alone with me?" he asked Annette.

"What do you want me to answer?" Annette replied, furious with her sister for setting such a trap and luring her into it.

Gerry asked if she would like to sit down.

"No, thank you," she snapped. Her dress was an old one with a split in the seam. She could not sit down even if she'd wanted to. But to Annette's surprise, Gerry's frankness disarmed her. He understood what she might be feeling and wasn't afraid to express it. Annette decided she was willing to meet him again.

The attraction was mutual. "I fell in love with those eloquent greenish-brown eyes, and those high Audrey Hepburn cheekbones, and the sweetest smile I had ever seen on a gentle girl's face," Gerry said. He was not as confident as Annette believed, though. "She was a famous celebrity, and me, I was a simple guy—and a poor one. It wasn't possible for her to be interested in me for too long."

Annette was just as unsure of herself. "I thought I wasn't able to love," she confessed later. Her emotionally sterile childhood, she secretly believed, had stunted her capacity to bond with others. Didn't her lack of affection toward her parents and other siblings prove that? "I thought my life had harmed me in some way," she recalled. But as Gerry gradually introduced her to the everyday joys of the world, teaching her to appreciate everything from philosophy and poetry to hockey games, Annette realized she had been mistaken. She had all the same feelings as anyone— the only thing she'd lacked was an opportunity to share them with someone whose affection was unsullied by decades of pain and resentment. "Being in love with him," Annette said, "was like being reborn."

CHAPTER 36

Boys? Million Dollars? Dionnes Shrug Shoulders

Lansing State Journal, May 5, 1955

On May 28, 1955, Yvonne, Annette, Cécile, and Marie turned twenty-one. That day everyone in the world wanted to know how the four sisters planned to spend the money that had been piling up in their trust fund for two decades. Only Yvonne consented to speak to the press.

"I don't know what to do with it," she said. "I'm not interested in it right now. First I want to finish my course, and that will be two more years." Maybe she would travel, she said. "There are many places I should like to see, but not now."

Such indifference bordered on offensive. In the midst of the Great Depression, quint fans had distracted themselves from their own financial woes with happy daydreams of the luxuries those five beautiful babies could one day buy with the millions of dollars they had seemed to earn effortlessly. But the girls themselves had never entertained such fantasies about their future fortune. They couldn't—no one had told them it existed.

The first they heard about a quint account was from a newspaper article not long after Émilie died. Her $171,000 share of the quintuplet fortune was to be split fourteen ways, the article said—among Oliva, Elzire, and their twelve surviving children. In addition to a $12,000 share of Émilie's estate, Yvonne, Annette, Cécile, and Marie realized, each of them was scheduled to inherit $171,000 within a matter of months, just as Émilie would have. The four of them were dumbfounded. Everyone

in the world knew the Dionne Quintuplets would one day be rich—
everyone but the sisters themselves. Émilie had died unaware. No wonder the principal at the Institut Familial had told them they could buy the
whole school if they wanted to.

The arithmetic was staggering: $183,000—equivalent to $1,306,498
US in 2017—seemed an enormous figure to the four sisters, accustomed
as they were to allowances of $5 each month. Yet they did not have
enough experience with money to know whether that was enough to
buy a bicycle, a car, or a fur coat. "I didn't know a nickel from a quarter
until I left home for the first time at age eighteen," Annette said.

Yvonne, Annette, Cécile, and Marie were indeed rich, just as the government of Ontario had promised. However, it wasn't as though they
were handed keys to four vaults full of money and invited to help themselves. Instead, an elaborate payout system had been structured to ensure that their fortune would last for decades to come.

The trust consisted of two kinds of money: principal and interest.
The principal was what nearly everyone imagined when they thought of
the quintuplet bank account: the thousands upon thousands of dollars
in royalties collected from advertisers, photographers, and filmmakers
during the heyday of Quint-mania. That principal had been invested in
real estate, government bonds, and stocks, and would remain invested so
it could generate income. That income was the interest.

For the first ten years, the Dionne sisters could not remove any of the
principal from their accounts. They would receive only interest, in payments of $500 a month (about $3,550 in US currency today). The sisters
would have three opportunities to withdraw lump sums from the principal, though their monthly payments would shrink accordingly every
time they did. At age thirty-one, they were entitled to 15 percent. At
thirty-nine, they could take 25 percent of the remaining balance. Finally,
at forty-five, they could take half of what was left—provided that each
sister's account never dropped below $30,000. That amount was perma-
nently reserved for their heirs.

The trust arrangement also specified that Yvonne, Annette, Cécile, and Marie would cover the expense of maintaining the Big House. Though the sisters technically owned it, Oliva and Elzire were granted the right to "enjoy and occupy" the mansion to the end of their days. When their parents ran short of funds, the girls agreed to deduct $75 apiece from their monthly allowances to funnel an additional $300 to their mother and father.

Yvonne, Annette, Cécile, and Marie remembered that first summer and fall of their adulthood as "a time of profound stirring, of self-searching, of adjustment." For the first time, they had total charge of their own lives, yet their circumstances made it difficult to revel in this new independence. Cécile and Yvonne were swamped with studies and hospital duties. Annette remained rudderless, craving direction. Music, her "special delight," was not the career she wanted after all. Nursing appealed to her, but on a visit home Elzire told Annette it was "out of the question." The thought of yet another of her daughters joining the ranks of the profession that had sliced her family in half was more than Elzire was willing to stomach without a fight. Annette, who had always striven to please her mother, did not have the heart to oppose Elzire now. She reapplied to the Institut Familial, where she began to explore teaching and psychology.

Marie gave them all cause for concern. "Something had changed," Cécile noticed. "Marie was very discouraged; she seemed disconnected. She had no expression on her face." She attempted to reenter Les Servantes du Très Saint Sacrement and failed. Her delicate health simply would not adapt to such a solitary, rigorous life. After two months at the convent, she was suffering from recurring chest pains and anemia. Annette and Gerry collected Marie from Quebec City and brought her to Montreal so she could recuperate under Yvonne and Cécile's watch in Hôpital Notre-Dame de l'Espérance.

When Marie was discharged in December, she and Annette rented a two-bedroom apartment in Montreal. It became "a kind of sanctuary" for all four sisters, the first place they could truly call home.

"We hoped to spend the holiday together in our delightful new hideaway, quietly and peacefully and restfully, doing very little but enjoying the chance to see one another without interruption for a day or so." The four of them signed a Christmas card for their parents and put it in the mail on December 22. They would go to Corbeil for New Year's—the traditional holiday for family reunions and gift-giving among French Canadian families.

Two days after Christmas, Phyllis Griffiths of the *Toronto Telegram* cornered Yvonne in the hospital and demanded to know why she and her sisters hadn't sent their parents a Christmas card. Yvonne was taken aback. She had not seen the morning's headlines. *PAPA DIONNE DECLARES QUINTS IGNORED FAMILY AT CHRISTMAS*, said the front page of the *Toronto Star*. Oliva Dionne had called Mort Fellman at the *North Bay Nugget* that morning and revealed that Yvonne, Annette, Cécile, and Marie had been absent from the family's festivities. The story "put the name Dionne back in more and bigger print than at any time since the birth of the famous quintuplets."

Tears streamed down Yvonne's face as the reporter read her father's statement:

"We were not surprised when the Quints did not come home for Christmas," Oliva had told the press. He and Elzire had sensed a widening separation for months, a separation they both blamed on "outside intruders." He would not identify these outsiders, however, not under any circumstances. "The Quints know who they are, and we know who they are, but that's all I'm going to say about them," he added cryptically. (Yvonne did indeed know. The "intruders" could only be Gerry and Philippe. Oliva had been keeping tabs on his daughters even from a distance—the bills for the private detectives showed up on their trust fund accounts.) "We didn't even receive a card from them," Oliva said.

"We did send one," Yvonne protested to Ms. Griffiths. "Can we help it if they didn't get it?"

The article went on as though Oliva were right there, arguing with his daughter. All the other Dionne children had at least telephoned to wish their parents a merry Christmas, he pointed out. Money, Oliva claimed, was at the root of the breach. "We suspected that outsiders were trying to influence the Quints some years ago, and we were sure of it by the way they acted towards us after they had left home, and then more so when they reached their 21st birthday and came into their money."

"Don't believe it!" Yvonne begged the reporter before running off in tears. "It's not true."

The four sisters said no more to the press. They appointed a spokesman and shut their apartment door, opening it only to those who knew a coded knock.

"They love their family," the spokesman explained. "But they do want a life of their own. Many sons and daughters move away from home and relish their independence. But they don't love their parents any less. This is the case with the quints."

The newspapers were not satisfied. Reporters camped outside the sisters' apartment, on the roof, and on the fire escape. On December 29, they reported the unmistakable sounds of a party going on inside as laughter and music came drifting beneath the Dionnes' closed door. Back in Corbeil that same day, Victor Dionne told the press, "My father is upstairs, half sick from this whole thing." The contrast was anything but flattering.

Yvonne, Annette, Cécile, and Marie could not hide out any longer. It was plain from the front-page headlines on the papers Philippe smuggled in with their groceries that the story was not fading away. On the contrary, it only mushroomed as their brothers publicly criticized them for acting like queens and treating the family like dirt. "Silence simply was not a sufficient response," the sisters decided. "For everyone's sake, we had to go to Corbeil, come what may, for a fair talk with Dad. Peace had to be restored somehow."

Aided by a sympathetic janitor who cut the lights in the apartment building around ten p.m., Yvonne, Annette, Cécile, and Gerry made a break for the service elevator and felt their way through the darkened garage to a waiting car. (Marie was deemed too fragile to make the trip and stayed behind.) "It was awful," Annette remembered. "We got down on the floor of the car so nobody could see us. We felt like thieves."

They drove through the night, crossing paths with a *Toronto Telegram* reporter and photographer at a gas station who thrust a camera into the car windows, leaving the girls "blinking like owls." More reporters and cameramen were stationed outside the Big House gate when the car arrived in Corbeil at four a.m. Flashbulbs popped and flared as the "shaken and weary" sisters scurried from the car to the house.

The next day, Oliva Dionne told the press that his family had exchanged kisses and presents and enjoyed a light meal before heading to bed. The whole affair, he said, had been due to "a misunderstanding somewhere, but it has all been ironed out."

Gerry Allard remembered receiving a very different greeting. "There was a feeling of tension as soon as we came in," he said. "A cold welcome," Gerry called it, with perfunctory remarks about the trip and the weather. The Dionnes opened their gifts and went upstairs to bed without a single word about the accusations that had prompted the awkward reunion.

The next day the family was all smiles for the camera. "There was absolutely no strain or tension," photographer Arthur Sasse, who had come to record the reconciliation, told the *Toronto Star*. "I didn't have to tell anybody to smile—they did it themselves."

Behind the doors of Oliva's office, however, there had been a heated exchange. Cécile led the barrage. "Why did you talk to the newspapers and start all this?" she demanded. "Why did you make trouble when we have never said a word about anything?"

To Yvonne, Annette, and Cécile's astonishment, their father did not thrust the blame back onto them. Oliva bore his daughters' anger "without flinching," and admitted his responsibility for manufacturing a crisis where there had been none. Others in the family had influenced him, he said, and he had acted on their bad advice.

The night before, as the car approached the Big House gate, the sisters had "half hoped there would be an accident, a skid, anything that would put us into hospital so we could avoid confronting Dad." Now they had the upper hand. "We could have said much more, you know, but we kept our mouths shut," Cécile admonished her father. They had never breathed even a hint to the press about the hard feelings and painful memories that could have justified a family rift. Oliva acknowledged this with a nod. For the first time in their lives, they had asserted themselves—and come out unscathed.

"There had never been a day like this," Yvonne, Annette, and Cécile said after it was over. It was as though each of them had grown up, all at once, in that room.

CHAPTER 37

The Dionnes: A Fight for Happiness

Chatelaine magazine, February 1962

Absent from the showdown at the Big House, Marie did her growing up in her own way the following spring. She, like Annette, had yet to find her niche in the world. Opportunities for women were limited in the mid-1950s, and the sisters' lack of knowledge and experience hampered their view even further. "So few doors seemed to stand open for us to enter," they recalled, "and each of them had to be reassuringly familiar or we were afraid to make the effort."

Marie—frail, iron-willed Marie—dared to look beyond those narrow boundaries and throw open a brand-new door. If she could not be a nun, Marie decided, she would be a businesswoman. A florist. She would open her own flower shop and earn her own living.

Annette's boyfriend arranged for Marie to spend two months learning the ins and outs of the floral business up close, at a shop his cousin owned. She practiced buying flowers wholesale, learning how to keep them fresh, display them, and arrange them. Cécile's boyfriend also took the project under his wing and spent a week or two observing alongside Marie so that he might lend a hand in the setup and day-to-day operations of her shop.

The only problem was money. When Marie appealed to the guardians of the trust—one of whom was her father—to release funds for her business, she was "turned down flat." Marie remained undaunted. "Whatever happens, I intend to go ahead," she insisted.

Yvonne, Annette, and Cécile contributed a few hundred dollars from savings accounts they held in North Bay. They also temporarily rerouted their parents' $300 allowance to Marie. It was not nearly enough—until Marie remembered her charge account at Eaton's department store. All four of them had one. They could buy whatever they liked, and the bills were sent to the trust committee at the end of the month. Marie boldly charged everything from the stationery to the counters and showcases to her Eaton's account.

"It was a wonderful adventure," her sisters remembered. "The other three of us had every bit as much fun as she did. For us, who had respected authority perhaps more than most people, Marie's defiant assertion of the right to do as she pleased was exhilarating. Her accounts of each day's excursions were listened to intently, often in peals of laughter. We could picture the faces of the trustees when the bills came home to roost."

Salon Émilie opened to great fanfare on Mother's Day of 1956. Newsreel cameras captured a quartet of smiles as Marie cut the ribbon and accepted congratulatory kisses from Yvonne, Annette, and Cécile. Everyone who walked in the door received a fat red rose. Some came again and again, accumulating a free bouquet before the doors closed for the night. At the end of the day, Marie had given away $600 worth of flowers.

Despite her customers' greed, Marie was thrilled—"too thrilled to complain," her sisters remembered. The shop revived Marie for the first time since Émilie's death. "She was not the same person after it opened," Philippe Langlois recalled. "She was still timid, but she could go up to people. She worked hard, very hard."

Nevertheless, Salon Émilie "refused to prosper." Marie could not resist giving flowers away to friends, and to churches for their altars. Nuns soliciting for charity often left the shop with cash donations straight from the register drawer. The shop lasted only six months—a "bitter blow" for Marie. "She was very discouraged, dispirited," Annette said. "She lost a lot of money from her trust allowance."

Yet her sisters refused to see Marie's business venture as a defeat. As far as Yvonne, Annette, and Cécile were concerned, Salon Émilie had broken Marie free of the frustrations and fears that being a quintuplet had instilled in her. "The experiment was worth far, far more than it cost," they said, "for who can set a cash price on freedom?"

Meanwhile, the way Gerry and Philippe had pitched in to help Marie drew Annette's and Cécile's hearts ever closer to the two young men. It had taken two years for Cécile to consider Philippe Langlois more than a friend. "I think the first thing that made me think of Phil this way was when I came in contact with babies in the hospital," she hinted. More and more, the idea of marriage occupied Annette's and Cécile's thoughts.

Annette left school in June of 1957. She and Gerry married that October, in a private Montreal ceremony conducted behind locked doors. Sixteen friends and relatives watched as the couple, dressed in coordinating brown suits, pledged their vows to each other.

Cécile and Philippe followed in November. Cécile envisioned her wedding day not only as the celebration of a new life with Philippe, but also as a chance to mend her family's old wounds. *This time,* she promised herself, *I'll get it right for Mom and Dad and me.* No expense was spared, and no one was shut out as Cécile floated down the aisle of Corbeil's Sacred Heart Church in her gown of silk, Swiss lace, and pearls—not even the press and the news cameras. "Blazing flashbulbs lit up the altar like a movie studio," the *Toronto Star* reported. Afterward the entire family—eighty guests in all—sat down together for a luncheon in North Bay. "I thought that all would be fixed," she said later, "that it would arrange communication between them and ourselves." (It didn't. The day consumed $10,000 from her trust account, and relations between the two halves of the family remained as awkward as ever.)

Before departing for her three-week honeymoon, Cécile stopped at the Sacred Heart cemetery and placed her bouquet of sweetheart roses, orchids, and mums on Émilie's grave.

◆ ◆ ◆

Cécile and Annette shared an ambition "to become the most suburban of housewives, indistinguishable from young brides anywhere." They learned to navigate beauty parlors, grocery stores, and department stores without hiding behind dark sunglasses and false names. They cooked and cleaned, painted and wallpapered, and mastered the trick of hanging the wash out to dry without cringing at the thought of neighbors' eyes upon them. "To Annette, that is a very real luxury—not to be stared at," Gerry said. His wife, he remembered, "was blooming." Within a few months, both sisters were pregnant.

It should have been joyous news. Annette had nurtured a dream of having a family of her own from the time she was a teenager. "Nothing has made me so happy in all my life as the thought of having a baby," she said. Like Annette, Cécile treasured the thought of having a little girl she could call Émilie. Instead, fear tainted their excitement. A French biologist had declared when the sisters were infants that quintuplets could not have children. Though he had never examined them and had no medical basis for his claim, a nurse who worked with Yvonne and Cécile at Hôpital Notre-Dame de l'Espérance agreed with the Frenchman's pronouncement. Their conviction left Cécile gripped with the certainty that she would die in childbirth. Annette lived in dread of delivering a freakish, misshapen baby. Neither of them could be convinced otherwise.

While Annette and Cécile brooded over their impending deliveries, Marie groped for a new foothold in the world. Bereft of her flower shop, she grappled with bouts of depression and frail health that put her in and out of the hospital as her weight dropped and she succumbed to fainting spells. For a time Marie managed to hold a job in another flower shop, under the name Denise Mousseau. It was under this name that she met Florian Houle, a civil servant in his forties, at Mass. The two began attending movies together. Only when Marie mentioned one night at dinner that she had weighed barely a pound at birth did Florian begin to realize who she was. The two were married in absolute secret on August 13, 1958. Out of respect for Marie's desperate wish for privacy from the press, Yvonne, Annette, and Cécile did not attend; their presence would only attract attention.

Cécile's one wish as the final weeks before her due date dwindled into days was simply to see her baby before she died, and so she chose to have no pain medications during her labor. She did not want to risk having her few precious moments with her child dulled by anesthesia. Yvonne would be by her side, for the hospital had granted her the special privilege of attending Cécile's delivery.

When the dreaded yet hoped-for moment came and the seven-pound, four-ounce baby boy was laid in his mother's arms, it was Yvonne, not Cécile, who "shook with sobs of exhaustion and joy." Cécile was almost too stunned by the fact that she was still alive to react. "How marvelous it is to watch the birth," she said weakly. She and Philippe named their son Claude. Another son, Patrice, would follow in 1960, then twins Bruno and Bertrand in 1961, and daughter Elisabeth in 1962.

Cécile's good fortune did little to ease Annette's worries. The fear of a grotesquely ill-formed baby consumed her for another six weeks—until little Jean-François Allard proved her entirely wrong when he arrived whole and handsome on November 2, 1958. Annette had two more sons: Charles in 1961, and Eric in 1962.

Only Marie entered into motherhood without fear. The miscarriages that claimed the lives of her first two babies did not sway her from the path she had set for herself, and Christmas Eve of 1960 brought Marie her greatest gift: a daughter. The little girl, "bright and gay as a bird," was christened Émilie. Another daughter, Monique, was born to Marie and Florian two years later.

◆ ◆ ◆

Though she doted on her nieces and nephews, Yvonne was not drawn toward marriage and children of her own. "She asked for little more than the immense satisfaction of serving the sick, most of all in the children's wards, and in observing the colors and shapes of the world for interpretation in her painting," her sisters said.

Yvonne spent her first summer after nursing school at a camp for disabled children, then took on private nursing jobs. For a few months she studied wood carving and sculpting. Despite her apparent potential, her teacher recalled her as "very bashful, having no confidence in herself." Like Émilie and Marie before her, Yvonne felt called to use her nursing skills in service to God. "I don't think I was ever good enough as a sculptor to become professional," she said. "My desire to be a nun became much stronger."

The Convent of the Little Franciscan Sisters, on the northern shore of the St. Lawrence River in Baie-Saint-Paul, became Yvonne's chosen community. The periods of silent reflection before Mass and during the Grand Silence each day dovetailed seamlessly with her quiet, interior nature. "It shaped me," she said of her experience there. Within the shelter of the convent, nothing and no one prompted her to dwell on the past— something Yvonne always assiduously avoided.

"I don't want to think about 'little Yvonne,'" she said of her childhood. "No. I put an end to it. I want to live in the present, that's all." Through the meditation she learned in Baie-Saint-Paul, Yvonne made a conscious effort to subdue the most painful of her memories, such as Émilie's funeral. "I want to go forward," she said, "and see the beautiful things in life. Because there is no use to put the knife into the wound."

Yvonne would have been happy to devote her life to the Little Franciscan Sisters, but it was not to be. When it was time for the novitiates to take their vows, the Mother Superior informed Yvonne that she would not be among them. No reason was given. "They just tell you it's not your place," Yvonne remembered. "What could I do? I didn't understand it, but there was nothing I could do about it. I was hurt. I thought I had the vocation, the calling. I thought I'd be happy there. I would have liked to stay, but that's life. I didn't want to become sick over it." She tried again, at the Convent of the Sacred Heart in Moncton, New Brunswick. After five years, she was told once more that she was not suited for life as a nun.

This time Yvonne accepted the decision and embraced the secular life as fully as she knew how. She alone of her sisters learned to drive. She indulged in a world tour, visiting India, Israel, Bethlehem, Italy, Germany, Belgium, France, and England. When she returned home, she treated herself to courses in art history, music history, and literature, eventually finding great satisfaction working as a mother substitute in a kindergarten, and later as a library clerk. "I worked a lot on myself, watching myself and trying not to hurt anyone," she said. "Work helped me a lot, and faith." Though the church had denied Yvonne one of her greatest desires, the loss did not weaken her devotion. "Just like someone needs food to go on," she explained, "I need the spirituality to go through all the things I face, to live."

CHAPTER 38

Quints' Story Causes New Wound

NORTH BAY NUGGET, SEPTEMBER 19, 1963

In 1963, the weight of the sisters' memories began to lift for the first time. Intent on setting the record straight about life behind the gates of the Dafoe Hospital and the Big House, Annette, Cécile, and Marie told the story of their lives to author James Brough in a series of thirty interviews. (Yvonne was still a novice in New Brunswick at that time and did not actively participate.) Brough then interwove their personal recollections with his own research to create a book that is half biography, half memoir. Called *We Were Five*, it reads as though spoken by the four sisters in unison. To whet the public's appetite and encourage sales, a shortened version of *We Were Five* appeared in *McCall's* magazine in October and November of 1963.

The *McCall's* articles shocked and dismayed the world more than Dr. Alfred Adler's controversial editorial had twenty-seven years earlier. Though Yvonne, Annette, Cécile, and Marie held back the most disturbing of their memories, barely hinting at any kind of abuse, the undercurrent of their lingering pain remained palpable. "Such bitterness," Nurse Yvonne Leroux said to the *Toronto Star*. "It is all so long ago. I am sorry for the whole bunch of them. . . ."

We Were Five struck the harshest blow to Oliva and Elzire Dionne. "There are two sides to every story," Oliva told the papers, "and Mrs. Dionne and I have ours." Indeed, they had already had their say. With their approval and cooperation, Lillian Barker had published two books telling Oliva and Elzire's side of the story—*The Quints Have a Family* in 1941, and *The Dionne Legend: Quintuplets in Captivity* in 1951. The second had been withdrawn from sale in Canada almost immediately, allegedly due to "certain inaccuracies discovered in the text." There's no doubt that Barker skewed some facts to magnify her readers' sympathy for the Dionnes, but the more likely reality is that Barker's bold criticism of Dr. Dafoe and the government of Ontario had shamed and angered the province. ("For Canada, the book is too true," she remarked to the American press, snorting "with ladylike elegance.")

"We have no intention of getting into a big controversy over this, except to say that the magazine article is full of untruths," Oliva Dionne maintained. "I hate to think it was for financial gain, but if it wasn't for that, what was it? Our conscience is clear. Mrs. Dionne and I may not have been the best parents in the world and we undoubtedly made many mistakes, but we tried our best under very trying circumstances." The phone never stopped ringing as Oliva gave his statement. "This is just like the old days," he remarked.

Publicly, Oliva reacted with cool dignity, but his private feelings were another matter. "Father's reaction was violent," Victor Dionne said. "That book really hurt them, hurt them deeply," Daniel's wife, Audrey, confirmed.

Marie's husband, Florian, had tried to soften the blow for his in-laws, telling Marie he disapproved of the tone of the book. Marie had surrendered to her husband's wishes and attended no more meetings with Brough. Not yet satisfied, Florian also attempted to convince Marie and her sisters to cut out the statements he felt were "most impolite and harsh" toward their parents. But Marie would not give that much ground.

"Everything we said in the magazine is true, true, true," she told a reporter. Annette likewise maintained for years to come that *We Were Five* was "a sensitive and accurate account." Unlike Florian Houle, Annette's husband firmly supported her decision to go public. Gerry knew how much more she and her sisters might have said, and how much good had come of confessing as much as they did. "You wouldn't know my wife now," he said. "She's not depressed. Before, everything was bottled up."

The revelations were nearly as difficult for the public to absorb as they had been for Yvonne, Annette, Cécile, and Marie to divulge. "People think that we are perfect," Annette reflected. "They want us always smiling."

"Now when I look back, it was a fairy tale," Genia Goelz, a lifetime quint fan, realized.

At the same time, Annette, Cécile, and Marie were noticing cracks in the fairy tales they'd hoped to fashion within their own lives. One of Cécile's twin boys, Bruno, had died at fifteen months, leaving a deep wound she had yet to recover from. "I cannot talk of him," she said. "That is a part of my life that belongs to nobody."

By the end of 1964, Cécile was permanently separated from her husband and seeking a divorce. "I didn't know anything about the world," Cécile reflected. "So I thought when I fell in love that everything was going to be beautiful and everything will be erased from my past." It was not the case. More challenging still, Philippe Langlois drank heavily. She soon learned he was also gay and unable to be faithful or honest with her, especially if he'd been drinking. After Cécile turned him out of the house, Philippe never asked to see his children. "It takes a lot of patience and courage to raise children without a father," Cécile discovered. The absence of Philippe's income posed a problem as well, for her trust fund interest payments were not enough to support her daughter and three sons. "I try hard to give them security, a sense of stability," she said. For Cécile, that meant temporarily relinquishing her children to foster homes when her emotional and financial burdens began taking a toll on her health.

Cécile considered it vital that her children experience normal family life—even if it meant she could visit them only on weekends. "I saw some parallels with my childhood and my mother's childhood," her son

Bertrand acknowledged. "But me, at least I had the chance to play with other children and neighbors," he said with a smile, fondly recalling how he collected empty bottles to trade in for candy money. "I consider that I had a normal childhood, even if I was separated from my mother for several years."

With no family of her own to support, Yvonne helped ease Cécile's responsibilities by brightening the children's birthdays with gifts. "Yvonne was my parent for me," Cécile said. "She was always there."

Meanwhile, Marie was struggling in more ways than her sisters realized. She, too, had separated from her husband, a man Annette remembered as "kind but very reserved." Behind closed doors, Marie later revealed, Florian Houle had turned out to be authoritarian and controlling. Her near-total ineptitude with housekeeping and handling money didn't help matters, and in 1964, Marie left with her daughters and rented an apartment in Montreal. For Monique and Émilie Houle, that time rang with laughter and glowed with love. Together the three of them would tumble down the hill in the park like rolling pins, or visit pet shops in search of the perfect parakeet to join their dog, Lassie, and two cats. Marie's doctor became fond of her, and the two began to date.

Yet Marie's friends were "deeply worried about both her physical condition and her attitude toward life." She had unaccountable fainting spells. Her moods fluctuated from gaiety to deep emotional hollows. Haunted by the feeling of having been brought up in a goldfish bowl, Marie sought out intensive therapy—including electroshock treatments—to soothe her unhealed wounds. Some therapies were more successful than others, and so there were also times when she turned to alcohol for relief. In 1969, she placed eight-year-old Émilie and six-year-old Monique in a foster home run by nuns.

"I knew that she had been treated for psychiatric care, but I didn't know she was so unhappy, so alone," Cécile said. Annette took to calling her sister every day so that Marie would not be so lonely without her daughters. When Marie did not pick up the phone one Monday in February of 1970, Annette thought little of it. By Thursday, Annette knew something was wrong. Marie had not answered, and just as alarming, she had not called all week. Usually she heard from her sister once a day, if not more. Annette called Marie's doctor friend, Marcel Bernier, and he went with Gerry to Marie's apartment.

Later that day, Annette's phone finally rang. "It's over," Dr. Bernier said. "That's it." The two men had found Marie dead on her bed. An empty cereal bowl and several bottles of medication stood on her night-stand.

Though Marie's official cause of death was undetermined, Florian Houle told the press his wife had died of an embolism—a blood clot in her brain. People were beginning to draw their own conclusions based on the reports of Marie's depression, the pill bottles in her bedroom, and rumors that exaggerated her drinking. For his daughters' sake, Houle needed that kind of talk to stop. The brutal truth was that Marie had been dead several days by the time Gerry and Dr. Bernier arrived—too long for the medical examiner to be certain of what had happened. Marie was thirty-five years old.

Oliva, Elzire, and six of Marie's eight brothers and sisters traveled to Montreal for her funeral. It was the first time the majority of the Dionnes had been together since Cécile's wedding twelve years earlier; Oliva and Elzire had not even met all of their grandchildren. Yet their shared sorrow did not bring the two halves of the family nearer. Everyone but Yvonne and Cécile refused Annette's invitation to return to her house for a sort of reunion after the funeral service.

"I would have given anything in the world to have them come to our home," Gerry said. "Not for me, but for Annette. She has been terribly upset by Marie's death—I wake up nights and find her crying."

◆ ◆ ◆

Yvonne, Annette, and Cécile took comfort in one another. Yvonne and Cécile moved to the same Montreal suburb where Annette and Gerry lived, and Annette's home, "the gravitational center for the Dionne sisters," became a tighter circle than ever. Daily rounds of phone calls began first thing in the morning. As the day progressed, the three of them inevitably ended up hopscotching from one house to another. Gerry had once quipped, "If more want to move in I just add rooms," but now Cécile and especially Yvonne's constant presence began to corrode his own relationship with Annette. "My husband thought he was married to three women," Annette explained.

It was more than that. Gerry, who had watched his wife blossoming like a bud in the early years of their marriage, sensed a disappointing change. "After the sisters came, the flower closed, they went to their old world, their private world," he said. In that world, Gerry always took second or third place. It infuriated him to find that plans he made with Annette in the morning were changed by Yvonne by the time he returned from work. At the time, Gerry neglected to take into account that Annette had no one but Yvonne and Cécile for company all day long. "I was working all the time, day and night," he eventually admitted. "I didn't realize what was going on." Gerry could only see that Yvonne held more sway in his home than he did himself.

"Finally I got fed up," Gerry said. The only solution he could see was to break Annette free of the circle of sisters and try to begin again with her, somewhere else. "I told Annette, *Your sister goes out of here or I go out myself.*" It was not a choice Annette could make, so Gerry made it for her. After sixteen years of marriage, he filed for divorce.

Two more irreversible losses followed. On November 14, 1979, word arrived that their father had died. He was seventy-six years old. "Oliva Dionne was not the plodding, backwoods farmer as he has often been portrayed," the *North Bay Nugget* eulogized the man the world had never

The Dionnes with their staff in 1936: Annette and Nurse Depue, Yvonne and Nurse Demar, Cécile and Nurse O'Shaughnessy, Émilie and Nurse Leroux, Marie and Nurse Noël.

Collection of the author

Nurse Noël watches Cécile, Émilie, Marie, Yvonne, and Annette playing by the nursery fence, September 1936.

Collection of the author

Marie, Annette, and Émilie play barber with Dr. Dafoe while Yvonne and Cécile distract him with picture books, April 1937.

Collection of the author

Three-year-old Cécile, Yvonne, Émilie, Marie, and Annette wreak havoc on the nursery's doll corner.

Collection of the author

The world's most famous five sisters—Annette, Yvonne, Cécile, Marie, and Émilie—in July 1937.

Collection of the author

Émilie, Annette, Marie, Cécile, and Yvonne tasting ice cream for the first time—on their fourth birthday.

Courtesy of Archives of Ontario, Fred Davis and Yvonne Leroux fonds, C-9-6-1

Four-year-old Annette, Yvonne, Cécile, Émilie, and Marie in a Christmas pose, likely staged weeks or months before the holiday.

Collection of the author

20th Century Fox film crews swarm around the children during the 1938 filming of *Five of a Kind*.

Courtesy of Callander Bay Heritage Museum

Émilie, Annette, Marie, Cécile, and Yvonne dressing for the grand finale of *Five of a Kind*.

Courtesy of Callander Bay Heritage Museum

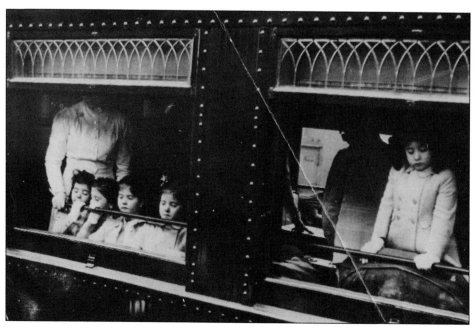

Gazing through the train windows at the royal spectacle in Toronto, May 1939.

Collection of the author

Annette, Émilie, Yvonne, Marie, and Cécile in the dresses they wore to meet King George VI and Queen Elizabeth in 1939.

Courtesy of Callander Bay Heritage Museum

Yvonne, Cécile, Annette, Marie, and Émilie on the train with their favorite playthings, en route to Corbeil after meeting the king and queen.

Collection of the author

Cécile, Marie, Annette, Émilie, and Yvonne, age six.

Collection of the author

Photographed with their daughters for the first time in six years, Oliva and Elzire revel in a rare moment of affection with Marie, Yvonne, Émilie, Annette, and Cécile.

Courtesy of Callander Bay Heritage Museum

While their sisters live behind barbed wire, Pauline, Daniel, Thérèse, and Ernest enjoy an outing to the family cottage on Trout Lake with their father in 1941.

Collection of the author

No one who received one of Dr. Dafoe's custom-made Christmas cards, like this one from the early 1940s, would have guessed he had a son of his own.

Courtesy of Callander Bay Heritage Museum

The "Big House," captured by a tourist in the mid-1940s.

Collection of the author

Yvonne, Cécile, Émilie, Marie, and Annette posing in the living room of the Big House around age twelve.

Collection of the author

The complete Dionne family in 1946. Rear: Yvonne, Pauline, Cécile, Rose-Marie, Émilie, Daniel, Thérèse, and Ernest. Center: Annette, Elzire, Marie, and Oliva with baby Claude.
Front: Oliva Jr. and Victor.

Collection of the author

Cécile crowns North Bay's winter carnival queen in February 1946 with Émilie, Yvonne, Annette, and Marie looking on.

Collection of the author

Cécile, Marie, Yvonne, Émilie, and Annette as teenagers, 1947.

Collection of the author

Émilie, Annette, Marie, Yvonne, and Cécile at Villa Notre Dame in the mid-1940s.

Courtsey of Callander Bay Heritage Museum

Three of the Dionne sisters—
likely Yvonne (second from left),
Cécile (center), and Émilie (far
right, looking down)—
studying with classmates at
Villa Notre Dame.

Collection of the author

Annette, Marie, Cécile,
Yvonne, and Émilie on
the Staten Island Ferry
during their 1950 tour of
New York City.

Collection of the author

Everywhere the Dionnes turned,
photographers blocked their view of
New York City.

Collection of the author

Annette, Cécile, Marie, Émilie, and Yvonne upon graduating from Villa Notre Dame on their eighteenth birthday in 1952.

Collection of the author

Yvonne, the first of the Dionnes to live apart from her sisters, in 1952.

Collection of the author

Émilie Dionne, as she appeared shortly before entering L'Accueil Gai.

Collection of the author

All smiles for the camera, following the Christmas scandal of 1955. Elzire embraces Yvonne while Annette and Cécile sit beside Oliva.

Collection of the author

Marie at the opening of her flower shop, Salon Émilie, on Mother's Day 1956.

Collection of the author

Cécile and Philippe on their wedding day, November 23, 1957.

Collection of the author

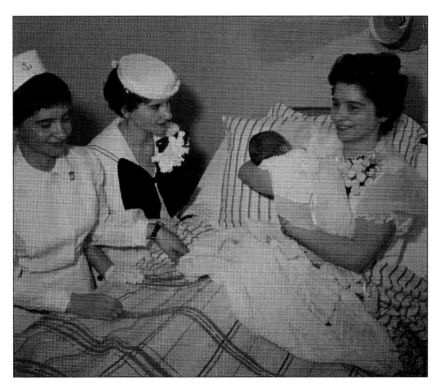

Yvonne and Annette congratulate Cécile on the birth of her first son,
Claude, in 1958.

Collection of the author

Gerry helps little Jean-François present Annette with ballet tickets for her twenty-fifth birthday in 1959.

Collection of the author

Elzire and Oliva Dionne in September 1979.
This was one of their last photographs together before Oliva's death.

Courtesy of Callander Bay Heritage Museum

Sisters triumphant: Annette, Cécile, and Yvonne Dionne in 1998.

Courtesy of the Getty Collection

Cécile and Annette Dionne, October 2016

Archives/Journal de Montréal

regarded as anything more than *Papa Dionne*. "Rather, he was intelligent, industrious and a gentleman who showed great courage in facing up to the many complex problems which arose when his family was suddenly thrown into world prominence in 1934." Oliva Dionne had spent most of his life in pursuit of two things he prized above almost all others: his five daughters and his dignity. Both had eluded his grasp.

Yvonne, Annette, and Cécile returned to Corbeil for their father's funeral. No one expressed any happiness at their return, including Elzire. "Mom said if our father was dead, it was our fault," Cécile remembered. "If he had so many worries, it was our fault."

Six years later, their mother was gone, too. "Her great love for her family is evident in her every action," the *Nugget* had said of Elzire Dionne in 1955. Yvonne, Annette, Cécile, Émilie, and Marie's greatest misfortune was perhaps that they had rarely experienced anything from their mother except the blunt force of Elzire's thwarted affection.

"I felt badly when Mom died," Annette said, "that we'd had no opportunity to straighten things out." Yvonne shared the same regret. "I would have liked that she asked for us," Yvonne reflected. "But she didn't. I saw the reality and I accepted it."

Oliva's and Elzire's wills contained identical clauses: "I declare that I have made no provision in my Will for my daughters, ANNETTE ALLARD, CÉCILE LANGLOIS and YVONNE DIONNE, by reason of the possession by them of their own adequate means."

But those clauses were entirely mistaken.

CHAPTER 39

The Babies of Quintland Now: Broke and Bitter

NEW YORK TIMES, MARCH 4, 1998

By the 1990s, the fortune that Welfare Minister David Croll had proudly decreed vast enough to provide for "all the normal needs of the Dionne family . . . for all time to come" had dwindled to nearly nothing. Yvonne, Annette, and Cécile were not rich, nor even comfortable. Instead, the three sisters were living together, pooling their three pensions so they could they get by on just $746 a month (about $850 US today).

Where had it all gone? A three-bedroom bungalow and a weekend lakeside chalet had consumed tens of thousands from Annette's account during the early years of her marriage. After Gerry left, she found that $40 in child support combined with her monthly interest payments of $345 were not enough to raise three boys, so Annette remortgaged her home for $40,000 to make up the difference. Twenty-five years later, she had a debt and a leaky roof.

Cécile's $10,000 wedding, her husband's "particularly lavish" spending, legal fees for her divorce, and a $16,000 house had drained her share of the trust fund to $6,000 by 1988. That money went toward an expansion of Annette's house in 1992, so that she could move in with her sister. Alone, Cécile had not the slightest hope of making ends meet on her monthly pension of $27.41.

A year later, Yvonne joined the household. Though she had enough money to live modestly, Yvonne's delicate bones, painful arthritis, and two hip replacements had left her feeling fragile enough to give up living alone. Besides, if her sisters needed her help, there was no question where Yvonne felt she belonged. Without her $5,000 savings and $399 pension, Annette and Cécile would have had only $347.93 to survive on each month. "I had no choice," Yvonne said.

Cécile's son Bertrand could not sit by and witness his mother's diminished circumstances. Something told him she and her sisters were entitled to much more. "I had a feeling that the quints had been robbed," Bertrand explained.

His hunch had been simmering for decades. When he was ten years old, he remembered, someone brought a Dionne Quintuplets pencil to school. Bertrand had recognized the images of his mother and aunts immediately. "My mother was struggling to pay the bills and I was wondering how come there's some pencil with their faces, and they don't receive any money from that?" he recalled. "That was the beginning of my fight."

Acting on his suspicions, Bertrand traveled to Toronto to launch his own investigation of the Dionne guardianship files in the Archives of Ontario. What he uncovered there sickened him. "I think it's more disgusting every time I think about it," he said. He accumulated suitcases full of documents, showing that the way his mother's and aunts' account had been managed, they might just as well have been robbed.

At age two their trust fund amounted to $500,000. At four it had swelled to $1.8 million. But by June 30, 1944, half of it had disappeared, leaving $945,000. Although a grand total of $2,086,747 had been collected from advertisers, photographers, and filmmakers during Yvonne, Annette, Cécile, Émilie, and Marie's childhood, $1,114,033 had been paid out over the years.

Nearly everyone involved had treated their trust fund as though it were a bottomless piggy bank. Each time Ontario's Official Guardian traveled north to review the Dionnes' accounting, he charged "every plate of fish and chips eaten in North Bay hotels to the quints' trust fund rather than his own government department." Yvonne, Annette, Cécile, Émilie, and Marie had paid for Dr. Blatz's research expenses—everything from the researchers' train fare to the camera, tripod, and film used to photograph them. In the 1930s Blatz's charges came to $1,998.12. Today the bill would amount to more than $26,000 in American currency. They paid for Dr. Dafoe's stamps—$18 in January of 1938—and picked up the tab for telephone calls and telegrams at a monthly rate that varied from $71.48 to $834 in today's US dollars. The nurses' tennis court? Courtesy of Yvonne, Annette, Cécile, Émilie, and Marie. On their seventh birthday the board of guardians donated a $1,750 ambulance to the Red Cross and funded $20,000 worth of war bonds in the sisters' names. As much as $15,000 went to furnish the Big House in 1943. Bertrand discovered that beginning in the 1940s his grandfather had charged the current equivalent of almost half a million dollars a year to the quintuplet account without ever providing receipts to justify his expenses. "Mom would tell us on August 27 that Dad was going out to get his birthday gift," Yvonne remembered, "and she would laugh and we would wonder why, and it was a new Cadillac." Annette recollected her brothers all had cars, too. Yvonne, Annette, Cécile, Émilie, and Marie had even borne the operating costs of their beloved Villa Notre Dame—$72,000 every year, or $618,000 US today.

When Bertrand discovered that the Province of Ontario had inflated its gasoline tax to six and eight cents a gallon at the height of Quintmania—a time when neighboring provinces were charging two or three cents a gallon—he had no doubt that his mother's and aunts' captivity had been deliberately prolonged to pump money into the province's pocket.

Fueled by disgust, Bertrand made it his full-time job to compel the Province of Ontario to right its wrongs against his mother and two surviving aunts. His first victory was teaming up with a Montreal lawyer, Daniel Payette, who took on the task of collecting unpaid revenue from advertising contracts. Nobody had paid the Dionnes so much as a dime for use of their names and faces since 1957. It took months, but eventually Payette won royalties on quint memorabilia and newsreel footage in Canada, the United States, Great Britain, France, and Australia, and gained a 10 percent share of profits from the Dionne Quints Museum in North Bay—more than tripling the sisters' monthly income. Payette also arranged for Yvonne, Annette, and Cécile to participate in the making of a miniseries and two documentaries about their lives, and brokered a deal with a Quebec publisher for a memoir of their teenage years, *Family Secrets,* that aired many of the disturbing memories they had held back from *We Were Five.*

As the untold story of their ruined childhood spread, compassion for Yvonne, Annette, and Cécile mounted. "It's beginning to seem more and more unpleasant and unsavory to me," lifetime quint fan Genia Goelz said in 1996. The fact that she had "loved them from afar" lent their suffering a personal quality. A similar sentiment had prompted a media advisor and a second lawyer to join Bertrand's crusade. "It was a moral obligation," Clayton Ruby said of his decision to represent the Dionnes, "that some lawyer ought to do it, that given their historical position, any Canadian ought to feel an obligation to them."

The government, however, appeared entirely unmoved by the sisters' plea. "We were a scientific curiosity, an object of exploitation for tourists, and we still carry the effects of that life," Yvonne, Annette, and Cécile had written to the premier of Ontario. "We have suffered all our life. . . . We are asking for compensation for past and present suffering." They requested $10 million. Months passed with no response—so many months that a new premier, Mike Harris, was elected in the meantime.

Bertrand was encouraged. He had written to Harris during the election and received a favorable reply. A resident of North Bay, Harris sympathized with the Dionnes' plight. If he was elected, Harris pledged, "your concern and request on behalf of the Dionne sisters will be given our full attention." Coming from a man who had assured voters over and over again, "I keep my promises," Harris's letter gave the Dionnes every reason to be hopeful.

And then? Nothing. Over a year passed before the attorney general of Ontario informed Yvonne, Annette, and Cécile that there would be no offer of compensation. As Harris's administration saw it, the province had no legal obligation toward the Dionnes. What had happened to them as children had nothing to do with their poverty as adults.

Bertrand knew better. If the trust fund had been properly managed, there would have been twice as much money in those accounts. The deeper he'd dug into the archives, the more suspicious things looked for the government. He knew the first three years' worth of minutes from the guardianship meetings were missing—everything from 1934 to 1937. It turned out that David Croll, Ontario's welfare minister and one of the sisters' first guardians, had refused to turn over the minutes when he stepped down from the board. Fishier still, Croll later burned the documents. Not only that, but the government lawyer who had negotiated film rights and advertising contracts on behalf of the Dionnes quit abruptly—and then went to work for the very companies he'd been haggling with.

Two months after that information went public, Harris's administration made an offer: $2,000 a month apiece for Yvonne, Annette, and Cécile, for the rest of their lives—as long as they signed a waiver absolving the government from all liability and kept the terms completely confidential. One word to the media and the deal was off.

The offer was an insult to the sisters. It felt to the Dionnes as though they were being placated with an allowance—as though they were still children. At that rate, they'd have to live another 138 years to be repaid what they believed had been stolen from them. "It's nowhere near what's owed and I want an inquiry," Cécile said.

Harris vocally opposed launching a financial inquiry. By the time it was over, he argued, millions of dollars would be wasted and "the three quints will be dead."

Affronted by such remarks, the Dionnes' team upped the stakes. On the recommendation of their media advisor, Carlo Tarini, the sisters traveled to Toronto and held a press conference. Summoning every ounce of the training they'd had as children, Yvonne, Annette, and Cécile braved the spectacle with a grace that just about knocked the wind out of Tarini. As he watched, the shyness and feebleness that had characterized all three women since the day he'd met them melted away for the few minutes that they calmly confronted a wall of cameras and reporters. "Every network, local news stations, three national networks—everybody has cameras, everybody's panning in, they're really in their faces," Tarini said. "It starts becoming unbelievable. It's a celebrity circus all over again. They're just sitting there, not upset."

"It is very painful for us to be here," Cécile read in a clear, steady voice. "After growing up in the spotlight it is the last place we now want to be. We have spent our lives hiding from it. Yet, Mr. Harris' conduct has forced us to come forward today to speak to you.

"We're not asking for one cent for the abuse," she continued. "There is not one cheque that has sufficient zeros to compensate us for having been kidnapped from our parents for nine and a half years and for wrecking our lives. We want only what was stolen from our trust fund. Instead, we received an offer which seems to be drawn to intimidate and bully us. Allow us our dignity."

The next day, front pages across the country featured a photo of the three sober-faced Dionnes dressed in sweatshirts and old coats and holding a sign between them:

Mr. Harris
WE WANT JUSTICE
NOT CHARITY

The image ignited an outcry in the public and the media that left Premier Harris "looking like a grinch." *Why Has Mike Harris Stiffed the*

Quints? demanded *Maclean's* magazine. While the *Toronto Star's* political cartoonist drew the premier as a scowling caveman tossing the three sisters a bone, a deluge of six thousand letters and faxes expressing support for Yvonne, Annette, and Cécile poured into the *Star's* newsroom.

Premier Harris's attitude implied that the three aging sisters were crass and greedy for attaching a dollar amount to their pain, all the while the Dionnes were insisting that what they wanted most of all was an acknowledgment of their suffering and the chance to understand where their money had gone.

By treating her and her sisters as a moneymaking entity rather than as five individuals, Cécile declared to the *New York Times,* the government had "stolen our souls."

"And they are still doing it," Yvonne added.

Premier Harris was at last suitably shamed. Within days, there was an offer on the table for $2 million. Yvonne, Annette, and Cécile turned it down. They shook their heads at $3 million, too. At $4 million—and an investigation of the trust accounts—they accepted.

The premier himself went to Annette's home to make amends. "It was an emotional meeting," Harris told the press afterward. "I apologized on behalf of the government of Ontario—all governments—and I apologized for our government's handling of the situation." As a token of humility, he brought a mocha coffee cake.

"So far as money is concerned the Quints owe the province of Ontario nothing," *MacLean's* had said in 1941. "They pay their own way. They have never been a public charge. Rather, the shoe is on the other foot. Citizens of Ontario owe the Dionne sisters a debt that cannot be accurately measured in currency." Fifty-seven years later, the province had finally acknowledged that debt.

Just as when they turned twenty-one, everyone in the world wanted to know what the Dionne sisters would do with their newfound millions. It was not a simple question to answer, for the fight had never been wholly about money. Four million dollars could not heal the shattered bonds, nor repay the years of turmoil that had riven the entire Dionne family beyond repair.

"I haven't given much thought to the future," Yvonne admitted. "There are so many emotions at the same time. It's difficult to absorb all this."

"I'm relieved," Annette said.

Cécile, too, was cautious with her emotions. "*Happy* is a big word," she said. "I am content."

In their hearts and minds, the victory was shared not three ways, but five. The triumph belonged just as much to Émilie and Marie as to Yvonne, Annette, and Cécile. "We feel they are looking down at us," Cécile mused. "And they might be smiling."

EPILOGUE

Dionne Visit Creates New Memories

North Bay Nugget, May 24, 1998

Stanley Anderson's cheeks flushed and his eyes began to water as the crowd made its way up the curving driveway. Alongside him, two other elderly residents of Nipissing Manor—the senior care center once known as the Big House—waited with bouquets. Anderson had never met the three women who had been invited to tour his residence, though he had seen them once before, sixty-some years earlier. Their graying hair had been brown then, done up in glossy ringlets.

As his guests approached, shadowed by two police officers and a throng of photographers, reporters, and TV cameras, Mr. Anderson presented his bouquet to Yvonne Dionne. His voice quavered with emotion, but his gaze and his handshake held firm. "Welcome home," he said.

Two days before, the sisters had been reluctant to call the visit a homecoming. "It's difficult to describe right now," Cécile said of her mixed emotions upon arriving in North Bay Thursday evening. This was a town whose business owners had once worried more about their profits than the health and well-being of Cécile and her sisters, the same town that had displayed the girls' clothes and toys to tourists in the house where they were born without ever offering the Dionnes themselves a nickel, whose residents had looked the other way in spite of sensing something amiss behind the Big House gate.

By the time Yvonne, Annette, and Cécile arrived at Nipissing Manor on Saturday afternoon, the welcomes they'd received had drastically altered their feelings toward the city. Outside the Dionne Quints Museum that morning, a plaque had been unveiled in the sisters' honor. Former schoolmates met them with hugs and joined them inside the farmhouse-turned-museum, sharing memories as they exclaimed over the photos and exhibits. At Nipissing Manor, cousins and in-laws gathered to greet them. Lifelong fans burst into tears at the touch of their hands, finally able to express what the survival of the Dionne Quintuplets had meant to them in the midst of the Great Depression. Moved by the reception, Yvonne, Annette, and Cécile wandered through the yellow brick mansion, once the scene of so many unhappy memories, "smiling and gushing like schoolgirls" as they explored their former bedrooms.

"They were not just smiling to be polite," Cécile's son Bertrand said. "When I looked at my mother's face, she had a shine."

With the melting of their trepidations, the Dionnes projected an air of graceful gentility to everyone they encountered, including the thirty reporters and photographers zooming in on their every move. To Annette, the media presence was perfectly natural. "Media was very close to us," she said. There was no simpler way of putting it. The newspapers had not only saved their lives as infants, but awakened fresh sympathy and awareness during the Dionnes' battle with the government six decades later, "Without you," Cécile told the reporters, "our voices would have been forever silenced, our plight all but forgotten, our lives and suffering in vain. You have changed our destiny and we are forever grateful."

Yvonne, Annette, and Cécile had determined to transform others' destinies as well, they announced that day, through their support of Kids Help Phone, a national hotline for abused and troubled children. As the Dionne Quintuplets, they had raised millions for tourism; now the world's most famous sisters pledged to use their celebrity for a much more worthy cause. "We were the children everyone looked at and nobody saw," Cécile explained. "Over the sadness inside, we had to smile and perform. I wish that we could have poured our hearts out to someone who knew that we were just children, like any others, and that we needed the same freedoms, the same understanding, the same love."

Later that night, Yvonne, Annette, and Cécile were the guests of honor at a gala charity dinner dance. Yvonne's usually serious face broke into a broad smile at the sight of a Black Forest cake baked in honor of their sixty-fourth birthday. All three sisters grinned at the crowd of 163 guests as they rose from their seats to blow out the candles. The evening culminated with the mayor's announcement that the North Bay street leading to their birthplace would be renamed Dionne Place. "This is overwhelming," Cécile said. "When you drive up Dionne Place, look up at the street sign and smile and know we are thinking of you." Émilie and Marie were part of the celebration, too, in spirit. "You will always be close to our hearts," Cécile promised her departed sisters in French.

The visit, Cécile reflected upon returning to Montreal, was like "opening the door on my youth." Unburdened by the worries of the past, she was able for the first time to see and enjoy the beauty of her birthplace. Annette found the trip every bit as transformative. Viewing the scenes of their childhood with a new compassion had brought peace and joy to her heart. "I have no more wounds," she said.

AFTERWORD

Yvonne Dionne died of cancer on June 24, 2001. Her sisters were at her side, just as they had always been. Annette and Cécile have requested that donations in Yvonne's memory be made to Kids Help Phone: kidshelpphone.ca.

In May of 1998, Cécile Dionne moved into a duplex her son Bertrand bought with a portion of his 15 percent share of the $4 million settlement. "I knew she would never feel secure enough to buy one for herself," he said of the purchase. They lived side by side until 2006, when Bertrand sold the house and moved his mother into a posh assisted-living facility. Six years later, Cécile's bank account was empty and Bertrand was gone. She has not heard from him since. In a cruel echo of her childhood, Cécile Dionne became a ward of the government, with no control over any aspect of her life. At first, all she could think of was how to escape the senior residence she was assigned to, but gradually she made an effort to become acquainted with the people around her in order to build a second family. "At my age it's difficult," she says. "But I clench my fists and I keep my head high." Once again, the media came to her rescue: reporter Marian Scott of the *Montreal Gazette* took up Cécile's cause and has been working to overturn the court's ruling and move her to a better place.

As of 2018, Annette lives independently in a condominium outside Montreal, where she occupies herself with her piano and her computer. Although she is unable to visit her sister as often as she'd like, Annette and

Cécile are constantly in touch. "When I realize that I start to miss her, I pick up the phone," Annette explains. That happens at least three times a day, for the comfort they bring to each other remains a vital part of their lives. "I thank God often to have Cécile," Annette says.

Of Yvonne, Annette, Cécile, Émilie, and Marie's eight siblings, two remain as of August 2018: Thérèse and Pauline. The Province of Ontario has yet to offer them an apology for the devastation it caused to the members of the Dionne family who lived outside the hospital gates.

A NOTE ON DIALOGUE

I have not invented any of the dialogue in this book. Everything rendered in quotation marks can be traced to diaries, correspondence, books, newspapers, magazines, newsreels, or film documentaries. Nevertheless, a note of caution is called for. I have no doubt that some of the lengthier conversations in these sources are composites or re-creations rather than precise word-for-word recollections. In several cases, I've abridged these conversations, snipping out what smacked of melodrama or stretched the limits of credulity where the speaker's memory was concerned.

It's also wise to keep in mind that in the race to capture public opinion, nearly everyone involved in the Dionne saga succumbed to the temptation to present an exaggerated picture of their own virtue and/or a distorted view of their opponents' flaws. I have made every effort to sift through the layers of boasts and accusations to present dialogue that comes as near the truth as possible, but in some instances, emotions ran too high and wounds too deep. Words were often spoken in pain or anger—on both sides of the Dionne/Dafoe divide.

In instances where the words themselves are not entirely verifiable, I believe a valuable measure of truth can still be found in the underlying emotion they convey. Lillian Barker, for example, is emphatically not someone to rely on for pinpoint accuracy, yet few other journalists managed to express the depth of Oliva and Elzire Dionne's yearning for sympathy and respect. On the other side of the fence—quite literally—Nurse de Kiriline's early accounts of her time at the Dafoe Hospital tended to mold the facts in Dr. Dafoe's favor, thus demonstrating her genuine devotion to him and to the ideals of scientific child care. In short, when I cannot be certain that the dialogue is objectively truthful, I believe that it conveys what the speaker most fervently wished to be heard.

REFERENCES

ARCHIVES

Leroux-Davis fonds, Archives of Ontario, York University.

Pierre Berton fonds, McMaster University.

W. E. Blatz Collection, Thomas Fisher Rare Book Library, University of Toronto.

BOOKS

Barker, Lillian. *The Dionne Legend: Quintuplets in Captivity*. New York: Doubleday, 1951.

Barker, Lillian. *The Quints Have a Family*. New York: Sheed & Ward, 1941.

Berton, Pierre. *The Dionne Years: A Thirties Melodrama*. New York: W. W. Norton & Company, 1977.

Blatz, William. *The Five Sisters: A Study in Child Psychology*. London, J. M. Dent & Sons Ltd., 1939. (Note: pagination of this British edition differs from the American edition published by William Morrow in 1938.)

Blatz, William, et al. *Collected Studies on the Dionne Quintuplets*. Toronto: University of Toronto Press, 1937.

Brough, James, with Annette, Cécile, Marie, and Yvonne Dionne. *We Were Five: The Dionne Quintuplets' Story*. New York: Simon & Schuster, 1963.

Corriveau, M. Louise. *Quints to Queens*. New York: Vantage Press, 1976.

de Kiriline, Louise. *The Quintuplets' First Year: The Survival of the Famous Five Dionne Babies and Its Significance for All Mothers*. Toronto: Macmillan, 1936.

De Kruif, Paul, and Rhea De Kruif. *Why Keep Them Alive?* New York: Harcourt, Brace and Co., 1936.

Gervais, Gaétan. *Les Jumelles Dionne et l'Ontario Français (1934–1944)*. Sudbury, Ontario: Prise de Parole, 2000.

Hunt, Frazier. *The Little Doc: The Story of Allan Roy Dafoe, Physician to the Quintuplets.* New York: Simon & Schuster, 1939.

Legros, Hector, and R. P. Joyal. "Memoire Sur les Parents et les Jumelles Dionne." In *North-Bay et les Jumelles Dionne.* Sudbury, Ontario: La Société Historique de Nouvel-Ontario Collège du Sacré-Coeur, 1950.

Legros, Madame, and Madame Lebel. *Administering Angels of the Dionne Quintuplets: A True Story of the Birth of the Dionne Quintuplets.* North Bay, Ont.: Northern Pub. Co., 1936.

Munro, Keith. "Full House: My Life with the Dionnes." In *The Aspirin Age: 1919–1941,* edited by Isabel Leighton. New York: Simon & Schuster, 1949.

Newman, Horatio Hackett. *Multiple Human Births: Twins, Triplets, Quadruplets and Quintuplets.* New York: Doubleday, Doran & Company, Inc., 1940.

Raymond, Jocelyn Moyer. *The Nursery World of Dr. Blatz.* Toronto: University of Toronto Press, 1991.

Slesinger, Stephen. *The Story of the Dionne Quintuplets.* Racine, WI: Whitman, 1935.

Soucy, Jean-Yves, with Annette, Cécile, and Yvonne Dionne. *Family Secrets: The Controversial and Shocking Story of the Dionne Quintuplets.* Toronto: Stoddart, 1996.

Strong-Boag, Veronica. "Intruders in the Nursery." In *Childhood and Family in Canadian History,* edited by Joy Parr. Toronto: McClelland and Stewart, 1982.

Tesher, Ellie. *The Dionnes.* Toronto: Doubleday Canada, 1999.

Tremblay, Claire. *Marcheuses Á l'Étoile: Les Soeurs de l'Assomption de la Sainte Vierge en Ontario 1910–1997.* Nicolet, Quebec: Éditions S.A.S.V., 1999.

Valverde, Maria. "Representing Childhood: The Multiple Fathers of the Dionne Quintuplets." In *Regulating Womanhood: Historical Essays on Marriage, Motherhood, and Sexuality,* edited by Carol Smart. London: Routledge, 1992.

FILMS

The Dionne Quintuplets. Canadian Broadcasting Corporation, 1978.

Full Circle: The Untold Story of the Dionne Quintuplets. BBC1, 1998.

Miracle Babies: The Story of the Dionne Quintuplets. Canadian Broadcasting Corporation, 1996.

Newspaper and periodical articles, too numerous to list individually here, may be found in the notes.

ACKNOWLEDGMENTS

Thanks to:

Naomi Balmer-Simpson, Therese Bulszewicz, Laura Colley, John Dufresne, Laura Mabee, Julietta McGovern, Charlotte and Gary Miller, Emily Wood Mitchell, Janice Murphy, Emily Paul, Cornelia Pokrzywa, Barry Torch, Amy Tureen, Anne-Marie Varga, and Heather Vlieg, for help in obtaining books, articles, photographs, and films.

Kathryn Brough and Carole Hébert, for kind permission to quote from works by their late husbands; also Christopher Aguirre, Christa Angelios, Daniel Novack, and Wendy Schmalz, my navigators through the permissions process.

Patricia Carr, North Bay Chamber of Commerce, for granting me access to the Dionne farmhouse, as well as glimpses of the artifacts in the Dionne Quints Museum collection, while both buildings were in transition.

Rachael Cole, for the perfect cover.

Pat Jones, for the first trip to North Bay—and for holding my sandwiches.

Annie Kelley, who knows that "Joan Crawford" has nothing to do with wire hangers.

Lani Pettit, for help with photo identification.

Joshua Pride, for his assistance on August 5, 2018.

Thelma Scaglione, for her recollections of the Leroux family and visits to Quintland.

Natasha Wiatr of Callander Bay Heritage Museum, for making the knowledge and resources in the museum's collection available—both in person and via email.

NOTES

EPIGRAPH

"We don't feel anyone can be fair to both sides": Ellie Tesher, *The Dionnes* (Toronto: Doubleday Canada, 1999), 223.

PROLOGUE

"The little girls are here": Jean-Yves Soucy with Annette, Cécile, and Yvonne Dionne, *Family Secrets: The Controversial and Shocking Story of the Dionne Quintuplets* (Toronto: Stoddart, 1996), 7.
"Bonsoir, Mom": Soucy, *Family Secrets*, 19 (French edition).
"Supper will be ready soon": Soucy, *Family Secrets*, 7.
"This side is for our family": Soucy, *Family Secrets*, 8.

CHAPTER 1

"Auntie, please hurry": Frazier Hunt, *The Little Doc: The Story of Allan Roy Dafoe, Physician to the Quintuplets* (New York: Simon & Schuster, 1939), 11. (Note: "Elzira" in original; altered for continuity.)
"Auntie, . . . I don't think," "Don't you worry, my dear," and *O God, inspire me in my work*: Douilda Legros and Mary-Jeanne Lebel, *Administering Angels of the Dionne Quintuplets: A True Story of the Birth of the Dionne Quintuplets* (North Bay, Ont.: Northern Pub. Co., 1936), 9. (Note: "Aunty" in original; altered for continuity.)
"weather-beaten": Lillian Barker, *The Dionne Legend: Quintuplets in Captivity* (New York, Doubleday, 1951), 46.
"a heart as big as a washtub": Hunt, *The Little Doc*, 14.
"Elzire's pulse is bad": Barker, *The Dionne Legend*, 34.
"melted away": Lillian Barker, "Tells of Offer to Exhibit Quints," *Des Moines Register*, September 22, 1935.
"the Little Doc": Hunt, *The Little Doc*, 237.
"My wife is very sick": Hunt, *The Little Doc*, 3.
"You go on back": Hunt, *The Little Doc*, 4.
"A few minutes": Barker, *The Dionne Legend*, 35.
"Good God, woman": Pierre Berton, *The Dionne Years: A Thirties Melodrama* (New York: W. W. Norton & Co., 1977), 37.
"My God, there are still more there": "Midwife 'Never Too Tired' to Tell of Dionnes Birth," *Pittsburgh Press*, May 27, 1935.
"Gosh!": Berton, *The Dionne Years*, 37.
"a little pressure": Allan Roy Dafoe, "The Dionne Quintuplets," *Journal of the American Medical Association* (September 1934), 674.
"Gosh!": Berton, *The Dionne Years*, 37.
"unreal and dreamlike": Dafoe, "The Dionne Quintuplets," 675.

"We just looked at each other with amazement": Legros and Lebel, 10.

"angel veils": Hunt, *The Little Doc,* 17.

"Auntie, have I twins, this time?": Legros and Lebel, 11.

"Yes, my dear": Legros and Lebel, 20.

"Cinq fillettes": Barker, *The Dionne Legend,* 38.

"What will I do with all them babies?": Legros and Lebel, 11.

"My God, what am I going to do": Legros and Lebel, 20.

"punched": Ira Wolfert, "Eternally Drawn Shades Shield Dionne Family," *Boston Globe,* September 13, 1936.

"As we did not anticipate his return": Legros and Lebel, 21.

"little mites": "Provide Hot-Water Incubator to Assist Dionne Quintuplets," *North Bay Nugget,* May 30, 1934.

"All we can do": Hunt, *The Little Doc,* 21.

"He told her to please herself": Legros and Lebel, 13.

"However, you can please yourself": Legros and Lebel, 21.

"Realizing this, near death as I was," "What do you think of," and "I don't know what to think": Lillian Barker, "'Give Us Your Babies or We'll Take Their Milk, Government Warned Me,'" *Des Moines Register,* September 15, 1935.

"What will people say": "Mother Dionne Sees Quintuplets as Divine Miracle," *Scranton Republican,* September 3, 1934.

CHAPTER 2

"either a mighty joke" and "Saw something this morning": Hunt, *The Little Doc,* 22.

"five little French frogs": Barker, *The Dionne Legend,* 41–42.

"Did you know you are the grandfather of five": Hunt, *The Little Doc,* 23.

"Oliva Dionne—5F": "Simple Notation Sufficed to Record Quintuplet Birth," *North Bay Nugget,* February 18, 1935.

"How much would it cost": Hunt, *The Little Doc,* 24; see also "Even Mother Incredulous When Five Infants Born," *North Bay Nugget,* May 27, 1935.

North Bay, May 28th:—Mrs. Oliva Dionne: Hunt, *The Little Doc,* 25. (Note: Elzire Dionne was twenty-five years old.)

"We couldn't believe it": Yvette Boyce, interviewed in *Miracle Babies: The Story of the Dionne Quintuplets,* Canadian Broadcasting Corporation, 1996.

"leave 'em alone": Hunt, *The Little Doc,* 21.

"Well, do you feel proud of yourself?": "Quintuplets Born to Farm Wife," *North Bay Nugget,* May 28, 1934.

"The way you talk": James Brough with Annette, Cécile, Marie, and Yvonne Dionne, *We Were Five: The Dionne Quintuplets' Story* (New York: Simon & Schuster, 1963), 15.

"I'm the kind of fellow": "Quintuplets Born to Farm Wife."

"He had not slept all night": Brough, *We Were Five,* 29.

"I'm so tired I could drop": Yvonne Leroux diary A, May 28, 1934, Leroux-Davis fonds, Archives of Ontario, York University, microfilm reel 3649. (Note: Nurse Leroux kept two diaries in 1934—one with brief daily notations and another containing more fleshed-out entries. For clarity, I have dubbed these "A" and "B" respectively, though no such designation exists at the Archives of Ontario.)

"Dr says Quintuplets": Yvonne Leroux diary B, May 28, 1934, Leroux-Davis fonds, Archives of Ontario, York University, microfilm reel 3649.

"Do whatever you can": Yvonne Leroux, "My Diary of Three Years with the Dionne Quintuplets," *Pittsburgh Press,* May 24, 1937.

"To this day I don't recall a thing": Leroux, "My Diary of Three Years."

"no decent dishes, no screens, doors, or cleanliness": Leroux diary B, May 28, 1934.

"What have I here": Leroux diary A, May 29, 1934.

"The largest seems to have difficulty": Leroux diary B, May 28, 1934.

CHAPTER 3

"one or two": Frazier Hunt, "The Little Doc: For the First Time in History," *Saturday Evening Post*, May 14, 1938.

"these marvelous Quintuplets?": Hunt, *The Little Doc*, 37.

"There was nothing in the house": Hunt, *The Little Doc*, 37.

"And good luck, and God bless 'em all": Hunt, *The Little Doc*, 38.

"How they doin'?": Hunt, *The Little Doc*, 206.

"hollow-eyed and worn": Hunt, *The Little Doc*, 38.

"They're still alive": Hunt, *The Little Doc*, 206–207.

"Bien, très bien": Hunt, *The Little Doc*, 207.

"Give them this from the eyedropper": Hunt, *The Little Doc*, 209.

"cocktail": Hunt, *The Little Doc*, 210.

"Well, these tiny little bits of humanity" and "Babes fought against the exposure": Leroux diary B, May 29, 1934.

"scrawny, spider-legged, horrible": Paul and Rhea De Kruif, *Why Keep Them Alive?* (New York: Harcourt, Brace and Co., 1936), 287.

"Like rats": Walter Winchell, "Quintuplets? Shucks!" *Liberty*, April 27, 1935, 41.

"Green's come out here," "frantic with worry," and "The thought of exhibiting the babies": Barker, "Tells of Offer to Exhibit Quints."

"We knocked on the door," "He says, 'Get out,'" "We thought we had him," "Will you fellas please go away," "He couldn't get the car started," and *When Mr. Dionne heard the news*: Berton, *The Dionne Years*, 52.

"Dig up an old-fashioned baby incubator": Hunt, *The Little Doc*, 213–214.

"gave him all the leads" and "Sure you haven't got one tucked away": Hunt, *The Little Doc*, 214.

"an old-timer" and "Get it downstairs": Hunt, *The Little Doc*, 215.

CHAPTER 4

"the telltale white lines": Hunt, *The Little Doc*, 217.

"Red Riding Hood dresses": Dafoe, "The Dionne Quintuplets," 676.

"coaxed along" and "Very thin": Leroux diary B, May 30, 1934.

"efficiently, punctually, and quietly": Louise de Kiriline, "Living Five Years in Twelve Months," *Manitowoc Herald Times*, July 15, 1935.

"Well, we will just have to keep up": Leroux diary B, May 30, 1934.

"turn any question over and over in his mind": Brough, *We Were Five*, 38.

"As long as he lived": Barker, *The Dionne Legend*, 55.

Make what you can, while you can: see Brough, *We Were Five*, 38; Hunt, *The Little Doc*, 218, 260; Berton, *The Dionne Years*, 60; Barker, *The Dionne Legend*, 57; Lillian Barker, "The Parents of the Quints Are Victims of a Smear Press," *America*, October 18, 1941.

Country Doctor Battling to Keep Quintuplets Alive: Pittsburgh Post-Gazette, May 30, 1934.

Progress of Quintuplets Amazes Medical World: Toronto Globe, May 30, 1934.

"no one could have been more poorly designed": Pierre Berton, "The Quints: Fabulous Flim-flam Years," *Detroit Free Press*, September 17, 1978.

"a funny-looking box" and "My name's Charlie Blake": Hunt, *The Little Doc*, 220.

"Those babies don't know": William Engle, "The Race to Save the Quints," *American Weekly*, May 9, 1948.

CHAPTER 5

"with particular thought to what might be tempting," "the other little Dionnes," and "a pretty little nurse": *"Star* Sends Assistance to Mother and Five Babes," *Toronto Star,* May 31, 1934.

"pathetically grateful" and "He was dressed," : Keith Munro, "Full House: My Life with the Dionnes," in *The Aspirin Age: 1919–1941,* edited by Isabel Leighton (New York: Simon & Schuster 1949), 299.

"The Little Doc was a newspaperman's dream," "I don't see how they can live," and "Our first impression of the place": Munro, 300.

"Do you want to see the babies?" and "We piled into the house": Munro, 301.

"She rolled back the white coverlet": "Five Baby Girl Sisters Smash 500-Year Record," *Toronto Star,* May 31, 1934.

"There was something terribly exciting": Munro, 301.

"the Quintuplet Disease": Charles E. Blake, "How They Got the Quints in Pictures," *Photoplay,* March 1936.

"It was like taking nature pictures": Fred Davis, letter of July 3, 1935, Leroux-Davis fonds, Archives of Ontario, microfilm reel 3649.

"Shattered glass flew all around": Munro, 301.

"The doctor even made some little joke about it": Munro, 302.

"Didn't you get the shock of your life": "Five Baby Girl Sisters."

CHAPTER 6

"very colorful, very adept": Berton, *The Dionne Years,* 58.

"luxurious private ward": Brough, *We Were Five,* 37.

"Ivan had a cheque made out": Berton, *The Dionne Years,* 59.

"the physicians in charge of the quintuplets": Charles Robert Morgan, "What Is the Menace Hanging over the Dionne Quintuplets?" *True Detective,* January 1936.

"They were talking back and forth in rapid French": Luis Kutner, interviewed in *The Dionne Quintuplets,* Canadian Broadcasting Corporation, 1978.

"Babes holding their own and that's all": Leroux diary B, May 31, 1934.

"Praying every minute": Leroux diary A, May 31, 1934.

CHAPTER 7

"I don't know what this town did": Hellen Allyn, "Father of Five Babies, Doctor Split over World's Fair Offer," *Pittsburgh Press,* June 2, 1934.

"a constant fight": Allan Roy Dafoe, "Care to Prevent Infection Highlight of Babies' Care," *Toronto Star,* January 23, 1935.

"Newshawks": "Fear One of Quintuplets Is Near Death," *Toronto Star,* June 2, 1934.

"We wanted some more shots of Papa Dionne": Ross Beesley, interviewed in *The Dionne Quintuplets.*

"Our little world was topsy-turvy": Brough, *We Were Five,* 14–15.

"Father of Five Babies, Doctor Split over World's Fair Offer": Allyn, "Father of Five Babies, Doctor Split."

"Told of the contract Dionne has signed": "Oliva Dionne Signs Handsome Contract to Exhibit Family at Chicago," *North Bay Nugget,* June 1, 1934; see also "Weakest of Babies Improves as First Trying Week Passes," *North Bay Nugget,* June 4, 1934.

"preposterous": "Quintuplets' Father to Get $100 a Week While All Live," *Toronto Star,* June 1, 1934.

"As long as I am boss": Helen Allyn, "Press Reporter Flies to Ontario and Tells How Five Babies Gain in Fight for Life," *Pittsburgh Press,* June 1, 1934.

"Public opinion wouldn't stand for it": "Doctor Vetoes Plan to Show 'Quints' at Fair," *Chicago Tribune*, June 1, 1934.

Father Silent About Plans to Show Babes: "Father Silent About Plans to Show Babes," *Muscatine Journal and News Tribune*, June 1, 1934.

"still in a daze" and "Who wouldn't be worried": Allyn, "Father of Five Babies, Doctor Split."

"Nothing doing": "Fear One of Quintuplets Is Near Death"; "Quintuplets' Mother Can't Get Excited; 'Babies Nothing New to Me,' She Insists," *Pittsburgh Press*, June 3, 1934.

"I will never go to the Chicago fair": "Incubator Sent by *Star* Shelters 4 of Quintuplets," *Toronto Star*, June 4, 1934.

"he might have been filling a fountain pen": De Kruif, 274.

"Doctor, if you do that it will kill them": Hunt, *The Little Doc*, 225.

"I think they deserve a little rum for that": Munro, 306.

"What a job": Leroux diary A, June 1, 1934.

"the faint dawn of something": Fred Davis, letter of July 3, 1935.

"Living had become a habit": Munro, 309.

"At that moment the world's greatest 'no' man was born" and "The next morning when we arrived": Munro, 302.

"He looked us right in the eye": Munro, 303.

"They are alive—that's about all I can say": "Fear One of Quintuplets Is Near Death"; see also Hunt, *The Little Doc*, 237.

"What had merely been a mildly sensational story": Fred Davis, letter of July 3, 1935.

CHAPTER 8

"The first week . . . was a nightmare": Dafoe, "The Dionne Quintuplets," 676.

"like an orphan": Barker, *The Dionne Legend*, 64.

"a task for a giant": Hunt, *The Little Doc*, 228.

"never was there a woman up here like Madame de Kiriline": Barker, *The Dionne Legend*, 70.

"We've got five babies out here": Hunt, *The Little Doc*, 229.

"Go out and get order," "No more was needed," and "conscious only of a fleeting feeling": Louise de Kiriline, "I Nursed the Quintuplets: Part One," *Chatelaine*, July 1936.

Are they really alive?: de Kiriline, "Living Five Years in Twelve Months," *Manitowoc Herald Times*, July 15, 1935.

"Pressed into the corner," "upset beyond recognition," "surgical cleanliness," "a shining white sheet," "the babies' sanctuary," and "their eventual survival": de Kiriline, "I Nursed the Quintuplets: Part One."

"arrogant taskmistress": James Brough, "We Were Five," *McCall's*, December 1963.

"We gave Madame de Kiriline and Mademoiselle Leroux": Lillian Barker, *The Quints Have a Family* (New York: Sheed & Ward: 1941), 137.

"chaos of the upset little home": Louise de Kiriline, *The Quintuplets' First Year: The Survival of the Famous Five Dionne Babies and Its Significance for All Mothers* (Toronto: Macmillan: 1936), 18.

"Boss Number One" and "Boss Number Two": Brough, *We Were Five*, 42; Berton, *The Dionne Years*, 71.

"the only five-baby incubator in all the world": "Baby Marie Grows Weaker Today in Incubator-Crib," *Toronto Star*, June 2, 1934.

"They are a wonderful thing": Leroux diary B, June 6, 1934.

"worse than seven funerals": "Incubator Sent by *Star* Shelters 4 of Quintuplets."

"I'll say they need water": Allyn, "Father of Five Babies, Doctor Split."

"If all crocks were changed at the same time": Louise de Kiriline, "I Nursed the Quintuplets: Part Two," *Chatelaine*, August 1936.

"Just to keep those five 'blue,' choking little creatures": Allan Roy Dafoe, "Quintuplets First Week Nightmare for Doctor," *Toronto Star*, January 24, 1935.

CHAPTER 9

"It was one of the banner days," "tiny roll of white," and "This is Émilie": Munro, 309.

"All of a sudden she opened her mouth and yawned": Munro, 309–310.

"Émilie weighs one pound, thirteen ounces": Munro, 310.

"The clothing was unwrapped," "Even the nurse seemed disturbed," "Marie, Marie," and "Movement began in one of the arms": Munro, 311.

"grieved over the loss of her doll-sized roommates": Barker, *The Dionne Legend*, 71.

"brute of a man": Berton, *The Dionne Years*, 70.

"I'd be lost without a baby in my arms": Lillian Barker, "The Most Unusual Mother I've Ever Known," *Extension*, January 1955.

"a super-death-fighting laboratory": De Kruif, 278.

"Holy of Holies": de Kiriline, "I Nursed the Quintuplets: Part Two."

"She always remarks on how cute they look": "Lethargy Strikes Quintet; Five Babies Are Given Rum," *Toronto Star*, June 12, 1934.

"too highly specialized": Barker, *The Dionne Legend*, 73.

"The nurses won't let me in to touch them": Eric Gibbs, "Mrs. Dionne Retains Faith in Births as God's Miracle," *Toronto Star*, August 31, 1934.

"Doctor Dafoe's heart was made of stone": De Kruif, 279.

"I long to hold my little jumelles": Barker, *The Dionne Legend*, 76.

"quick-spoken where her children were concerned": Barker, *The Dionne Legend*, 78.

"They're doing everything for the babies": Barker, *The Dionne Legend*, 77–78.

"We were helpless": Tesher, *The Dionnes*, 224.

CHAPTER 10

"like ladies": Barker, *The Dionne Legend*, 77.

"with the abstracted manner" and "master in the cow barn and hay field": Forrest Davis, "Action Taken to Guard Babes from Epidemic," *Pittsburgh Press*, August 10, 1934.

"We have had no trouble": "Government Intervenes in Dionne-Chicago Deal," *North Bay Nugget*, June 18, 1934.

"There have been so many other promoters": "New Light Thrown on Baby Contract," *North Bay Nugget*, June 20, 1934.

"They have offered me money": "Quintuplets for Hospital If Showmen Don't Ease Up," *Toronto Star*, June 5, 1934.

"I'm not denying it; I'm not saying it's true": "Quintuplets for Hospital."

"strenuous efforts to break the contract": "Fear One of Quintuplets Is Near Death."

"You know, Oliva has been alone here for ten years": "Government Intervenes in Dionne-Chicago Deal."

"We are quite willing": "New Light Thrown on Baby Contract."

"Turning over custody": Barker *The Dionne Legend*, 80.

"more than a little gruff": Hunt, *The Little Doc*, 137.

"In a sickroom": Hunt, *The Little Doc*, 283–284.

"He treated them with disdain": George Sinclair, interviewed in *The Dionne Quintuplets*.

"We were raking hay" and "His face looked": Barker, *The Quints Have a Family*, 142.

"Brace yourself for a shock" and "Why, with such an unnatural arrangement": Barker, *The Quints Have a Family*, 143.

"To me they were" and "If I live to be a hundred": Barker, "Tells of Offer to Exhibit Quints."

"How can I accept it?": Barker, *The Quints Have a Family*, 144.

"Then there was an ominous lull": Barker, "Tells of Offer to Exhibit Quints."

"As far as we are aware": "No Interference with Quintuplets Says Children's Aid Society Head," *North Bay Nugget*, July 11, 1934.

"fit and worthy parents": Barker, *The Dionne Legend*, 78.

"shook like a leaf": Barker, *The Quints Have a Family*, 148.

"I would tell them": Barker, "Tells of Offer to Exhibit Quints."

CHAPTER 11

"Dionne Highway" and "Quintuplet Drive": "Dionne Homestead Now Well Guarded," *Toronto Globe*, August 16, 1934.

"They want to know 'How far'": "Dionnes Now Have to Guard Quintuplets from Tourist Horde," *Chicago Tribune*, August 2, 1934.

"Mrs. Oliva Dionne, the Miracle Mother, North Woods, Canada": "The Miracle Mother," *Toronto Globe*, June 14, 1934.

"with the excitement of a sporting event": "Rum, Milk, Corn Syrup, Quintuplets First Meal," *Toronto Star*, January 22, 1935.

"What is there about these babies": "The Quintuplets," *Pittsburgh Press*, August 12, 1934.

"Of course, they have no right to be alive at all": "Quintuplets Come Near Being Six, Dionnes' Family Physician States," *Wilkes-Barre Record*, June 6, 1934.

"Not 'How are the quintuplets?'" and "She is so tiny": "Nature, Attendants Alike Single Out Marie for Favor," *Toronto Star*, June 7, 1934.

"never could lose its entrancing novelty": de Kiriline, *The Quintuplets' First Year*, 74.

"I remember one of the first times": de Kiriline, *The Quintuplets' First Year*, 61–62.

"But gradually . . . there began to be characteristic differences": de Kiriline, *The Quintuplets' First Year*, 63.

"In many ways I would say": de Kiriline, *The Quintuplets' First Year*, 64–65.

"A more perfectly shaped child," "a shade rounder," and "nature was a distinctly placid one": de Kiriline, *The Quintuplets' First Year*, 65.

"pathetically patient" and "acquired the disposition": de Kiriline, *The Quintuplets' First Year*, 66.

"a small duckling": de Kiriline, *The Quintuplets' First Year*, 67.

"the little Madonna": de Kiriline, "Living Five Years in Twelve Months," *Manitowoc Herald Times*, July 18, 1935.

"Parents are not quite sure": Leroux diary B, July 27, 1934.

"The hospital is under way": Leroux diary B, August 6, 1934.

"a jumbling noise at the window" and "heard the noise of someone running": "Kidnapping Plot Is Feared; Prowler Disturbs Dionnes," *Toronto Star*, August 8, 1934.

"the watchdog of the household": "First Reporter Is Admitted to the Quintuplets' Bedroom," *Toronto Globe*, August 17, 1934.

"The grandfather quivered with rage," "but that dread was in everyone's mind," and "Underneath the routine in nursery": "Kidnapping Plot Is Feared."

"Calamity in nursery" and "She grabbed them all to her breast": Leroux diary B, August 6, 1934.

"Any prowler daring those lights": Leroux diary B, August 10, 1934.

"The older, singly born Dionne young ones" and "He grumbles daily": Davis, "Action Taken to Guard Babes from Epidemic."

CHAPTER 12

"Can you imagine": Leroux diary B, August 13, 1934.

"the observation tower": Barker, *The Dionne Legend*, 90.

"L'hôpital temporaire": Barker, *The Quints Have a Family*, 148.

"Dear Doctor": De Kruif, 285, and Berton, *The Dionne Years*, 216 (footnote 78–24).

"Scraps of wood and stone": "Hunt for Souvenirs Around Dionne Home," *Toronto Star*, August 22, 1934.

"Look here!" and "We'll give the baby an enema": Hunt, *The Little Doc*, 250.

"I became convinced": Dafoe, "Care to Prevent Infection."

"Babes are all losing weight": Leroux diary B, September 12, 1934.

"That whole time was a nightmare": de Kiriline, "Living Five Years in Twelve Months," *Manitowoc Herald Times*, July 17, 1935.

"Babes still sick": Leroux diary B, September 14, 1934.

"The situation did not bear discussion" and "It was evident to us all": de Kiriline, "Living Five Years in Twelve Months," *Manitowoc Herald Times*, July 17, 1935.

"We've got to move them today": Hunt, *The Little Doc*, 251.

"Naturally, they were afraid" and "The radiators began to warm the air": de Kiriline, "Living Five Years in Twelve Months," *Manitowoc Herald Times*, July 17, 1935.

"It was a cold, rainy, miserable day": Oliva Dionne, "Whose Children Are the Quintuplets?" *True Story*, February 1939.

"The Little Doctor followed": Hunt, *The Little Doc*, 254.

"We stood at the door a moment": de Kiriline, "Living Five Years in Twelve Months."*Manitowoc Herald Times*, July 17, 1935.

"eyes that had been wrung dry": Dionne, "Whose Children Are the Quintuplets?"

"This will never seem like home again": Barker, *The Dionne Legend*, 92.

"If we had expected drama": de Kiriline, "Living Five Years in Twelve Months," *Manitowoc Herald Times*, July 17, 1935.

"Those children were as pale" and "For Dr. Dafoe to move those babies": de Kiriline, "Living Five Years in Twelve Months," *Manitowoc Herald Times*, July 17, 1935.

"The day of the moving": de Kiriline, *The Quintuplets' First Year*, 75.

"As if by the touch of a fairy's wand": de Kiriline, *The Quintuplets' First Year*, 76.

"much improved": Transcription from "The Dionne Quintuplets—Daily weights and records." Pierre Berton fonds, McMaster University.

"In general their condition is satisfactory": "Babies Moved to Hospital," *North Bay Nugget*, September 21, 1934.

"In short, . . . they took up life again": de Kiriline, "Living Five Years in Twelve Months," *Manitowoc Herald Times*, July 17, 1935.

"the rats' nest": de Kiriline, *The Quintuplets' First Year*, 157.

"soon became vigorously kicking youngsters": de Kiriline, *The Quintuplets' First Year*, 75–76.

"the exact shade of the old-fashioned cinnamon rose": Marguerite Mooers Marshall,"The Private Life of the Dionne Quintuplets," *Liberty*, June 29, 1935.

"with their dark velvety sparkling eyes": de Kiriline, *The Quintuplets' First Year*, 88–89.

"Whatever she does is done with all her might": de Kiriline, "Living Five Years in Twelve Months," *Manitowoc Herald Times*, July 18, 1935.

"scrap": Ernest Lynn, "Nurse Describes Personalities of Quintuplets as They Reach Age of Antics (And Scraps, Too)," *Pittsburgh Press*, February 22, 1935.

"She is interested in everything," "Almost the most upset she ever got," "athlete of the crowd," "To make her laugh and frolic," and "You felt as though": de Kiriline, "Living Five Years in Twelve Months," *Manitowoc Herald Times*, July 18, 1935.

"Hello, bums!": "Soft Voice Often Stills Babies' Tiny Troubles," *Toronto Star*, January 19, 1935;

Marguerite Mooers Marshall, "The Fairy Godfather and the Dionne Quintuplets Cinderellas," *Liberty,* April 18, 1936.

"How's my gang this morning?": "Simple Notation Sufficed to Record Quintuplet Birth."

"his voice, his smile, his eyes": Marshall, "The Fairy Godfather."

"I know of no greater treat in the world": Brough, *We Were Five,* 54.

"It never occurred to us": Genia Goelz, interviewed in *Miracle Babies.*

CHAPTER 13

"That was a sad time": Yvette Boyce, interviewed in *Miracle Babies.*

"I would sooner do a big washing": "Quintuplets' Mother Plans Direct Action," *Pittsburgh Post-Gazette,* March 15, 1935.

"a luxurious fortress": Phyllis Griffiths, "Papa and Mama Dionne," *Chatelaine,* March 1936.

"like we had committed some crime": Harry E. Taylor, "Parents of Dionne Quints Bitterly Resent the Removal of the Girls from the Dionne Household and Care," *Humboldt Republican,* October 9, 1936; see also "Parents Saddened as Noted Infants Celebrate Birthday," *North Bay Nugget,* May 27, 1935.

"She looked down at the adorable children": Dionne, "Whose Children Are the Quintuplets?"

"They belong to them, . . . not to us": Dionne, "Whose Children Are the Quintuplets?"

"That is not so": Dionne, "Whose Children Are the Quintuplets?"

"Kodak pests": Lillian Barker, "Quintuplets' Mother Tells Story of Romance and Marriage," *Des Moines Register,* September 29, 1935.

"He keeps his eyes downward": Wolfert, "Eternally Drawn Shades."

"As the weeks passed": Dionne, "Whose Children Are the Quintuplets?"

"Dr. Dafoe says our other children": Phyllis Griffiths, "Mrs. Dionne, Troubled and Worried over Quintuplets' Future, Wants Her Babies," *Winnipeg Tribune,* May 28, 1935; see also "Doctor Encourages Parents to See Quintuplets Often," *Toronto Star,* January 21, 1935, and Dafoe, "Care to Prevent Infection."

"Crowds came to see the quintuplets" and "It is only for two years": Dionne, "Whose Children Are the Quintuplets?"

"In order to house them properly": Lillian Barker, "Mrs. Dionne Tells of First Son's Birth When She Was 17," *Des Moines Register,* October 13, 1935.

"wonder parents": "Ma and Pa Dionne in U.S.," *Paramount Newsreel,* 1935 (in *The Dionne Quintuplets*).

"We just want to show them a real good time": "Dionnes Reach Toronto Today," *North Bay Nugget,* February 4, 1935.

"This is just a visit": "Dionnes May Earn $12,00 for Theatrical Appearances," *El Paso Herald-Post,* February 9, 1935.

"But as we got nearer and nearer": Barker, "Mrs. Dionne Tells of First Son's Birth."

"I am sure, if it had been possible" and "Events followed one another": Dionne, "Whose Children Are the Quintuplets?"

"These are not actors, folks": "Oliva Is Philosophic, Mrs. Dionne in Tears over $1,000,000 Action," *Toronto Star,* February 9, 1935.

"Mrs. Dionne and myself": "Dionnes Cheered on Stage, Named in $1,000,000 Suit," *Pittsburgh Post-Gazette,* February 9, 1935.

"Merci beaucoup et que Dieu vous bénisse": Lillian Barker, "Don't My Babies Need Me?" *Modern Romances,* October 1936.

"They eat them three times a day": "Dionnes Beam in Stage Debut," *Des Moines Register,* February 9, 1935.

That Little Shrimp There, Yep, That's Papa Dionne and "would never be big enough": "That Little Shrimp There, Yep, That's Papa Dionne," *Milwaukee Journal,* February 7, 1935.

"stooge": "Parents of Quintuplets Buy Five Dolls, Drink 20 Bottles of Soda Pop," *Decatur Herald*, February 7, 1935.

"backwoods": "Strawberries in February Send Dionne Bill Upward," *Pittsburgh Press*, February 11, 1935.

"Dionne Tour a Flop": "Dionne Tour a Flop," *Toronto Globe*, February 11, 1935.

"circus tour": "Mrs. Dionne Buys but Papa Never Passes Up Pop as Chicago Crowds Gape," *Pittsburgh Press*, February 7, 1935.

"It's nauseating to Canadians": "Exploitation of Quintuplets Will Become Illegal," *Evening Times* (Sayre, PA), February 9, 1935.

"I want my babies to have the best possible chance": "Touring to Build a Home, Says Quintuplets' Mother," *Toronto Star*, February 15, 1935.

"They are far from destitute": "Dionnes Lose Fight to Control Trust," *Pittsburgh Press*, February 23, 1935.

"They have no value": "Exploitation of Quintuplets Will Become Illegal."

"You can rest assured": "Dionnes Lose Fight to Control Trust."

CHAPTER 14

"We returned to Corbeil" and "Elzire could not speak": Dionne, "Whose Children Are the Quintuplets?"

"They can do that in Russia" and "Do you think the quintuplets could have lived": "'God Picked Us,' Says Dionne; 'He Will Do What Is Right,'" *Toronto Star*, March 1, 1935.

"I know that we are not the smartest": "Dionnes Revise View of Hepburn Position," *North Bay Nugget*, March 6, 1935.

"Special Guardian" and "natural guardian": The Dionne Quintuplet Guardianship Act, 1935.

"to go back to my farm" and "All we want is a chance": "Dionnes Oppose State Control of Babes," *North Bay Nugget*, March 11, 1935.

"to prevent professional, quick-talking exploiters," "We don't want them exhibited," and "You must protect the father and mother": "Dionne Bill Moves On; Price Fears Parents Bereft of Children," *Toronto Star*, March 12, 1935.

"I never saw such drastic legislation": "Dionne Guardians' Bill Draws Attack," *Indianapolis Star*, March 15, 1935.

"Extreme cases require extreme measures": "Dionne Bill Moves On."

"Who would like to have their children taken away" and "If the bill goes through": "Quintuplets' Mother Plans Direct Action."

"hateful": Leroux diary, March 3, 1935, and mid-March, 1935 (precise date not noted by Leroux).

"I often wonder": Louise de Kiriline, "Should They Have a State-Mother?" *Chatelaine*, June 1936.

"bitter controversy": "Quintuplets' Mother Plans Direct Action."

"The Dionne quintuplets nearly caused a riot": "Quintuplets' Mother Plans Direct Action."

"What a mess" and "The trouble is": Leroux diary, March 18, 1935. (Note: Nurse Leroux's dating of this entry is almost certainly mistaken, as the *North Bay Nugget* reported the Dionnes' move to the hospital on March 15.)

"eloquence": Britt Jessup, interviewed in *The Dionne Quintuplets*.

CHAPTER 15

"extraordinarily adequate": Hunt, *The Little Doc*, 283.

"You know it is only just good luck": de Kiriline, "I Nursed the Quintuplets: Part Two."

"the continent's best known baby doctor": *The Dionne Quintuplets*, 1978.

"To the whole world": William Blatz, *The Five Sisters: A Study in Child Psychology* (London: J. M. Dent & Sons Ltd.: 1939), 187–188.

"bickering or misunderstanding," "peevish and petulant," and "Now there is the strictest rule": Lotta Dempsey, "What Will Become of Them?" *Chatelaine*, June 1937.

"not only the physical hygiene": Allan Roy Dafoe, "Warns Against Picking Babies Up Needlessly," *Toronto Star*, February 9, 1935.

"It is necessary to control even your voice": Marguerite Mooers Marshall, "The Hidden Lives of the Quintuplets," *Liberty*, January 4, 1936.

"The babies were never picked up": de Kiriline, "I Nursed the Quintuplets: Part Two."

"a kind of gold standard": Eunice Fuller Barnard, "Science Designs a Life for the Dionnes," *New York Times Magazine*, October 10, 1937.

"There, surrounded by a retinue": Barnard, "Science Designs a Life for the Dionnes."

"that the care and effort": Blatz, *The Five Sisters*, 187.

"Then all at once the enormity": Louise de Kiriline, "I Nursed the Quintuplets: Part Seven," *Chatelaine*, January 1937.

"The work was made easy": "Rendons les Dionelles à leur mère," *La Patrie*, February 15, 1936.

"The hospital is a sanitary glass cage": Lee B. Hartshorn, "Quintuplets Entertain," *The Nation*, June 19, 1935.

"We had to be cautious": Cecile Michaud in Berton, *The Dionne Years*, 116.

"no longer friendly": Griffiths, "Mrs. Dionne, Troubled and Worried."

"Don't you come up those steps": "Refused Mother of Quintuplets View of Babies," *Ottawa Journal*, May 25, 1935.

"I am glad that my babies": Griffiths, "Mrs. Dionne, Troubled and Worried."

"brusque drama": "Refused Mother of Quintuplets View of Babies."

"They felt that they had been ousted": Berton, *The Dionne Years*, 65.

"She is very excitable": Leroux diary, June 1, 1935.

"I made a conscious effort" and "Mrs. Dionne is a charming woman": "Rendons les Dionelles à leur mère."

CHAPTER 16

"As a burnt child dreads the fire": Lillian Barker, "Dionne Wins Control over His Five Girls," *America*, October 25, 1941.

"They tell lies about us": Evelyn Seeley, "Green-Eyed Monster Rises over Quintuplets' Cradles," *Pittsburgh Press*, May 24, 1935.

"unspoiled, clean-bred stock": "Quintuplets' Life Chances Better Far from Cities," *Toronto Star*, January 8, 1935.

"primitive": Marguerite Mooers Marshall, "How the Dionne Quintuplets Are Getting Rich," *Liberty*, September 28, 1935.

"ramshackle": Stephen Slesinger, *The Story of the Dionne Quintuplets* (Racine, WI: Whitman: 1935), 6; Roy Tash, "Shooting the 'Quints,'" *The International Photographer*, December 1935.

"dingy": Marshall, "How the Dionne Quintuplets Are Getting Rich."

"the miserable Dionne shack": De Kruif, 285.

"unpretentious": Slesinger, 6.

"modest": "The Quins: The Story of the Famous 'Dionne Quintuplets,'" *Pathé*, 1934.

"decidedly handsome" and "A kitchen apron": Barker, *The Quints Have a Family*, 33.

"From the very day the quints were born": Barker, *The Quints Have a Family*, 34.

"printed unkind and untrue things" and "Whether you let me": Barker, *The Quints Have a Family*, 36.

Most Famous of Mothers One of the Unhappiest: Lillian Barker, "Most Famous of Mothers One of the Unhappiest," *New York Daily News*, May 26, 1935.

"Tell him, tell him": Gibbs, "Mrs. Dionne Retains Faith in Births."

"emphatic way" and "lightning-quick intelligence": Barker, "Most Famous of Mothers One of the Unhappiest," *New York Daily News*, May 26, 1935.

"daily torture" and "Separation by death": Lillian Barker, "My Life and Motherhood," *Des Moines Register*, September 8, 1935.

"more and more a crucifixion": Barker, "Most Famous of Mothers One of the Unhappiest," *New York Daily News*, May 26, 1935.

"How could I . . . present myself": Barker, "My Life and Motherhood"; see also "Irate Dionne May Not Go to Quints' Party," *Detroit Times*, May 26, 1935, Lucile F. Nobach scrapbook, North Bay Public Library.

"To every one who has ever done": Barker, "My Life and Motherhood."

"So many people don't understand" and "Don't, I beg you": Barker, "Most Famous of Mothers One of the Unhappiest," *New York Daily News*, May 26, 1935.

"perfectly disgusting," "almost unthinkable," and "Baby Lorraine might have lived": "Should Parents of Dionne Quintuplets or Canadian Government Rear Famous Tots?" *Des Moines Register*, September 1, 1935.

"I'm sure I could have raised them all": Marshall Smith, "Her Quintuplets Starved to Death 40 Years Ago!" *El Paso Herald-Post*, November 26, 1935.

CHAPTER 17

"the happiest, least complicated years of our lives" and "We had everything we wanted": Brough, *We Were Five*, 55.

"a compendium of Lilliput luxury": Eunice Fuller Barnard, "Home or Science? The Dionnes' Case Debated," *New York Times Magazine*, October 17, 1937.

"a certain gladness": Brough, *We Were Five*, 70.

"The overwhelming memory": Brough, *We Were Five*, 58.

"Above all else, we had each other" and "We were a club, a society": Brough, *We Were Five*, 56.

"We had bicycles, we had dolls": Annemarie O'Neil and Natasha Sotynoff, "Sisters Triumphant," *People*, May 4, 1998.

"They were not supposed to": Cécile Dionne, interviewed in *Miracle Babies*.

"But I do remember": Annette Dionne, interviewed in *Miracle Babies*.

"We knew that there was one visitor": Brough, *We Were Five*, 55.

"A normal child, a mother presses to her breast": Ellie Tesher, "We'll Keep on Fighting, Dionne Sisters Promise," *Toronto Star*, March 2, 1998.

"It was not possible," "They were always there," and "a kind of composite mother": Brough, *We Were Five*, 55.

"To a child, a mother is only": "Dionne Quins Face Third Birthday as Miraculously Normal Children," *Winnipeg Tribune*, May 28, 1937.

"Always, those babies clamoured": "Tragedy of the Young Dionnes," *Maclean's*, January 1, 2000; see also "Note by D.A.M. during week of January 24, 1937," Thomas Fisher Rare Book Library, W. E. Blatz Collection, Box 36.

"In the nursery itself": Doreen Chaput, interviewed in *The Dionne Quintuplets*.

"We didn't know at that time": Tesher, *The Dionnes*, 109.

CHAPTER 18

"the baby show": Allan Roy Dafoe, "Butcher's Meat Basket Quintuplets' First Crib," *Toronto Star*, January 10, 1935.

"Visitors still coming by the hundreds": Leroux diary, April 2, 1935.

"The babes seem to feel the excitement": Leroux diary, April 8, 1935.

"It wasn't a public you wanted to turn away": Dorothy Millichamp, interviewed in *Full Circle: The Untold Story of the Dionne Quintuplets*, BBC1, 1998.

"We are showing the babies": Leroux diary, June 15, 1935.

"The babes clap and coo": Leroux diary, June 11, 1935.

"snaps and crackles": Jane Williams, "Dollars Flow In but Papa Dionne Still Angry About Famed Quintuplets," *Ithaca News-Journal*, September 16, 1936; see also Brough, *We Were Five*, 48.

"Not only did those babies 'play up'": Yvonne Leroux, "The Five Unluckiest Children," handwritten draft circa 1939, Leroux-Davis fonds, Archives of Ontario, microfilm reel 3650. (Note: a condensed version of this essay was published in *Liberty* magazine under the byline of Marguerite Mooers Marshall on January 27, 1940.)

"When you know people have driven": Allan Roy Dafoe, "The Quintuplets: Trick Screen to Hide Visitors," *Pittsburgh Press*, April 7, 1936.

"Sometimes it seems to me": "Come On, Let's Sing," Colgate-Palmolive-Peet CBS radio broadcast, December 23, 1936, Leroux-Davis fonds, Archives of Ontario, microfilm reel 3650.

"eighth wonder of the world": de Kiriline, "Should They Have a State-Mother?"

"inspired immediate confidence": "Corbeil Quintuplets Reach 108 Hour Age; Improving Rapidly," *North Bay Nugget*, June 1, 1934.

"How will they be prepared": Alfred Adler, "Separate the Quins!" *Cosmopolitan*, March 1936.

"In city after city": "'Separating Quints' Reacts on Adler," *Toronto Globe*, February 29, 1936.

"Why not divide Dr. Adler": "Humorist vs. Psychologist," *Marion* (Iowa) *Sentinel*, August 13, 1936.

"He was sore": Berton, *The Dionne Years*, 126.

"But to use them as a dumping place": de Kiriline, "Should They Have a State-Mother?"

"Whether they like it or not": Chester Matthews, "Will They Be Radio Stars Tomorrow?" *Radio Guide*, April 18, 1936.

"We have found": "Expropriating Dionne Land Due to Failure to Agree, Says Croll," *Toronto Star*, February 10, 1936.

"These children are the treasures of the world": "Providing Ample Playground for Dionne Quintuplets," *Toronto Star*, February 15, 1936.

"Those babies have a right": "Taking Dionnes 'Out Of Goldfish Bowl' Says Croll," *Toronto Star*, February 10, 1936.

"blurred silent shadows": Henry Albert Phillips, "The Quints," *Woman's World*, November 1936.

"This at first seems like cold-blooded exploitation": Blatz, *The Five Sisters*, 61.

"One cannot help but feel": William Blatz et al., "Routine Training," in *Collected Studies on the Dionne Quintuplets* (Toronto: University of Toronto Press, 1937), 8.

CHAPTER 19

"Couldn't even get across the road": Callander gas station attendant, interviewed in *The Dionne Quintuplets*.

"A line, orderly and quiet": Willis Thornton, "Let's Visit the Quintuplets," *Pittsburgh Press*, August 24, 1936.

"Already legend has endowed these pebbles": Betty M. Snyder, "In Canada You See the Quints," *Baltimore Sun*, September 20, 1936.

"passion pebbles": Bruce McLeod, "My Neighbors the Quints," *Maclean's*, December 1950.

"Up and down the restless line": Snyder, "In Canada You See the Quints."

"seemingly filled with a common sense of awe": Phillips, "The Quints."

"It was like viewing a litter of kittens": Mrs. Pat Thompson, interviewed by Barbara Sears, Pierre Berton fonds, McMaster University.

"breathtaking": Virginia Irwin, "Getting Famous with Dionne Quintuplets," *St. Louis Post-Dispatch*, August 17, 1936.

"Right along there, ladies": Snyder, "In Canada You See the Quints."
"Take a last look now, and hop it!" "I thank my Almighty God," "We drove 590 miles to see this," and "Long before you cover the 2½ miles": Thornton, "Let's Visit the Quintuplets."
"Quinstore": "Quinstore Ready to Serve Visitors," *North Bay Nugget*, May 27, 1935.
"long and patient": Wolfert, "Eternally Drawn Shades."
"He has been the butt of yokel humor" and "Leave your car for a minute": Snyder, "In Canada You See the Quints."
"sprang up like dandelions": Tesher, *The Dionnes*, 50.
"We had a big house": Jack Adams, interviewed in *Miracle Babies*.
"Everything here was new": Thornton, "Let's Visit the Quintuplets."
"The Dafoe Hospital, the Dionne homestead": Snyder, "In Canada You See the Quints."
"People are coming in here": "Quintuplets at Play," *Pathe News*, 1936.

CHAPTER 20

"the famed quintuplets go about their daily routine": Thornton, "Let's Visit the Quintuplets."
"Of course we knew": Brough, *We Were Five*, 62.
"I remember that we laughed": Annette Dionne, interviewed in *Miracle Babies*.
"Those one-way screens were, in truth, two-way screens": Brough, *We Were Five*, 12.
"Most of the time we yelled and shrieked": Brough, *We Were Five*, 61.
"the children would scamper through the gates": Blatz, *The Five Sisters*, 64.
"They couldn't see them": Berton, *The Dionne Years*, 163.
"But most of the time": Blatz, *The Five Sisters*, 61.
"To the observer at first glance": Claire Tremblay and Jacqueline Noël letter of March 1938. (http://www.crccf.uottawa.ca/passeport/IV/IVB1d/IVB1d01-3-4-1_b.html).
"uncooperative": Jocelyn Moyer Raymond, *The Nursery World of Dr. Blatz* (Toronto: University of Toronto Press: 1991), 139.
"almost pathological": Raymond, 140.
"the dirty man": Jacqueline Noël diary, July 25, 1938, Bibliothéque et Archives Nationales du Québec, Jacqueline Noël Collection, P574.
"If you go near him, Little Jesus will cry": Berton, *The Dionne Years*, 171.
"Daily the children run to the adult": Tremblay and Noël letter of March 1938.
"the thrill of my childhood," "awestruck," "stiff, sterile nurses," and "I had the eerie feeling": Gladys Bailey, interviewed by Barbara Sears, April 14, 1976, Pierre Berton fonds, McMaster University.
"As the Venetian blinds are raised": Barnard, "Science Designs a Life for the Dionnes."
"only as long as they are unconscious of it": Phyllis Griffiths, "Showing of Quints May Be Ended This Year," *Los Angeles Times*, May 20, 1938.
"The children's health and education come first": Phyllis Griffiths, "Old Ex-Judge Guards Quints," *Los Angeles Times*, May 23, 1938.

CHAPTER 21

"human nuggets": Brough, *We Were Five*, 64.
"The Dionne Quintuplet fund": David Croll radio broadcast in *Miracle Babies*.
"a case of jitters and general irritability" and "Life in a 'goldfish bowl'": "Life in 'Goldfish Bowl' Too Much for Dionnes; Colds Are Aggravated by Bad Case of Jitters," *Pittsburgh Press*, August 13, 1937.
"We poked our heads through cardboard Valentine hearts": Brough, *We Were Five*, 64.
"Picture-taking sessions were as good as parties": Brough, *We Were Five*, 65.

"For publicity's sake we were called on": James Brough, "Dear Quints . . . With Love from the Quints," *McCall's*, February 1962.

"Every small event, they needed a picture": Yvonne Dionne, interviewed in *Full Circle*.

"The gifts were all empty boxes": Cécile Dionne, interviewed in *Miracle Babies*.

"We were obliged to do so many things": Cécile Dionne, interviewed in *Full Circle*.

"fool antics" and "active as a bunch of crickets": Tash, "Shooting the 'Quints.'"

"Not even for all the millions": Fred Davis, "My Quintuplet Scrapbook," *Pittsburgh Press*, February 5, 1936.

"We've been having grand days": Letter of Nora Rousselle, March 10, 1938, Thomas Fisher Rare Book Library, W. E. Blatz Collection, Box 35.

"Moving picture staff most cooperative" and "amusing, coaxing, directing and interfering": Memorandum to Dionne Staff, September 1936, Thomas Fisher Rare Book Library, W. E. Blatz Collection, Box 36.

"They can't live the normal life of ordinary individuals": Dempsey, "What Will Become of Them?"

"There was a terrible tendency": Brough, *We Were Five*, 64.

"a tidal wave" and "It is not possible to imagine its force": Brough, "Dear Quints . . ."

"the Province's national resource": *Toronto Evening Telegram*, September 2, 1936, quoted in Raymond, 115.

CHAPTER 22

"Government bulletins and other authorities": Barnard, "Science Designs a Life for the Dionnes."

"My mother fed me": Connie Vachon, interviewed in *Miracle Babies*.

"made super-babies": De Kruif, 262.

"Rubbish": William Corbin, "Babes in the Woods," *The American Magazine*, September 1934; see also Slesinger, 15.

"Anyone who ever spent": Blake, "How They Got the Quints in Pictures."

"I wasn't especially bright at school": Newsreel footage of Allan Roy Dafoe in *The Dionne Quintuplets*.

"Thank God he is not so small": Leroux diary, April 22, 1935.

"does not really care for the children": Noël diary, June 27, 1937.

"He was in fact the loneliest man": George Sinclair, interviewed in *The Dionne Quintuplets*.

"He may unconsciously have come": Brough, *We Were Five*, 54.

"They know his car": Leroux diary, April 16, 1936.

"I remember Dr. Dafoe": Annette Dionne, interviewed in *Miracle Babies*; see also Annette Dionne with Frank Rasky, "Annette Dionne Today," *The Canadian*, May 27, 1967.

CHAPTER 23

"One of the supreme satisfactions": Allan Roy Dafoe, "Latest Methods of Care Available to All Mothers," *Toronto Star*, January 29, 1935.

"If ever the question": Matthews, "Will They Be Radio Stars Tomorrow?"

"If, at the end of eighteen years": Barnard, "Home or Science?"

"They should never become 'guinea pigs'": Dafoe in foreword to Blatz, *Collected Studies*.

"We were weighed, measured, tested, studied": Brough, *We Were Five*, 50.

"nearly indistinguishable": Blatz, "Biological Study," in *Collected Studies*, 46.

"*any* physical or other contact": Blatz, "Social Development," in *Collected Studies*, 4.

"by gesture, touch, or word": Blatz, "Social Development," in *Collected Studies*, 7.

"whose unpredictable behavior delights her sisters": "The Five Sisters," *Life*, January 16, 1939.

"Annette seeks an audience": Blatz, Social Development," in *Collected Studies,* 16.
"happy-go-lucky," "to give and take on a fifty-fifty basis," and "the unknown quantity": Blatz, "Social Development," in *Collected Studies,* 16.
"One thing is certain": Blatz, "Social Development," in *Collected Studies,* 16–17.
"artificial": "Why Do the Quints Differ? A Puzzle for Science," *The Science News-Letter,* November 13, 1937.
"Anyone watching them play together": Horatio Hackett Newman, *Multiple Human Births: Twins, Triplets, Quadruplets and Quintuplets* (New York: Doubleday, Doran & Co., 1940), 116.
"I was sure I would be able": Gladys Shultz, "Scientists of a Continent Discuss the Quints' Future," *Better Homes and Gardens,* January 1938.
"is about as poor as it could possibly be made": Newman, 199.
"Indeed, a wider variety": Newman, 120.
"Ah": "Parents Oppose Adler in Separating Quints," *Detroit Times,* February 27, 1936, Lucile F. Nobach scrapbook, North Bay Public Library.
"Quintalk": "The Quintuplets Round Out Their First Three Years," *Life,* May 17, 1937.
"apparent retardation": Blatz, "Mental Growth," in *Collected Studies,* 9.
"It's the most natural thing in the world": Shultz, "Scientists of a Continent Discuss."
"backward": Newman, 114; see also "The Five Sisters," *Life.*
"The quintuplets already provide": Barnard, "Science Designs a Life for the Dionnes."
"in actual fact . . . the equivalent": Raymond, 120.
"the machinery of their pleasantly ordered lives": Dempsey, "What Will Become of Them?"
"Dionne jail": "The Five Sisters," *Life.*
"It was in no sense uncomfortable": Brough, *We Were Five,* 66–67.
"emotional episodes": Blatz, "Self-Discipline," in *Collected Studies,* Table IX, Graph VIa, VIb, VIc.
"non-compliance behavior": Blatz, "Self-Discipline," in *Collected Studies,* Graph III.

CHAPTER 24

"When [Mrs. Dionne] came over": Raymond, 136.
"The mother and father felt": Mollie O'Shaughnessy, interviewed in *The Dionne Quintuplets.*
"If they look like anybody": Phyllis Griffiths, "Still Bitter," *Des Moines Register,* May 29, 1937.
"there was always some dispute": Ian Parker, "The Dark Side of the Famous Five," *The Independent,* November 5, 1995.
"You will listen to me": Gerald Clark, "Just One Great Big Unhappy Family," *St. Louis Post-Dispatch,* April 12, 1942.
"greenish mush": "Dr. Dafoe Answers Parents' Criticism of Care of Babes," *North Bay Nugget,* April 27, 1936.
"The Dionne family . . . are accustomed to lumberjack meals": Charles E. Blake, "Dr. Dafoe Makes Answer to Charges of Parents of Dionne Quintuplets," *New Castle News,* April 29, 1936.
"Their hair was so long and so heavy": Doreen Chaput, interviewed in *The Dionne Quintuplets.*
"I am the Most Unhappy Mother in the World": Lillian Barker, "I Am the Most Unhappy Mother in the World," *Liberty,* October 3, 1936.
"Don't My Babies Need Me?": Barker, "Don't My Babies Need Me?" *Modern Romances,* September 1936.
"This being cut off from my baby girls": Oliva Dionne, "Why My Wife and I Are Unhappy," *Liberty,* September 26, 1936.
"Even pigs are allowed": Claire Wallace, "What's Ahead for the Quints?" *Maclean's,* November 15, 1935.
"This baby is fine": Phyllis Griffiths, "Happiness of Yule for Other Homes Adds to Bitterness in Dionne Hearts," *Indianapolis Star,* December 23, 1936.

"Why should I cooperate with them": Wolfert, "Eternally Drawn Shades."

"Not for the government": "No More Babies for Government, Mrs. Dionne Says, Longing for Quintuplets," *Sedalia Democrat*, April 30, 1935.

"Does or does not the best interest of these children": Barnard, "Home or Science?"

"Just visit any orphanage": Barker, "I Am the Most Unhappy Mother."

"a kind of emotional vitamin": Barnard, "Home or Science?"

"They have wealth, they have money": "And How They Grow," *La Crosse Tribune and Leader-Press*, March 1, 1937.

"It is obvious that the quintuplets": Barnard, "Home or Science?"

"They are so sweet": Noël diary, June 7, 1937.

"It was too much": Clark, "Just One Great Big Unhappy Family."

"We could not help weeping": Brough, *We Were Five*, 55.

"I left a piece of myself there": "Rendons les Dionelles à leur mère."

"just resigned and walked out": Letter of Nora Rousselle, July 19, 1938, Thomas Fisher Rare Book Library, W. E. Blatz Collection, Box 35.

"I feel certain": Berton, *The Dionne Years*, 188.

"Mom could not understand": Brough, *We Were Five*, 55.

"The babies will grow away from us": Williams, "Dollars Flow In but Papa Dionne Still Angry About Famed Quintuplets"; see also Brough, *We Were Five*, 48.

"Will the five ordinary Dionne children": Mary Dougherty, "What About the Other Five Dionnes?" *Pictorial Review*, May 1935.

"To have glory somewhere in the family": Kathleen Norris, "Will the Bigger Dionnes Resent the Littler Dionnes?" *Arizona Republic*, June 30, 1935.

CHAPTER 25

"We had a normal family life": Ellie Tesher, "The Tragic Saga of the Dionne Quintuplets," *Toronto Star*, May 17, 1984.

"My youth ended": Tom Fennell, "The Forgotten Dionnes," *Maclean's*, November 21, 1994.

"litter": Berton, *The Dionne Years*, 70.

"Don't you think it would be a good idea": Berton, *The Dionne Years*, 70.

"They took my father's pride": Tesher, "The Tragic Saga of the Dionne Quintuplets."

"All well and good": "Rendons les Dionelles à leur mère."

"buying back Marie": Barker, "Don't My Babies Need Me?" *Modern Romances*, October 1936.

"Nobody would believe what we suffered": Tesher, "The Tragic Saga of the Dionne Quintuplets."

"intelligent culture" and "scientific training": Maria Valverde, "Representing Childhood: The Multiple Fathers of the Dionne Quintuplets," in *Regulating Womanhood: Historical Essays on Marriage, Motherhood, and Sexuality*, edited by Carole Smart (London: Routledge, 1991), 134.

"the forgotten five" and "the forgotten six": Griffiths, "Happiness of Yule for Other Homes."

"Callander madonna": Undated clipping in Callander Bay Heritage Museum collection. (https://www.cityofnorthbay.ca/quints/digitize/LOCATION/NHMUS/13120172.jpg).

"This one will never go away": Tesher, *The Dionnes*, 237.

CHAPTER 26

"dissipated": "Dr. Dafoe Suspects Outside Interests Seek Gain Control of Dionne Quintet," *North Bay Nugget*, April 22, 1938.

"extravagance": "Probe into Supervision of Quints by DaFoe Asked," *Pittsburgh Post-Gazette*, April 22, 1938.

"schemes to divorce the affections": "Probe into Supervision of Quints."

"as Catholic and French children": Berton, *The Dionne Years*, 169.

"dream home": Gregory Clark, "'Dream Home' for Dionnes May Be Built at Corbeil," *Toronto Star*, May 20, 1938.

"Well, . . . that's the first time I was given": "Guardians of Quintet Consent to Reunion of All Dionne Family," *North Bay Nugget*, May 20, 1938.

"a new spirit of cooperation": "Guardians of Quintet Consent to Reunion."

"outside interests": "Dr. Dafoe Suspects Outside Interests."

"That $600,000 bank account": "Dafoe Planning New Home for Quintuplets," *Detroit Times*, April 24, 1938, Lucile F. Nobach scrapbook, North Bay Public Library.

"When the children were poor": "Dr. Dafoe Suspects Outside Interests."

"We, the people, are with you!": Berton, *The Dionne Years*, 172.

"As with most primitive people": Edith Johnson, "Have the Dionnes Won or Lost?" unidentified magazine article of May 1938, quoted in Berton, *The Dionne Years*, 150–151.

"surprisingly little": Gladys Schultz, "Mrs. Schultz Visits the Quints," *Better Homes and Gardens*, February 1938.

"the five little sisters stand": Clara Savage Littledale, "My Visit to the Quintuplets," *The Parents' Magazine*, January 1937.

"that deadliest scourge of childhood": "Dionne Quintuplets Get Toxoid Injections to Protect Them from Diphtheria," *Pittsburgh Press*, January 8, 1936.

"Today they are five splendid physical specimens": Dempsey, "What Will Become of Them?"

"the greatest tourist attraction Canada has ever known": E. C. Phelan, "Dionne Suit May Bring Showdown," *Toronto Globe*, July 14, 1939.

"the quintuplets haven't the stamina": Dempsey, "What Will Become of Them?"

"The excessive care to protect them from infection": Sidonie Matsner Gruenberg, "Will 'Hothouse' Life Weaken Dionne Quins?" *Physical Culture*, January 1938.

"Those poor quintuplets": Barnard, "Home or Science?"

CHAPTER 27

"Cow!"; "Sheep! Horse!" and "Faster!": "Quints Cry 'Faster' New World Unfolds," *Toronto Star*, May 22, 1939.

"Pass them, pass them!": "Chat with King Boast of Yvonne," *North Bay Nugget*, May 22, 1939.

"dirty rotten trick": "Police to Blame for Sly Getaway of Dionne Girls," *North Bay Nugget*, May 22, 1939.

"Hello, Monsieur le Judge": "Chat with King Boast of Yvonne."

"playing 'King and Queen'": "Quints Shun Sleep as Train Brings Them to Toronto," *Toronto Globe and Mail*, May 22, 1939.

"As though the judge were the King himself" and "neither nervous nor worried": "Quints Cry 'Faster.'"

"bounced up and down," "Such great big sighs they gave," "The quints regard sharing a room," "But to sleep?" "saucer-eyed and excited," and "Little Émilie lies there": "Quints Shun Sleep."

"the Dionne daughters spent their first night away from home": "Quints Cry 'Faster.'"

"I don't know whether the newspaper people will go to bed" and "Now we are in Toronto": "Quints Shun Sleep."

"sweet little dresses" and "delightful": "Marie and Émilie Topple While Rehearsing Their Bow," *Toronto Globe and Mail*, May 20, 1939.

"the other Dionne children": "Quints Cry 'Faster.'"

"Les journalistes!": Barker, *The Dionne Legend*, 177.

"The Quints blew kisses": M. Louise Corriveau, *Quints to Queens* (New York: Vantage Press, 1976), 40.
"It's crazy, the doctor's hat": Barker, *The Dionne Legend*, 178.
"began dancing and yelling 'Voiture, voiture!' ": "Quints Cry 'Faster.' "
"the children shrieked": "Quints Cry 'Faster.' "
"The girls were especially entranced": Corriveau, 40.
"Now we had a much better idea": Brough, *We Were Five*, 85–86.
"On their way to the legislative building" and "the happiest in the entire group": "Quints Cry 'Faster.' "
Your Majesty: Barker, *The Dionne Legend*, 173.
"a word of astonishment": Barker, *The Dionne Legend*, 174.
"Don't go away": Barker, *The Dionne Legend*, 178.
"the last word in little-girl loveliness": " 'Berries' Says Dan Dionne of Quint Sisters' Special," *Toronto Star*, May 20, 1939.
"As the children walk": "Quints Shun Sleep."
"We're going to meet the King": " 'Berries' Says Dan Dionne."
"they had been told": "Flirtatious Quint Caused Sovereign to Display Blush," *North Bay Nugget*, May 24, 1939.
"Keep your fingers crossed": Barker, *The Dionne Legend*, 179.
"La belle Reine": "Dr. Dafoe Tells About It," *New York Times*, May 23, 1939.
"This is Canada's most famous doctor": "Quintuplets Kiss Queen at Meeting," *New York Times*, May 23, 1939.
"But I was only halfway down": "Quints Hug and Kiss the 'Beautiful Lady'; Fascinated by the King," *Toronto Globe and Mail*, May 23, 1939.
"came to the royal audience": "Her Majesty Is Hugged, Kissed by Famous Five," *Toronto Star*, May 22, 1939.
"and then took a headlong rush": "Quints Hug and Kiss the 'Beautiful Lady.' "
"kicked up their heels": "Five Loveliest Sub-Debs Have 'Coming-Out' Party," *Australian Women's Weekly*, June 3, 1939.
"Wherever will I put them all": "Quints Hug and Kiss the 'Beautiful Lady.' "
"His Majesty stooped over": "Her Majesty Is Hugged, Kissed."
"mechanics or gadgets" and "Just like Mr. Ouellette's buckle!": Corriveau, 43.
"Kisses are for the Queen": "Flirtatious Quint Caused Sovereign to Display Blush."
"There was no majesty stuff in that room": "Quints Home After Big Day," *Des Moines Register*, May 23, 1939.
"What a scene it was": Corriveau, 43.
"You must be proud": Barker, *The Dionne Legend*, 181.

CHAPTER 28

Dionne Accuses Dafoe of Libel: "Dionne Accuses Dafoe of Libel," *Toronto Globe*, May 27, 1939.
Rural Free Delivery: "N.Y. Club Confers Doctor of Litters Degree on Dafoe," *Chicago Tribune*, April 13, 1939.
Dr. A. R. Dafoe—Mass Deliveries: "Dionnes Suing Dr. Dafoe for Libel for Posing as 'Doctor of Litters,' " *Winnipeg Tribune*, May 26, 1939.
Dr. Dafoe unfair to organized storks: "N.Y. Club Confers Doctor of Litters."
Matrimonial Slot Machine Co., "Yvonne! Marie! Émilie! Annette! Cécile!" and *There are men who just love babies:* Newsreel footage in *The Dionne Quintuplets*.
"Doctor of Litters": "Club Initiates Dafoe as 'Doctor of Litters,' " *Toronto Globe*, April 13, 1939.
"Well, do you feel proud of yourself?": "Quintuplets Born to Farm Wife."

"And any man can get pretty sick": Llewellyn Miller, "On the 'Five of a Kind' Location," *Hollywood*, August 1938.

"nasty remarks" and "to break one's spirit": "Being Quintuplets' Parents No Fun, Says Dr. A. R. Dafoe," *North Bay Nugget*, March 6, 1936.

"We are insulted by the affiliation": "Dionne Files Suit Against Dr. Dafoe," unidentified newspaper clipping circa May 1939 in "Scrap Book No. 2. Quintuplets," author's collection.

"Is it fair that Mr. Dionne should be compelled": "Dionne Files Suit."

"the sixth quintuplet": Merrill Denison, "Infant Industry: The Quintuplets," *Harper's Magazine*, November 1938.

Dionne Suit May Bring Showdown: "Dionne Suit May Bring Showdown," *Toronto Globe*, July 14, 1939.

"in sole charge of their health and hygiene," "The physical, intellectual, moral," "The doctor declares," and "This is the best New Year's news": "Reunion Is Slated of Quints, Parents; Dafoe Resigns Post," *Toronto Globe*, December 29, 1939.

"A curious lack of reality": Brough, *We Were Five*, 90.

"So we were only too happy": Brough, *We Were Five*, 91.

"She put her hand close to my ear": Francis Talbot, "The Quints Are Now Seven and They Long to Go Home," *America*, August 16, 1941.

"and thus save them": *America*, August 16, 1941 (table of contents).

"eager to please anybody and everybody": Brough, *We Were Five*, 90.

"They were fine until the parents came": Doreen Chaput, interviewed in *The Dionne Quintuplets*.

"Yvonne and Émilie whispered to me": Barker, *The Dionne Legend*, 194.

"It would be fitting to say": Brough, *We Were Five*, 94.

"Émigrees from our home": Brough, *We Were Five*, 101.

"We knew instinctively the emotions": Brough, *We Were Five*, 95.

"People on the program drilled us": Brough, *We Were Five*, 96.

"I don't want to speak English": Frederick Edwards, "The Quint Question," *Maclean's*, July 15, 1941.

"Five little chins became stubborn": "Quint Broadcast Causes Big Stir," *North Bay Nugget*, May 15, 1941.

"We, the English-speaking peoples of Canada": "The Quints' Broadcast," *Toronto Star*, May 17, 1941.

"If the quints won't speak English": "A Little of Everything," *Toronto Star*, May 27, 1941.

"insurrection": Edwards, "The Quint Question."

"a private little chuckle": "Quints Birthday Ends at 'Mike,'" *North Bay Nugget*, May 29, 1941.

"I do not know what got into them" and "in excellent English": Edwards, "The Quint Question."

"They just wouldn't go near him": Doreen Chaput, interviewed in *The Dionne Quintuplets*.

"He looked much older": Brough, *We Were Five*, 98.

"Do you think . . . that there was a better way": McLeod, "My Neighbors the Quints."

"I feel that my usefulness" and "They were sweet children": "Dafoe Bids Quints Good-by; 'I've Done My Best,' He Says," *Toronto Star*, February 16, 1942.

CHAPTER 29

"I was disappointed in them": Clark, "Just One Great Big Unhappy Family."

"exactly the sort of place": Marshall, "Private Life of the Dionne Quints."

"I wouldn't want children of my own": Marguerite Mooers Marshall, "The Five Unluckiest Children in the World," *Liberty*, January 27, 1940. (Note: Yvonne Leroux's handwritten draft entitled "The Five Unluckiest Children" can be found in the Leroux-Davis fonds, Archives of Ontario, microfilm reel 3650.)

"The guards wouldn't let me in the enclosure": Clark, "Just One Great Big Unhappy Family."
"Among ourselves, there was obviously never any question": Brough, *We Were Five*, 51.
"We were treated as five": Brough, *We Were Five*, 120.
"I suffered a lot when young": Cécile Dionne, interviewed in *Miracle Babies*.

CHAPTER 30

"We will ask God": "Dr. Dafoe Is Dead; End Comes Suddenly," *North Bay Nugget*, June 2, 1943.
"because we knew, without being told": Brough, *We Were Five*, 104.
"It cost me $75,000": Brough, *We Were Five*, 99.
"The fable was": Brough, *We Were Five*, 101.
"It was a haven to us": Brough, *We Were Five*, 102.
"Like that" and "Without being prepared": Cécile Dionne, interviewed in *Miracle Babies*.
"the little girls": Soucy, 7.
"Now, we're one big family": Soucy, 12.
"Every instinct urged us" and "We clearly seemed as strange": Brough, *We Were Five*, 103.
"These were very hurt people": Connie Vachon, interviewed in *The Dionne Quintuplets*.
"If we spanked one of those kids": Griffiths, "Showing of Quints May Be Ended This Year."
"In each other's presence, they competed": Brough, *We Were Five*, 117.
"For sure, the grief ruined her health": Soucy, 24.
"Did a nurse tell you to do that?": Soucy, 70.
"I think sometimes she didn't realize": Tesher, *The Dionnes*, 168.
Brat: Soucy, 52.
Stupid: Soucy, 57.
Crazy: Soucy, 5.
Dirty pig: Soucy, 70.
"If I'd raised you, you'd be normal": Soucy, 37.
"The most important lesson": Brough, *We Were Five*, 102.
"We were convinced that we had brought misery": Brough, *We Were Five*, 119.
"behaved toward each other": Brough, *We Were Five*, 118; for Elzire Dionne's own acknowledgment of guilt, see also "Parents Saddened as Noted Infants Celebrate Birthday," *North Bay Nugget*, May 27, 1935, and Taylor, "Parents of Dionne Quints Bitterly Resent the Removal of the Girls."
"If only I could have been a single child": Brough, *We Were Five*, 119.
"Their return was a true celebration": Tesher, *The Dionnes*, 225.
"My mother didn't have a lot of education": Tesher, *The Dionnes*, 226.
"Despite all that she had to endure": Tesher, *The Dionnes*, 227.
"Yet there was lots of joy": Tesher, *The Dionnes*, 235.
"Christmas—that was real family life": Berton, *The Dionne Years*, 209.
"We had been ordered to mix": Brough, *We Were Five*, 120.
"We were raised to live a normal life": Fennell, "The Forgotten Dionnes."
"The girls grew up in captivity": Fennell, "The Forgotten Dionnes."
"Our first instinct": Brough, *We Were Five*, 106.
"My god! . . . The grand mal!": Soucy, 56.
"Now, no one will know" and "If anyone found out": Soucy, 58.
"How do you feel?" and "As long as you're with me": Soucy, 60.
"any stormy scene from which she could not escape" and "The cry coming from her bedroom": Brough, *We Were Five*, 107.
"It is lovely": "Dionnes Reunited Under Single Roof," *Toronto Star*, November 17, 1943.
"truth and falsehood.": Brough, *We Were Five*, 105.
"like sheep": " 'Papa' Dionne's Own Story," *Detroit Free Press*, December 5, 1954.

"We were caught": Brough, *We Were Five*, 120.

"the strong one, the decisive one": Soucy, 38.

"You are no longer children": Soucy, 37.

"I would like to put light": Tesher, *The Dionnes*, 145.

"During difficult moments": Sarah-Maud Lefebvre, "Encore traumatisées plusieurs décennies après," *Le Journal de Montreal*, October 22, 2016.

"My mother said that I had the same eyes": Tesher, *The Dionnes*, 209.

"I think Cécile, in the Big House": Annette Dionne, interviewed in *Full Circle*.

"the one quickest to show kindness" and "her nature seemed to turn in on itself": Brough, *We Were Five*, 68.

"the most sober-minded": Brough, *We Were Five*, 136.

"Most of whatever happiness": Brough, *We Were Five*, 113.

"And we were already short": Cécile Dionne, interviewed in *Full Circle*.

"rare adventure": Brough, *We Were Five*, 114.

"never failed to dampen the pleasure": Brough, *We Were Five*, 115.

"Petticoat Patrol": McLeod, "My Neighbors the Quints."

"I wouldn't be my sisters for anything": Brough, "We Were Five," *McCall's*, October 1963.

"The old newspapers contain many a story": Brough, *We Were Five*, 104.

CHAPTER 31

"It was impossible to enroll the Quintuplets" and "At the start of the school year": Brough, *We Were Five*, 122.

"Barbed wire" and "They kept to themselves": Connie Vachon, interviewed in *The Dionne Quintuplets*.

"You're smart enough": Soucy, 91.

"I remember being very surprised": Anthony Depalma, "St. Bruno Journal; The Babies of Quintland Now: Broke and Bitter," *New York Times*, March 4, 1998.

"It surprised me at first": Simone Boileau, interviewed in *Miracle Babies*.

"No one was" and "They would ask us questions": Connie Vachon, interviewed in *Miracle Babies*.

"We hung on every word": Brough, *We Were Five*, 123.

"Didn't it bother you": Soucy, 97.

"We were happy": Soucy, 98.

"a kind of bond": Brough, *We Were Five*, 135.

"It was a state of affairs": Brough, *We Were Five*, 123.

"Morally, those people are taking you farther": Soucy, 109; see also Brough, *We Were Five*, 124.

"For the second time, we were bundled off": Brough, *We Were Five*, 124.

"learn a new way to live": Soucy, 113.

"But what the problem was": Jacqueline Giroux Filion, interviewed in *Miracle Babies*.

"Many times I felt there was a subtle strangeness": Connie Vachon, interviewed in *Miracle Babies*.

"more relaxed, not as strict" and "How are my little girls?": Soucy, 73.

"Keep them for yourselves": Soucy, 74.

"Why didn't you answer right away," "I was swallowing my chocolate," and "You're still coughing": Soucy, 78.

"excellent for chest colds," "I'll rub you down myself," and "Are you shy in front of your own father?": Soucy, 79.

Let it be over quickly! and "Feels good, eh?": Soucy, 80.

"I'm getting cold" and "Your turn, Émilie": Soucy, 81.

"Who wants to go with Dad" and "I was afraid for them": Tesher, *The Dionnes*, 197.

"He put his finger into my blouse": Tesher, *The Dionnes*, 143.

"I always saw when something was coming": Tesher, *The Dionnes*, 169.

"It's over, Émilie": Soucy, 108.

"We must never leave Em all alone": Soucy, 108–109.

"going downstairs at night": Soucy, 72.

"Oh, no, . . . That was private": Annette Dionne, interviewed in *Full Circle*.

"It would have been very difficult": Yvonne Dionne, interviewed in *Full Circle*.

"I think I would tell her": Cécile Dionne, interviewed in *Full Circle*.

"First of all, I didn't know where to go": Annette Dionne, interviewed in *Miracle Babies*.

"And sharp": Cécile Dionne, interviewed in *Miracle Babies*.

"customary calm": Soucy, 105.

"These sisters, the nuns, lived through hell in there": Tesher, *The Dionnes*, 106.

"her father loved her only": Tesher, *The Dionnes*, 107.

"They would have been fired": Tesher, *The Dionnes*, 106.

"Even if we are not in the confessional": Soucy, 106.

"We assert that we had good parents" and "a lot of trash": "Dionne Siblings Say Sex Abuse Claim False," *Toronto Star*, September 26, 1995.

"How could it happen": "Life with Father," *People*, October 16, 1995.

"Never": Tesher, *The Dionnes*, 227.

"Is this why I was uncomfortable?": Connie Vachon, interviewed in *Full Circle*.

CHAPTER 32

"I like Shirley Temple" and "found much satisfaction": Jack Karr, "The Fabulous Five Are 14," *Toronto Star Weekly*, May 22, 1948.

"I don't remember the girls ever saying": Connie Vachon, interviewed in *Full Circle*.

"We had our new names": Brough, *We Were Five*, 135.

"In that time, . . . there was only two choices": Cécile Dionne, interviewed in *Full Circle*.

"When Dad told us": Brough, *We Were Five*, 138.

"Half pleased, half disappointed": Brough, *We Were Five*, 139.

"There was still that finger": Brough, *We Were Five*, 141.

"Dad was a great one": Brough, *We Were Five*, 142.

"Pat him on the back": McLeod, "My Neighbors the Quints."

"I felt free like a bird": Annette Dionne, interviewed in *Full Circle*.

"They saved us": Tesher, *The Dionnes*, 171.

"The interview had us all trembling" and "You are rich enough": Brough, *We Were Five*, 140.

CHAPTER 33

"I have an announcement to make": Soucy, 160.

Does that mean I might be able: Soucy, 162.

"I have chosen this particular order": "Marie Dionne Admired Nuns Who Supervised Schooling," *Ottawa Journal*, August 24, 1954.

"I am very grateful" and "How do you feel": Soucy, 166.

"But she's letting go of us!": Soucy, 163.

"It will be too emotional for you": Soucy, 168.

"It was a big shock": Tesher, *The Dionnes*, 171.

"Are you taking good care of her?" and *Do what you must*: Soucy, 169.

"a new serenity": Soucy, 171.

"the slightest hesitation": Soucy, 174.

"It was very severe": Cécile Dionne, interviewed in *Full Circle*.

"She was too young": Annette Dionne, interviewed in *Full Circle*.

"hurt her as if she were cutting into her own flesh" and "superhuman effort": Soucy, 174.

"It touched the other sisters": "Mother Superior Thought Marie Dionne 'Too Delicate,'" *Ottawa Journal*, July 20, 1954.

"As time slipped by": Brough, *We Were Five*, 150–151.

"I prefer to remain a child": Brough, *We Were Five*, 151.

"robust health": "Emilie Dionne Considers Joining Secular Convent," *Catholic Advance*, July 3, 1954.

"took to it heartily," "so quiet we could not tell," and "She wanted to work": John Belliveau, "Those Five Never Knew Much Real Happiness, Family Member Says," *Toronto Star*, August 7, 1954.

"I decided the only intelligent thing": "Mother Superior Thought Marie Dionne 'Too Delicate.'"

"I was very confused": Brough, *We Were Five*, 152.

"appeared dazed and ill": "Dionne Quintuplet Leaves Convent," *Bristol Daily Courier*, July 19, 1954.

"They thought I was stupid": Brough, *We Were Five*, 153.

"all kinds of rumors": "Marie Dionne Quits Convent; Two Explanations Are Given," *Gettysburg Times*, July 19, 1954.

"I do not intend to go back home": Brough, *We Were Five*, 154.

CHAPTER 34

"Take hold of yourselves": Brough, *We Were Five*, 157.

QUINT DIES OF STROKE: Don Delaplante, "Quint Dies of Stroke," *Toronto Globe*, August 7, 1954.

"They were all talking and laughing": "Emilie's Body Arrives at Callander, ONT," *Lowell Sun*, August 8, 1954.

"I looked in on her": Brough, *We Were Five*, 157.

"frequent weak spells": Belliveau, "Those Five Never Knew."

"We had no idea": Brough, *We Were Five*, 158.

"Cécile, you will never feel so bad again": Soucy, 193; see also Parker, "The Dark Side of the Famous Five."

"like widows and orphans": Soucy, 200.

"It was like a nightmare": Cécile Dionne, interviewed in *Miracle Babies*.

"a flame that would never again be revived": Soucy, 195.

"Inside, there's a voice that said": Tesher, *The Dionnes*, 124.

"broke the spell": Soucy, 197.

"Just one, then" and "Émilie is still playing the part": Soucy, 197.

"persons genuine in their grief": "Bury Émilie Monday Near Grandparents," *Toronto Star*, August 7, 1954.

"The way everyone has been so kind": Brough, *We Were Five*, 161.

"She is stronger than I am": Angela Burke, "Émilie 'So Good, Gay Had Not Seemed Ill,' Says Sister Yvonne," *Toronto Star*, August 7, 1954.

"It was very dark": Cécile Dionne, interviewed in *Miracle Babies*.

"that they were still part": Soucy, 200.

"face haggard with grief": Don Delaplante, "Émilie Goes to Her Last Rest; Long Struggle with Illness Told," *Toronto Globe*, August 10, 1954.

"almost in a state of collapse": John Breil, "Priest Won't End Rite Until Curious Leave; Many Grab for Roses," *Toronto Star*, August 9, 1954.

"bitterly": C. M. Fellman, "Hundreds Watch as Émilie Dionne Buried," *Lethbridge Herald*, August 9, 1954.

"senseless" and "to keep Émilie alive within her soul": Soucy, 200.

"We are not lowering the body" and "Have you no respect": Breil, "Priest Won't End Rite."

"All gone. And the grass": Leo Voyer, interviewed in *The Dionne Quintuplets*.

CHAPTER 35

The cage is open: Soucy, 203.
"I remember feeling": Parker, "The Dark Side of the Famous Five."
If only being a quint was a secret: Soucy, 188.
"I knew it was better like that": Cécile Dionne, interviewed in *Full Circle.*
"I like everything about nursing": "Boys? Million Dollars? Dionnes Shrug Shoulders," *Lansing State Journal,* May 5, 1955.
"a touch of lipstick": Brough, *We Were Five,* 165.
"An inexplicable weariness": Soucy, 208.
"I think she wants to be friendly": "Boys? Million Dollars?"
"two by two": Brough, *We Were Five,* 165.
"The feeling is as deep": Brough, *We Were Five,* 165–66.
"Nobody had thought fit": Brough, *We Were Five,* 167.
"We had been raised": Brough, *We Were Five,* 168.
"represented a riddle": Brough, *We Were Five,* 169.
"sequestered": Brough, *We Were Five,* 175.
"That is absolutely false": Soucy, 213.
"Oh, . . . And I had hoped": Soucy, 214.
"sparkling eyes and an attractive smile": Soucy, 215.
"The first few times I met her": Robert J. Levin, "Two Dionne Quintuplets: From Loneliness to Love," *Redbook,* September 1958.
"From the smile on her face": Brough, *We Were Five,* 175.
"Annette says good-bye" and "So in my next letter I put down": Levin, "Two Dionne Quintuplets."
"spic and span": Brough, *We Were Five,* 176.
"Someone is expecting you": Soucy, 221.
"Finally Cécile walked out": Levin, "Two Dionne Quintuplets."
"Are you afraid to be alone": Brough, *We Were Five,* 177.
"I fell in love": Annette Dionne with Frank Rasky, "I'm Out of the Cocoon," *The Canadian,* June 3, 1967.
"She was a famous celebrity," "I thought I wasn't able to love," and "I thought my life had harmed me": Levin, "Two Dionne Quintuplets."
"Being in love with him": Dionne with Rasky, "I'm Out of the Cocoon."

CHAPTER 36

"I don't know what to do with it": "Boys? Million Dollars?"
"I didn't know a nickel from a quarter": Tesher, *The Dionnes,* 89.
"enjoy and occupy": Brough, *We Were Five,* 184.
"a time of profound stirring": Brough, *We Were Five,* 190.
"special delight": Brough, *We Were Five,* 191.
"out of the question": Tesher, *The Dionnes,* 142.
"Something had changed": Tesher, *The Dionnes,* 130.
"a kind of sanctuary": Brough, *We Were Five,* 196.
"We hoped to spend the holiday together": Brough, *We Were Five,* 196.
PAPA DIONNE DECLARES QUINTS: "Papa Dionne Declares Quints Ignored Family at Christmas," *Toronto Star,* December 27, 1955.
"put the name Dionne back": John Keasler, "Dionne Quints and Their Troubles," *St. Louis Post-Dispatch,* January 8, 1956.
"We were not surprised," "We did send one," "We suspected that outsiders," and "Don't believe it!": "'It's Not True,' Sobs Quint," *Ottawa Journal,* December 27, 1955.

"They love their family": "Quints Now 'Having Fun' on Their Own," *Des Moines Register*, December 29, 1955.

"My father is upstairs": Keasler, "Dionne Quints and Their Troubles."

"Silence simply was not a sufficient response": Brough, *We Were Five*, 199.

"It was awful": Levin, "Two Dionne Quintuplets."

"blinking like owls": Brough, *We Were Five*, 202.

"shaken and weary": Brough, *We Were Five*, 203.

"a misunderstanding somewhere": "Quints 'Happy' as Rift Healed," *North Bay Nugget*, December 31, 1955.

"There was a feeling of tension": Berton, *The Dionne Years*, 202.

"There was absolutely no strain": Peter Dunlop, "Quints All Smiles; Papa Happy, Relaxed as Hatchet Buried," *Toronto Star*, December 31, 1955.

"Why did you talk to the newspapers": Brough, *We Were Five*, 204; see also Soucy, 251.

"without flinching": Brough, *We Were Five*, 204.

"half hoped there would be an accident": Brough, *We Were Five*, 202.

"We could have said much more": Brough, *We Were Five*, 204.

"There had never been a day like this": Brough, *We Were Five*, 204.

CHAPTER 37

"So few doors seemed to stand open": Brough, *We Were Five*, 191.

"turned down flat" and "Whatever happens, I intend to go ahead": Brough, *We Were Five*, 209.

"It was a wonderful adventure": Brough, *We Were Five*, 212.

"too thrilled to complain": Brough, *We Were Five*, 213.

"She was not the same person": Levin, "Two Dionne Quintuplets."

"refused to prosper": Brough, *We Were Five*, 219.

"bitter blow": Brough, *We Were Five*, 220.

"She was very discouraged": Tesher, *The Dionnes*, 133.

"The experiment was worth": Brough, *We Were Five*, 220.

"I think the first thing": Levin, "Two Dionne Quintuplets."

This time . . . I'll get it right: Tesher, *The Dionnes*, 189.

"Blazing flashbulbs lit up the altar": Frank Teskey, "Cecile Dionne Wed, Trousseau Worth $10,000," *Toronto Star*, November 23, 1957.

"I thought that all would be fixed": Tesher, *The Dionnes*, 190.

"to become the most suburban of housewives": Brough, *We Were Five*, 236.

"To Annette, that is a very real luxury": Marie Grebenc, "Life No Bed of Roses for 'The Poor Quints,'" *Arizona Republic*, June 12, 1969.

"was blooming": George Dewan, "Surviving Dionnes Still Seek an Elusive Privacy," *Indianapolis Star*, May 13, 1984.

"Nothing has made me so happy": Levin, "Two Dionne Quintuplets."

"shook with sobs of exhaustion and joy" and "How marvelous it is": Brough, *We Were Five*, 240.

"bright and gay as a bird": Brough, *We Were Five*, 242.

"She asked for little more": Brough, *We Were Five*, 189.

"very bashful, having no confidence in herself" and "I don't think I was ever good enough": Tesher, *The Dionnes*, 174.

"It shaped me": Tesher, *The Dionnes*, 165.

"I don't want to think about 'little Yvonne'": Yvonne Dionne, interviewed in *Full Circle*.

"I want to go forward": Yvonne Dionne, interviewed in *Miracle Babies*.

"They just tell you it's not your place": Tesher, *The Dionnes*, 177.

"I worked a lot on myself" and "Just like someone needs food": Tesher, *The Dionnes*, 179.

CHAPTER 38

"Such bitterness": Vaun Wilmott, "Dionnes 'Bitterly Resentful' Recalls Quints' Nurse," *Toronto Star*, September 19, 1963.

"There are two sides to every story": " 'True, True, True,' Says Marie; Quintuplets' Story 'Full of Lies' Says a Shocked Papa Dionne," *Ottawa Journal*, September 19, 1963.

"certain inaccuracies discovered in the text": "It's Not for Canada: Publishers Withdraw Book on Quints," *Toronto Globe*, March 13, 1951.

"For Canada, the book is too true": "Book on Dionne Quints Disputed," *San Bernardino County Sun*, April 16, 1951.

"We have no intention.": " 'True, True, True,' says Marie."

"This is just like the old days": Bob Lewis, "Papa Hurt, 'Sad,' " *Ottawa Citizen*, September 19, 1963.

"Father's reaction was violent": " 'True, True, True,' says Marie."

"That book really hurt them": Berton, *The Dionne Years*, 208.

"most impolite and harsh": Berton, *The Dionne Years*, 204.

"Everything we said": "Dionne Quints Tell of Childhood: 'The Saddest Home We Ever Knew,' " *Star Tribune* (Minneapolis), September 19, 1963. (Note: This article misattributes the quote to Annette. However, all others indicate Marie as the speaker. See, for instance, "Dionne Blasts Story Quints Were Unhappy," *Chicago Tribune*, September 20, 1963.)

"a sensitive and accurate account": Dionne with Rasky, "Annette Dionne Today."

"You wouldn't know my wife now": " 'True, True, True,' says Marie."

"People think that we are perfect": Annette Dionne, interviewed in *Miracle Babies*.

"Now when I look back": Genia Goelz, interviewed in *Miracle Babies*.

"I cannot talk of him": Grebenc, "Life No Bed of Roses."

"I didn't know anything about the world": Cécile Dionne, interviewed in *Miracle Babies*.

"It takes a lot of patience and courage": Grebenc, "Life No Bed of Roses."

"I saw some parallels": Bertrand Langlois, interviewed in *Full Circle*.

"Yvonne was my parent for me": Tesher, *The Dionnes*, 181–182.

"kind but very reserved": Tesher, *The Dionnes*, 134.

"deeply worried about both her physical condition": Marie Grebenc, "Four Surviving Dionnes Are Near Their 35th Birthday," *Pittsburgh Press*, May 25, 1969.

"I knew that she had been treated": Cécile Dionne, interviewed in *Miracle Babies*.

"It's over": Tesher, *The Dionnes*, 139.

"I would have given anything": Marie Grebenc, "Sorrow of Sister's Funeral Fails to Heal Dionne Family Wounds," *Pittsburgh Press*, March 8, 1970.

"the gravitational center for the Dionne sisters": Grebenc, "Life No Bed of Roses."

"If more want to move in": "Happiness for Dionnes Is Being Together," *Detroit Free Press*, December 27, 1965.

"My husband thought he was married to three women": Annette Dionne, interviewed in *Full Circle*.

"After the sisters came": Dewan, "Surviving Dionnes Still Seek an Elusive Privacy."

"I was working all the time": Tesher, *The Dionnes*, 155.

"Finally I got fed up": Berton, *The Dionne Years*, 211.

"Oliva Dionne was not the plodding": "Oliva Dionne's Quiet Funeral Contrasts with Hectic Days as Quintuplets' Father," *North Bay Nugget*, November 15, 1979.

"Mom said if our father was dead": Tesher, *The Dionnes*, 207.

"Her great love for her family": C. M. Fellman, "Their Million Dollar Birthday," *Orlando Sentinel*, May 22, 1955.

"I felt badly when Mom died": Tesher, *The Dionnes*, 157.

"I would have liked that she asked for us": Tesher, *The Dionnes*, 184.

"I declare that I have made no provision": Tesher, *The Dionnes*, 92–93.

CHAPTER 39

"all the normal needs": David Croll radio broadcast in *Miracle Babies.*
"particularly lavish": Berton, *The Dionne Years,* 211.
"I had no choice": Tesher, *The Dionnes,* 187.
"I had a feeling": Tesher, *The Dionnes,* 248.
"My mother was struggling" and "I think it's more disgusting": Bertrand Langlois, interviewed in *Miracle Babies.*
"every plate of fish and chips": Valverde, 127.
"Mom would tell us on August 27": Tesher, *The Dionnes,* 87.
"It's beginning to seem": Genia Goelz, interviewed in *Miracle Babies.*
"It was a moral obligation": Tesher, *The Dionnes,* 285.
"We were a scientific curiosity": Tesher, *The Dionnes,* 266.
"your concern and request": Tesher, *The Dionnes,* 270.
"I keep my promises": Tesher, *The Dionnes,* 270.
"It's nowhere near what's owed": Tesher, *The Dionnes,* 80.
"the three quints will be dead": "Harris Against Dionne Inquiry," *Toronto Globe,* February 20, 1998.
"Every network, local news stations": Tesher, *The Dionnes,* 283.
"It is very painful for us": Daniel Girard and Joel Ruimy, "Province Won't Raise Its Offer, Premier Says," *Toronto Star,* February 27, 1998.
"looking like a grinch": Richard Mackie, "The Quints Versus the Premier," *Toronto Globe,* March 4, 1998.
Why Has Mike Harris Stiffed the Quints?: Allan Fotheringham, "Why Has Mike Harris Stiffed the Quints?" *Maclean's,* March 9, 1998.
"stolen our souls": Depalma, "St. Bruno Journal."
"It was an emotional meeting": Mike Harris in *Full Circle.*
"So far as money is concerned": Edwards, "The Quint Question."
"I haven't given much thought," "I'm relieved," and "*Happy* is a big word": Brenda Branswell, "Quest for Truth," *Maclean's,* March 23, 1998.
"We feel they are looking down at us": O'Neil and Sotynoff, "Sisters Triumphant."

EPILOGUE

"Welcome home": Carolyn Samuel, "Dionne Visit Creates New Memories," *North Bay Nugget,* May 23, 1998.
"It's difficult to describe right now": John Size and Carolyn Samuel, "Dionnes Arrive for Busy Weekend," *North Bay Nugget,* May 22, 1998.
"smiling and gushing like schoolgirls": Keith Howell and Caroyln Samuel, "Quints Make Royal Homecoming," *North Bay Nugget,* May 23, 1998.
"They were not just smiling to be polite": Keith Howell, "Quint Homecoming a New Start," *North Bay Nugget,* May 25, 1998.
"Media was very close to us": Samuel, "Dionne Visit Creates New Memories."
"Without you, . . . our voices": Howell and Samuel, "Quints Make Royal Homecoming."
"We were the children": Tesher, *The Dionnes,* 301.
"This is overwhelming": Howell, "Quint Homecoming a New Start."
"You will always be close to our hearts": Howell, "Quint Homecoming a New Start."
"opening the door on my youth": Howell and Samuel, "Quints Make Royal Homecoming."
"I have no more wounds": Annette Dionne, interviewed in *Full Circle.*

AFTERWORD

"I knew she would never feel secure enough": Tesher, *The Dionnes*, 296.

"At my age it's difficult": Marian Scott, "Dionne Quint Penniless, 18 Years After Ontario Settled with 3 Sisters for $4 Million," *Montreal Gazette*, October 23, 2016.

"When I realize that I start to miss her": Sidhartha Banerjee, "As They Turn 83, Surviving Dionne Quintuplets Seek Protections for Children," *Montreal Gazette*, May 26, 2017.

"I thank God often to have Cécile": Annette Dionne, interview with Vanessa Lee, CTV News, May 26, 2017. http://www.ctvnews.ca/video?clipId=1133815.

INDEX